India of My Dreams

Mahatma Gandhi

rajpal

Price : **Rupees Two hundred fifty only (Rs. 250.00)**
Edition : 2008 © Navjeewan Trust, Ahmedabad
ISBN : 978-81-7028-740-7
INDIA OF MY DREAMS by *Mahatma Gandhi*

RAJPAL & SONS, Kashmere Gate, Delhi-110006
Website : www.rajpalpublishing.com
E-mail : mail@rajpalpublishing.com

TO THE READER

I would like to say to the diligent reader of my writings and to others who are interested in them that I am not at all concerned with appearing to be consistent. In my search after Truth I have discarded many ideas and learnt many new things. Old as I am in age, I have no feeling that I have ceased to grow inwardly or that my growth will stop at the dissolution of the flesh. What I am concerned with is my readiness to obey the call of Truth, my God, from moment to moment, and, therefore, when anybody finds any inconsistency between any two writings of mine, if he has still faith in my sanity, he would do well to choose the later of the two on the same subject.

Harijan, 29.4.1933   **M. K. Gandhi**

FOREWORD

It is a happy idea to place before the world and the country at the present moment when we are entering upon a new era a picture of the India of Mahatma Gandhi's dreams. The freedom which we have won is throwing upon us the responsibilities of making or marring the future of India. It is in no small measure the achievement of Mahatma Gandhi's leadership. The matchless weapon of truth and non-violence which he has used is needed by the world to cure it of many of its ills. We are aware how imperfect have been the instruments that had to be used by Gandhiji, and yet history will record that our object has been gained with the least possible sacrifice which any other country similarly situated could have been called upon to make. As the weapon has been unique, the opportunities which the achievement of freedom offers are equally unique. In our hour of victory and rejoicings we cannot afford to ignore either the leader who has led us or the undying principles which have inspired him. Freedom is only the means to a greater and nobler end, and the achievement of India of Mahatma Gandhi's dreams will be the fitting consummation of all that he has worked for and stands for. At this juncture we need to be reminded of the basis and fundamentals of his teachings. A book, which places before the reader not only those basic and fundamental principles, but also indicates how we can help to fulfil them through our freedom by establishing a polity and social life, and through the instrumentality of a constitution and the dedication of the human material which this vast country will now throw up to work without any external fetters or internal inhibitions, will be welcomed by all. Shri R. K. Prabhu has proved his skill in making a selection of the most telling and significant passage from Mahatma Gandhi's writings and I have no doubt that this volume will be a useful addition to the literature on the subject.

New Delhi,   **Dr. Rajendra Prasad**
8th August 1947   (First President of India)

PREFACE TO THE FIRST EDITION

In this work an attempt has been made, by assembling together passages from writings and speeches of Mahatma Gandhi, to give the reader an idea of the part which he expects a completely free and independent India of his conception to play in her own domestic affairs as well as in her relations with the rest of the world. On 15th August, 1947, India will have finally shaken off the yoke of foreign rule which for the past century and a half had held her soul in bondage and well-nigh ruined her materially, morally and spiritually. In the process of achieving her independence, however, her unity has been broken in many places and her soul has been badly bruised, owing to internecine quarrels, and the shape of 'Swaraj' that is emerging is not at all what her patriotic sons and daughters had ardently longed for and struggled for all these decades. It is quite natural, therefore, that Gandhiji, the Father of Indian Independence, should feel little inclined to enthuse over the Independence that is drawing; and cry out, like the Vedic seer, 'Lead us from darkness unto Light'.

Gandhiji has refused to subscribe to the fantastic theory that the Muslims of India are 'a separate nation'. 'My whole soul rebels against the idea that Hinduism and Islam represent two antagonistic cultures and doctrines,' he has said. 'To assent to such a doctrine is for me a denial of God. For I believe with my whole soul that the God of the Quran is also the God of the Gita, and that we are all, no matter by what name designated, children of the same God. I must rebel against the idea that millions of Indians who were Hindus the other day changed their nationality on adopting Islam as their religion.' He refuses to believe that India will remain for ever partitioned, either geographically or spiritually, in the manner that is being sought to be done at present. 'India does not become two nations,' he says, 'because it has been cut up into two sovereign States.' He lives in the hope and will work in the hope that with the removal of the most serious obstacle in the way of her unity—the wedge driven by her alien rulers—and the healing of the wounds recently inflicted on her, the India of his dreams will yet emerge into reality in the not so distant future.

The compiler of the present work, cognizant of the onerousness of the task before him and of his own shortcomings, is fully aware of the risks involved in trying to convey to the readers a conception of 'India of Gandhiji's dreams' which may fall short, far short, of the picture which the master artist has drawn in the immortal pages of *Young India* and *Harijan* and in other collections of his writings and speeches. The compiler expresses the hope that he may not have deviated far from the correctness as well as comprehensiveness of that picture, inasmuch as the attempt to redraw the picture, on a reduced scale, has been made in Gandhiji's own words. For whatever shortcomings there still remain in the present work the compiler tenders his profuse apologies both to Gandhiji and to the reader.

August, 1947   **R. K. Prabhu**

CONTENTS

1

INDIA OF MY DREAMS

Everything in India attracts me. It has everything that a human being with the highest possible aspirations can want.[1]

India is essentially *karmabhumi* (land of duty) in contradistinction to *bhogabhumi* (land of enjoyment).[2]

India is one of the few nations on the earth which have retained some of their ancient institutions although they have been overlaid with superstition and error. But she has hitherto shown an inherent capacity for purging herself of error and superstition. My faith in her ability to solve the economic problems that face her millions has never been so bright as it is today.[3]

I feel that India's mission is different from that of others. India is fitted for the religious supremacy of the world. There is no parallel in the world for the process of purification that this country has voluntarily undergone. India is less in need of steel weapons, it has fought with divine weapons, it can still do so. Other nations have been votaries of brute force. The terrible war going on in Europe furnishes a forcible illustration of the truth. India can win all by soul force. History supplies numerous instances to prove that brute force is as nothing before soul force. Poets have sung about it and seers have described their experiences.[4]

If India takes up the doctrine of the sword, she may gain momentary victory. Then India will cease to be the pride

> India is essentially karmabhumi *(land of duty)* in contradistinction to bhogabhumi *(land of enjoyment)*

of my heart. I am wedded to India because I owe my all to her. I believe absolutely that she has a mission for all the world. She is not to copy Europe blindly. India's acceptance of the sword will be the hour of my trial. I hope I shall not be found wanting. My religion has no geographical limits. If I have a living faith in it, it will transcend my love for India herself. My life is dedicated to service of India through the religion of non-violence.[5]

If India makes violence her creed, and I have survived, I would not care to live in India. She will cease to evoke any pride in me. My patriotism is subservient to my religion. I cling to India like a child to its mother's breast, because I feel that she gives me the spiritual nourishment I need. She has the environment that responds to my highest aspirations. When that faith is gone, I shall feel like an orphan without hope of ever finding a guardian.[6]

I would like to see India free and strong so that she may offer herself a willing and pure sacrifice for the betterment of the world. India's freedom must revolutionize the world's outlook upon peace and war. Her impotence affects the whole of mankind.[7]

I am humble enough to admit that there is much that we can profitably assimilate from the West. Wisdom is no monopoly of one continent or one race. My resistance to Western civilization is really a resistance to its indiscriminate and thoughtless imitation based on the assumption that Asiatics are fit only to copy every thing that comes from the West.... I do believe that if India has patience enough to go through the fire of suffering and to resist any unlawful encroachment upon her own civilization which, imperfect though it undoubtedly is, has hitherto stood the ravages of time, she can make a lasting contribution to the peace and solid progress of the world.[8]

India's destiny lies not along the bloody way of the West, of which she shows signs of tiredness, but along the bloodless way of peace that comes from a simple and godly life. India is in danger of losing her soul. She cannot lose it and live. She must not, therefore, lazily and helplessly say, "I cannot escape the onrush from the West." She must be strong enough to resist it for her own sake and that of the world.[9]

European civilization is no doubt suited for the Europeans but it will mean ruin for India, if we endeavour to copy it. This is not to say that we may not adopt and assimilate whatever may be good and capable of assimilation by us as it does not also mean that even the Europeans will not have to part with whatever evil might have crept into it. The incessant search for material comforts and their multiplication is such an evil, and I make bold to say that the Europeans themselves will have to remodel their outlook, if they are not to perish under the weight of the comforts to which they are becoming slaves. It may be that my reading is wrong, but I know that for India to run after the Golden Fleece is to court certain death. Let us engrave in our hearts the motto of a Western Philosopher, 'plain living and high thinking'. Today it is certain that the millions cannot have high living and we the few who profess to do the thinking for the masses run the risk, in a vain search after high living, of missing high thinking.[10]

I shall strive for a constitution, which will release India from all thraldom and patronage, and give her, if need be, the right to sin. I shall work for an India, in which the poorest shall feel that it is their country in whose making they have an effective voice; an India in which there shall be no high class and low class of people; an India in which all communities shall live in perfect harmony. There can be no room in such an India for the curse of untouchability or the curse of the intoxicating drinks and drugs. Women will enjoy the same rights as men. Since we shall be at peace with all the rest of the world, neither exploiting, nor being exploited, we should have the smallest army imaginable. All interests not in conflict with the interests of the dumb millions will be scrupulously respected, whether foreign or indigenous. Personally, I hate distinction between foreign and indigenous. This is the India of my dreams.... I shall be satisfied with nothing less.[11]

2
THE MEANING OF SWARAJ

The word 'Swaraj' is a sacred word, a Vedic word, meaning self-rule and self-restraint, and not freedom from all restraint which 'independence' often means.[1]

By Swaraj I mean the government of India by the consent of the people as ascertained by the largest number of the adult population, male or female, native-born or domiciled, who have contributed by manual labour to the service of the State and who have taken the trouble of having registered their names as voters.... Real Swaraj will come not by the acquisition of authority by a few but by the acquisition of the capacity by all to resist authority when it is abused. In other words, Swaraj is to be obtained by educating the masses to a sense of their capacity to regulate and control authority.[2]

Self-government depends entirely upon our internal strength, upon our ability to fight against the heaviest odds. Indeed, self-government which does not require that continuous striving to attain it and to sustain it is not worth the name. I have, therefore, endeavoured to show both in word and deed, that political self-government, that is, self-government for a large number of men and women, is no better than individual self-government, and, therefore, it is to be attained by precisely the same means that are required for individual self-government or self-rule.[3]

Self-government means, continuous effort to be independent of government control, whether it is foreign government or whether it is national. Swaraj government will be a sorry affair if people look up to it for the regulation of every detail of life.[4]

My Swaraj is to keep intact the genius of our civilization. I want to write many new things but they must all be written on the Indian slate. I would gladly borrow from the West when I can return the amount with decent interest.[5]

> The word 'Swaraj' is a sacred word, a Vedic word, meaning self-rule and self-restraint, and not freedom from all restraint which 'independence' often means

Swaraj can be maintained, only where there is majority of loyal and patriotic people to whom the good of the nation is paramount above all other considerations whatever including their personal profit. Swaraj means government by the many. Where the many are immoral or selfish, their government can spell anarchy and nothing else.[6]

The Swaraj of my...our...dream recognizes no race or religious distinctions. Nor is it to be the monopoly of the lettered persons nor yet of moneyed men. Swaraj is to be for all, including the farmer, but emphatically including the maimed, the blind, the starving toiling millions.[7]

It has been said that Indian Swaraj will be the rule of the majority community, i.e. the Hindus. There could not be a greater mistake than that. If it were to be true, I for one would refuse to call it Swaraj and would fight it with all the strength at my command, for to me Hind Swaraj is the rule of all people, is the rule of justice.[8]

If Swaraj was not meant to civilize us, and to purify and stabilize our civilization, it would be nothing worth. The very essence of our civilization is that we give a paramount place to morality in all our affairs, public or private.[9]

Poorna Swaraj.... 'Poorna' complete because it is as much for the prince as for the peasant, as much for the rich landowner as for the landless tiller of the soil, as much for the Hindus as for the Musalmans, as much for Parsis and Christians as for the Jains, Jews and Sikhs, irrespective of any distinction of caste or creed or status in life.[10]

The very connotation of the word and the means of its

> ## My Swaraj is to keep intact the genius of our civilization

attainment to which we are pledged—truth and non-violence—precludes all possibility of that Swaraj being more for some one than for the other, being partial to some and prejudicial to others.[11]

The Swaraj of my dream is the poor man's Swaraj. The necessaries of life should be enjoyed by you in common with those enjoyed by the princes and the moneyed men. But that does not mean that you should have palaces like theirs. They are not necessary for happiness. You or I would be lost in them. But you ought to get all the ordinary amenities of life that a rich man enjoys. I have not the slightest doubt that Swaraj is not Poorna Swaraj until these amenities are guaranteed to you under it.[12]

My notion of Poorna Swaraj is not isolated independence but healthy and dignified independence. My nationalism, fierce though it is, is not exclusive, is not devised to harm any nation or individual. Legal maxims are not so legal as they are moral. I believe in the eternal truth of *'sic utere tuo ut alienum non laedas'* ('Use thy own property so as not to injure thy neighbour's').[13]

It all depends upon what we mean by and want through Poorna Swaraj. If we mean an awakening among the masses, a knowledge among them of their true interest and ability to serve that interest against the whole world and if through Poorna Swaraj we want harmony, freedom from aggression from within or without, and a progressive improvement in the economic condition of the masses, we can gain our end without political power and by directly acting upon the powers that be.[14]

Let there be no mistake about my conception of Swaraj. It is complete independence of alien control and complete economic independence. So at one end you have political independence, at the other the economic. It has two other ends. One of them is moral and social, the corresponding end is Dharma, *i.e.* religion in the highest sense of the term. It includes Hinduism, Islam, Christianity, etc., but is superior to them all.... Let us call this the square of Swaraj, which will be out of shape if any of its angles is untrue.[15]

The Swaraj of my conception will come only when all of us are firmly persuaded that our Swaraj has got to be won, worked and

> *The Swaraj of my ... our ... dream recognizes no race or religious distinctions*

maintained through truth and Ahimsa alone. True democracy or Swaraj of the masses can never come through untruthful and violent means, for the simple reason that the natural corollary to their use would be to remove all opposition through the suppression or extermination of the antagonists. That does not make for individual freedom. Individual freedom can have the fullest play only under a regime of unadulterated Ahimsa.[16]

In Swaraj based on Ahimsa people need not know their rights, but it is necessary for them to know their duties. There is no duty but creates a corresponding right, and those only are true rights which flow from a due performance of one's duties. Hence rights of citizenship accrue only to those who serve the State to which they belong. And they alone can do justice to the rights that accrue to them. Everyone possesses the right to tell lies or resort to goondaism. But the exercise of such a right is harmful both to the exerciser and society. But to him who observes truth and non-violence comes prestige, and prestige brings rights. And people who obtain rights as a result of performance of duty, exercise them only for the service of society, never for themselves. Swaraj of a people means the sum total of the Swaraj (self-rule) of individuals. And such Swaraj comes only from performance by individuals of their duty as citizens. In it no one thinks of his rights. They come, when they are needed, for better performance of duty.[17]

Under Swaraj based on non-violence nobody is anybody's enemy, everybody contributes his or her due quota to the common goal, all can read and write, and their knowledge keeps growing from day to day. Sickness and disease are reduced to the minimum. No one is a pauper and labour can always find employment. There is no place under such a government for gambling, drinking and immorality or for class hatred. The rich will use their riches wisely and usefully, and not squander them in increasing their pomp and worldly pleasures. It should not happen that a handful of rich people should live in jewelled palaces and the millions in miserable hovels devoid of sunlight or ventilation. In non-violent Swaraj there can be no encroachment upon just rights; contrariwise no one can possess unjust rights. In a well-organized State, usurpation should be an impossibility and it should be unnecessary to resort to force for dispossessing an usurper.[18]

3
IN DEFENCE OF NATIONALISM

For me patriotism is the same as humanity. I am patriotic because I am human and humane. It is not exclusive. I will not hurt England or Germany to serve India. Imperialism has no place in my scheme of life. The law of a patriot is not different from that of the patriarch. And a patriot is so much the less a patriot if he is a lukewarm humanitarian. There is no conflict between private and political law.[1]

Just as the cult of patriotism teaches us today that the individual has to die for the family, the family has to die for the village, the village for the district, the district for the province, and the province for the country, even so a country has to be free in order that it may die, if necessary, for the benefit of the world. My love, therefore, of nationalism or my idea of nationalism is that

> For me patriotism is the same as humanity. I am patriotic because I am human and humane. It is not exclusive

my country may become free, that if need be the whole of the country may die, so that the human race may live. There is no room for race hatred there. Let that be our nationalism.[2]

I want India's rise so that the whole world may benefit. I do not want India to rise on the ruin of other nations.[3]

An India prostrate at the feet of Europe can give no hope for humanity. An India awakened and free has a message of peace and goodwill to a groaning world.[4]

It is impossible for one to be inter-nationalist without being a nationalist. Internationalism is possible only when nationalism becomes a fact, *i.e.* when people belonging to different countries have organized themselves and are able to act as one man. It is not nationalism that is evil, it is the narrowness, selfishness, exclusiveness which is the bane of modern nations which is evil. Each wants to profit at the expense of, and rise on the ruin of, the other. Indian nationalism has struck a different path. It wants to organize itself or to find full self-expression for the benefit and service of humanity at large.[5]

God having cast my lot in the midst of the people of India, I should be untrue to my Maker if I failed to serve them. If I do not know how to serve them I shall never know how to serve humanity. And I cannot possibly go wrong so long as I do not harm other nations in the act of serving my country.[6]

My patriotism is not an exclusive thing. It is all-embracing and I should reject that patriotism which sought to mount upon the distress or exploitation of other nationalities. The conception of my patriotism is nothing if it is not always, in every case without exception, consistent with the broadest good of humanity at large. Not only that, but my religion and my patriotism derived from my religion embrace all life. I want to realize brotherhood or identity not merely with the beings called human, but I want to realize identity with all life, even with such things as crawl upon earth... because we claim descent from the same God, and that being so, all life in whatever form it appears must be essentially one.[7]

Our nationalism can be no peril to other nations inasmuch as we will exploit none, just as we will allow none to exploit us. Through Swaraj we will serve the whole world.[8]

After nearly 50 years of public life, I am able to say today that my faith in the doctrine that the service of one's nation is not inconsistent with the service of the world has grown. It is a good doctrine. Its acceptance alone will ease the situation in the world and stop the mutual jealousies between nations inhabiting this globe of ours.[9]

4

DEMOCRACY IN INDIA

The highest form of freedom carries with it the greatest measure of discipline and humility. Freedom that comes from discipline and humility cannot be denied, unbridled licence is a sign of vulgarity injurious alike to self and one's neighbours.[1]

There is no human institution but has its dangers. The greater the institution the greater the chances of abuse. Democracy is a great institution and therefore it is liable to be greatly abused. The remedy, therefore, is not avoidance of democracy but reduction of possibility of abuse to a minimum.[2]

A popular State can never act in advance of public opinion. If it goes against it, it will be destroyed. Democracy disciplined and enlightened is the finest thing in the world. A democracy prejudiced, ignorant, superstitious, will land itself in chaos and may be self-destroyed.[3]

I have repeatedly observed that no school of thought can claim a monopoly of right judgement. We are all liable to err and are often obliged to revise our judgements. In a vast country like this, there must be room for all schools of honest thought. And the least, therefore, that we owe to ourselves as to others is to try to understand the opponent's view-point and, if we cannot accept it, respect it as fully as we expect him to respect ours. It is one of the indispensable tests of a healthy public life and therefore fitness for Swaraj. If we have no charity, and no tolerance, we shall never settle our

The highest form of freedom carries with it the greatest measure of discipline and humility

differences amicably and must, therefore, always submit to the arbitration of a third party, *i.e.* to foreign domination.[4]

When people come into possession of political power, the interference with the freedom of the people is reduced to a minimum. In other words a nation that runs its affairs smoothly and effectively without much State interference is truly democratic. Where such a condition is absent, the form of Government is democratic in name.[5]

Democracy and violence can hardly go together. The States that are today nominally democratic have either to become frankly totalitarian or, if they are to become truly democratic, they must become courageously non-violent. It is a blasphemy to say that non-violence can only be practised by individuals and never by nations which are composed of individuals.[6]

The very essence of democracy is that every person represents all the varied interests which compose the nation. It is true that it does not exclude and should not exclude special representation of special interests, but such representation is not its test. It is a sign of its imperfection.[7]

The democracy or the Swaraj of the masses can never come through untruthful and violent means, for the simple reason that the natural corollary to their use would be to remove all opposition through the suppression or extermination of the antagonists. That does not make for individual freedom. Individual freedom can have the fullest play only under a regime of unadulterated Ahimsa.[8]

> *The greater the institution the greater the chances of abuse. Democracy is a great institution and therefore it is liable to be greatly abused. The remedy, therefore, is not avoidance of democracy but reduction of possibility of abuse to a minimum*

A free democratic India will gladly associate herself with other free nations for mutual defence against aggression and for economic co-operation. She will work for the establishment of a real world order based on freedom and democracy, utilizing the world's knowledge and resources for the progress and advancement of humanity.[9]

My notion of democracy is

that under it the weakest should have the same opportunity as the strongest. That can never happen except through non-violence. No country in the world today shows any but patronizing regard for the weak....Western democracy, as it functions today, is diluted Nazism or Fascism. At best it is merely a cloak to hide the Nazi and the Fascist tendencies of imperialism.... India is trying to evolve true democracy, *i.e.*, without violence. Our weapons are those of *satyagraha* expressed through the *charkha*, the village industries, removal of untouchability, communal harmony, prohibition, and non-violent organization of labour as in Ahmedabad. These mean mass effort and mass education. We have big agencies for conducting these activities. They are purely voluntary, and their only sanction is service of the lowliest.[10]

A born democrat is a born disciplinarian. Democracy comes naturally to him who is habituated normally to yield willing obedience to all laws, human or divine.... Let those who are ambitious to serve democracy qualify themselves by satisfying first this acid test of democracy. Moreover, a democrat must be utterly selfless. He must think and dream not in terms of self or party but only of democracy. Only then does he acquire the right of civil disobedience....I value individual freedom but you must not forget that man is essentially a social being. He

> A born democrat is a born disciplinarian. Democracy comes naturally to him who is habituated normally to yield willing obedience to all laws, human or divine....

has risen to his present status by learning to adjust his individualism to the requirements of social progress. Unrestricted individualism is the law of the beast of the jungle. We have to learn to strike the mean between individual freedom and social restraint. Willing submission to social restraint for the sake of the wellbeing of the whole society, enriches both the individual and the society of which one is a member.[11]

Rights accrue automatically to him who duly performs his duties. In fact the right to perform one's duties is the only right that is worth living for and dying for. It covers all legitimate

> *True democracy cannot be worked by twenty men sitting at the centre. It has to be worked from below by the people of every village*

rights. All the rest is grab under one guise or another and contains in it seeds of Himsa.[12]

In a democracy the individual will is governed and limited by the social will which is the State, which is governed by and for democracy. If every individual takes the law into his own hands there is no State, it becomes anarchy, *i.e.* absence of social law or State. That way lies destruction of liberty. Therefore, they should subdue their anger and let the State secure justice.[13]

People in a democracy should be satisfied with drawing the Government's attention to mistakes, if any. They could remove the Government if they wished to. But they should not obstruct them by agitating against them. Ours is not a foreign Government having a mighty army and navy to support them. They have to derive their strength from the people.[14]

True democracy cannot be worked by twenty men sitting at the centre. It has to be worked from below by the people of every village.[15]

Mobocracy

Personally I do not mind Governmental fury as I mind mob fury. The latter is a sign of national distemper and therefore more difficult to deal with than the former which is confined to a small corporation. It is easier to oust a Government that has rendered itself unfit to govern than it is to cure unknown people in a mob of their madness.[16]

Nothing is so easy as to train mobs, for the simple reason that they have no mind, no premeditation. They act in a frenzy. They repent quickly. Non-co-operation I am using in order to evolve democracy.[17]

> *If the individual ceases to count, what is left of society?*

We must train these masses of men who have a heart of gold, who feel for the country, who want to be taught and led. But a few intelligent, sincere workers are needed, and the whole nation can be organized to act intelligently and democracy can be evolved out of mobocracy.[18]

The spirit of democracy cannot be established in the midst of terrorism whether governmental or popular. In some respects popular terrorism is more antagonistic to the growth of the democratic spirit than the governmental. For the latter strengthens the spirit of democracy, whereas the former kills it.[19]

Majority and Minority

If we want to cultivate a true spirit of democracy, we cannot afford to be intolerant. Intolerance betrays want of faith in one's cause.[20]

Claiming the right of free opinion and free action as we do, we must extend the same to others. The rule of majority when it becomes coercive, is as intolerable as that of a bureaucratic minority. We must patiently try to bring round the minority to our view by gentle persuasion and argument.[21]

The rule of majority has a narrow application, *i.e.* one should yield to the majority in matters of detail. But it is slavery to be amenable to the majority, no matter what its decisions are. Democracy is not a state in which people act like sheep. Under democracy, individual liberty of opinion and action is jealously guarded. I therefore, believe that the minority has a perfect right to act differntly from the majority.[22]

If the individual ceases to count, what is left of society? Individual freedom alone can make a man voluntarily surrender himself completely to the service of society. If it is wrested from him, he becomes an automaton and society is ruined. No society can possibly be built on a denial of individual freedom.[23]

> *Democracy is not a state in which people act like sheep. Under democracy, individual liberty of opinion and action is jealously guarded*

5

INDIA AND SOCIALISM

Socialism was not born with the discovery of the misuse of capital by capitalists. As I have contended, socialism, even communism, is explicit in the first verse of *Ishopanishad*. What is true is that when some reformers lost faith in the method of conversion, the technique of what is known as scientific socialism was born. I am engaged in solving the same problem that faces scientific socialists. It is true, however, that my approach is always and only through unadulterated non-violence. It may fail. If it dies, it will be because of my ignorance of the technique of non-violence. I may be a bad exponent of the doctrine in which my faith is daily increasing. The A.I.S.A. and the A.I.V.I.A. are organizations through which the technique of non-violence is being tested on an all-India scale. They are special autonomous bodies created by the Congress for the purpose of enabling me to conduct my experiments without being fettered by the vicissitudes of policy to which a wholly democratic body like the Congress is always liable.[1]

Real socialism has been handed down to us by our ancestors who taught: "All land belongs to Gopal, where then is the boundary line? Man is the maker of that line and he can, therefore, unmake it." Gopal literally means shepherd; it also means God. In modern language it means the State, *i.e.* the People. That the land today does not belong to the people is true. But the fault is not in the teaching. It is in us who have not lived up to it. I have no doubt that we can make as good an approach to it as is possible for any nation, not excluding

Russia, and that without violence. The most effective substitute for violent dispossession is the wheel with all its implications. Land and all property is his who will work for it. Unfortunately the workers are or have been kept ignorant of this simple fact.[2]

I have always held that social justice, even to the least and the lowliest is impossible of attainment by force. I have further believed that it is possible by further training of the lowliest by non-violent means to secure redress of the wrongs suffered by them. That means is non-violent non-co-operation. At times non-co-operation becomes as much a duty as co-operation. No one is bound to co-operate in one's own undoing or slavery. Freedom received through the effort of others, however benevolent, cannot be retained when such effort is withdrawn. In other words, such freedom is not real freedom. But the lowliest can feel its glow as soon as they learn the art of attaining it through non-violent non-co-operation.... I am quite sure that non-violent non-co-operation can secure what violence never can, and this by ultimate conversion of the wrong-doers. We in India have never given non-violence the trial it has deserved. The marvel is that we have attained so much even with our mixed non-violence.[3]

No man should have more land than he needs for dignified sustenance. Who can dispute the fact that the grinding poverty of the masses is due to their having no land that they can call their own?

But it must be realized that the reform cannot be rushed. If it is to be brought about by non-violent means, it can only be done by education both of the 'haves' and the 'have-nots'. The former should be assured that there never will be force used against them. The have-nots must be educated to know that no one can really compel them to do anything against their will, and that they can secure their freedom

Real socialism has been handed down to us by our ancestors who taught: "All land belongs to Gopal, where then is the boundary line? Man is the maker of that line and he can, therefore, unmake it." Gopal literally means shepherd; it also means God by learning the art of non-violence, *i.e.* self-suffering. If the end in view is to be achieved, the education I have adumbrated has to be commenced now. An atmosphere of mutual respect and trust has to be established as the preliminary step. There can then be no violent conflict between the classes and the masses.[4]

Who is a Socialist?

Socialism is a beautiful word and so far as I am aware in socialism all the members of society are equal—none low, none high. In the individual body, the head is not high because it is the top of the body, nor are the soles of the feet low because they touch the earth. Even as members of the individual body are equal, so are the members of society. This is socialism.

In it the prince and the peasant, the wealthy and the poor, the employer and employee are all on the same level. In terms of religion there is no duality in socialism. It is all unity. Looking at society all the world over there is nothing but duality or plurality. Unity is conspicuous by its absence. This man is high, that one is low, that is a Hindu, that a Muslim, third a Christian, fourth a Parsi, fifth a Sikh, sixth a Jew. Even among these there are sub-divisions. In the unity of my conception there is perfect unity in the plurality of designs.

In order to reach this state we may not look on things philosophically and say that we need not make a move until all are converted to socialism. Without changing our life we may go on giving addresses, forming parties and hawk-like seize the game when it comes our way. This is no socialism. The more we treat it as game to be seized, the farther it must recede from us.

Socialism begins with the first convert. If there is one such, you can add zeroes to the one and the first zero will count for ten and every addition will count for ten times the previous number. If,

> *None low, none high. In the individual body, the head is not high because it is the top of the body, nor are the soles of the feet low because they touch the earth. Even as members of the individual body are equal, so are the members of society. This is socialism*

however, the beginner is a zero, in other words, no one makes the beginning, multiplicity of zeroes will also produce zero value. Time and paper occupied in writing zeroes will be so much waste.

This socialism is as pure as crystal. It, therefore, requires crystal-like means to achieve it. Impure means result in an impure end. Hence the prince and the peasant will not be equalized by cutting off the prince's head, nor can the process of cutting off equalize the employer and the employed. One cannot reach truth by untruthfulness. Truthful conduct alone can reach truth. Are not non-violence and truth twins? The answer is an emphatic 'no'. Non-violence is embedded in truth and *vice versa*. Hence has it been said that they are faces of the same coin. Either is inseparable from the other. Read the coin either way. The spelling of words will be different. The value is the same. This blessed state is unattainable without perfect purity. Harbour impurity of mind or body and you have untruth and violence in you.

Therefore, only truthful, non-violent and pure-hearted Socialists will be able to establish a socialistic society in India and the world. To my knowledge there is no country in the world which is purely socialist. Without the means described above the existence of such a society is impossible.[5]

6

INDIA AND COMMUNISM

I must confess that I have not yet been able to fully understand the meaning of Bolshevism. All that I know is that it aims at the abolition of the institution of private property. This is only an application of the ethical ideal of non-possession in the realm of economics and if the people adopted this ideal of their own accord or could be made to accept it by means of peaceful persuasion, there would be nothing like it. But from what I know of Bolshevism it not only does not preclude the use of force, but freely sanctions it for the expropriation of private property and maintaining the collective State ownership of the same. And if that is so, I have no hesitation in saying that the Bolshevik regime in its present form cannot last for long. For it is my firm conviction that nothing enduring can be built on violence. But, be that as it may, there is no questioning the fact that the Bolshevik ideal has behind it the purest sacrifice of countless men and women who have given up their all for its sake, and an ideal that is sanctioned by the sacrifices of such master spirits as Lenin cannot go in vain; the noble example of their renunciation will be emblazoned for ever and quicken and purify the ideal as time passes.[1]

Socialism and communism of the West are based on certain conceptions which are fundamentally different from ours. One such conception is their belief in the essential selfishness of human nature. I do not subscribe to it for I know that the essential difference between man and the brute is that the former can respond to the call of the spirit in him, can rise superior to the passions that he owns in common with the brute and, therefore, superior to selfishness and violence, which belong to the brute nature and not to the immortal spirit of man. That is the fundamental conception of Hinduism, which has years of penance and austerity at the back of discovery of this truth. That is why, whilst we have had saints who have worn out their bodies and laid down their lives in order to explore the secrets of the soul, we have had none, as in the West, who laid down their lives in exploring the remotest or the highest regions of the earth. Our socialism or communism should, therefore, be based on non-violence and on harmonious co-operation of labour and capital, landlord and tenant.[2]

What does communism mean in the last analysis? It means a classless society—an ideal that is worth striving for. Only I part company with it when force is called to aid for achieving it. We are all born equal, but we have all these centuries resisted the will of God. The idea of inequality, of 'high and low', is an evil, but I do not believe in eradicating evil from the human breast at the point of the bayonet. The human breast does not lend itself to that means.[3]

Communism of the Russian type, that is communism which is imposed on a people, would be repugnant to India. If communism came without any violence, it would be welcome. For then no property would be held by anybody except on behalf of the people and for the people. A millionaire may have his millions but he will hold them for the people. The State could take charge of them, whenever they would need them for the common cause.[4]

The Socialists and Communists say they can do nothing to bring about economic equality today. They will just carry on propaganda in its favour and to that end they believe in generating and accentuating hatred. They say, when they get control over the State they will enforce equality. Under my plan the State will be there to carry out the will of the people, not to dictate to them or force them to do its will. I shall bring about economic equality through non-violence, by converting the people to my point of view by harnessing the forces of love as against hatred. I will not wait till I have converted the whole society to my view but will straight away make a beginning with myself. It goes without saying that I cannot hope to bring about economic equality of my conception, if I am the owner of fifty motor cars or even of ten *bighas* of land. For that I have to reduce myself to the level of the poorest of the poor. That is what I have been trying to do for the last fifty years or more, and so I claim to be a foremost Communist although I make use of cars and other facilities offered to me by the rich. They have no hold on me and I can shed them at a moment's notice, if the interests of the masses demand it.[5]

We must have the ability and courage to subsist on what our soil can give us rather than depend on foreign charity. Otherwise we shall not deserve to exist as an independent country. The same applies to foreign ideologies. I would accept them only to the extent that I can assimilate them and adapt them to the Indian scene. But I must refuse to go under them.[6]

7
THE CURSE OF INDUSTRIALISM

There is a growing body of enlightened opinion which distrusts this civilization which has insatiable material ambition at one end and consequent war at the other. But whether good or bad, why must India become industrial in the Western sense? The Western civilization is urban. Small countries like England or Italy may afford to urbanize their systems. A big country like America with a very sparse population, perhaps, cannot do otherwise. But one would think that a big country, with a teeming population with an ancient rural tradition which has hitherto answered its purpose, need not, must not copy the Western model. What is good for one nation situated in one condition is not necessarily good enough for another differently situated. One man's food is often another man's poison. Physical geography of a country has a predominant share in determining its culture. A fur coat may be a necessity for the dweller in the polar regions, it will smother those living in the equatorial regions.[1]

I would categorically state my conviction that the mania for mass-

> *When production and consumption both become localized, the temptation to speed up production, indefinitely and at any price, disappears. All the endless difficulties and problems that our present-day economic system presents, too, would then come to an end*

production is responsible for the world crisis. Granting for the moment that machinery may supply all the needs of humanity, still, it would concentrate production in particular areas, so that you would have to go about in a roundabout way to regulate distribution; whereas, if there is production and distribution both in the respective areas where things are required, it is automatically regulated, and there is less chance for fraud, none for speculation.

You see that these nations (Europe and America) are able to exploit the so-called weaker or unorganized races of the world. Once these races gain an elementary knowledge and decide that they are no more going to be exploited, they will simply be satisfied with what they can provide themselves. Mass-production, then at least where the vital necessities are concerned, will disappear.

> Machinery has its place; it has come to stay. But it must not be allowed to displace necessary human labour

When production and consumption both become localized, the temptation to speed up production, indefinitely and at any price, disappears. All the endless difficulties and problems that our present-day economic system presents, too, would then come to an end.[2]

Machinery has its place; it has come to stay. But it must not be allowed to displace necessary human labour. I would welcome every improvement in the cottage machine, but I know that it is criminal to displace hand labour by the introduction of power-driven spindles unless one is at the same time ready to give millions of farmers some other occupation in their houses.[3]

I refuse to be dazzled by the seeming triumph of machinery. I am uncompromisingly against all destructive machinery. But simple tools and instruments and such machinery as saves individual labour and lightens the burden of the millions of cottages, I should welcome.[4]

Dead machinery must not be pitted against the millions of living machines represented by the villagers scattered in the seven hundred thousand villages of India. Machinery to be well used has to help and ease human effort. The present use of machinery tends more and more to concentrate wealth in the hands of a few in total disregard of millions of men and women whose bread is snatched by it out of their mouths.[5]

Industrialization on a mass scale will necessarily lead to passive or active exploitation of the villagers as the problems of competition and marketing come in. Therefore, we have to concentrate on the village being self-contained, manufacturing mainly for use. Provided this character of the industry is maintained, there would be no objection to villagers using even the modern machines and tools that they can make and can afford to use. Only they should not be used as a means of exploitation of others.[6]

I do not believe that industrialization is necessary in any case for any country. It is much less so for India. Indeed, I believe that Independent India can only discharge her duty towards a groaning world by adopting a simple but ennobled life by developing her thousands of cottages and living at peace with the world. High thinking is inconsistent with complicated material life based on high speed imposed on us by Mammon worship. All the graces of life are possible only when we learn the art of living nobly.

There may be sensation in living dangerously. We must draw the distinction between living in the face of danger and living dangerously. A man who dares to live alone in a forest infested by wild beasts and wilder men without a gun and with God as his only Help, lives in the face of danger. A man who lives perpetually in mid-air and dives to the earth below to the admiration of a gaping world lives dangerously. One is a purposeful, the other a purposeless life.

Whether such plain living is possible for an isolated nation, however large geographically and numerically in the face of a world, armed to the teeth, and in the midst of pomp and circumstance, is a question open to the doubt of a sceptic. The answer is straight and simple. If plain life is worth living, then the attempt is worth making, even though

> *I do not believe in armchair or armed socialism. I believe in action according to my belief, without waiting for wholesale conversion*

only an individual or a group makes the effort.

At the same time I believe that some key industries are necessary. I do not believe in armchair or armed socialism. I believe in action according to my belief, without waiting for wholesale conversion. Hence, without having to enumerate key industries, I would have State ownership, where a large number of people have to work together. The ownership of the products of their labour, whether skilled or unskilled, will vest in them through the State. But as I can conceive such a State only based on non-violence, I would not dispossess moneyed men by force but would invite their co-operation in the process of conversion to State ownership. There are no *pariahs* of society, whether they are millionaires or paupers. The two are sores of the same disease. And all are men "for a' that".

And I avow this belief in the face of the inhumanities we have witnessed and may still have to witness in India as elsewhere. Let us live in the face of danger.[7]

8

CLASS WAR

I do not teach the masses to regard the capitalists as their enemies, but I teach them that they are their own enemies.[1]

The class war is foreign to the essential genius of India which is capable of evolving communism broad-based on fundamental rights of all on equal justice. The Ramarajya of my dream ensures the right alike of prince and pauper.[2]

I never said that there should be co-operation between the exploiter and the exploited so long as exploitation and the will to exploit persists. Only I do not believe that the capitalists and the landlords are all exploiters by an inherent necessity, or that there is a basic or irreconcilable antagonism between their interests and those of the masses. All exploitation is based on co-operation, willing or forced, of the exploited. However much we may detest admitting it, the fact remains that there would be no exploitation if people refuse to obey the exploiter. But self comes in and we hug the chains that bind us. This must cease. What is needed is not the extinction of landlords and capitalists, but a transformation of the existing relationship between them and the masses into

> All exploitation is based on co-operation, willing or forced, of the exploited. However much we may detest admitting it, the fact remains that there would be no exploitation if people refuse to obey the exploiter. But self comes in and we hug the chains that bind us. This must cease

something healthier and purer.

The idea of class war does not appeal to me. In India a class war is not only not inevitable, but it is avoidable if we have understood the message of non-violence. Those who talk about class war as being inevitable have not understood the implications of non-violence or have understood them only skin-deep.

Let us not be obsessed with catchwords and seductive slogans imported from the West. Have we not our distinct Eastern tradition? Are we not capable of finding our own solution to the question of labour and capital? What is the system of Varnashrama but a means of harmonizing the difference between high and low, as well as between capital and labour? All that comes from the West on this subject is tarred with the brush of violence. I object to it because I have seen the wreckage that lies at the end of this road. The more thinking-set even in the West today stand aghast at the abyss for which their system is heading. And I owe whatever influence I have in the West to my ceaseless endeavour to find a solution which promises an escape from the vicious circle of violence and exploitation. I have been a sympathetic student of the Western social order and I have discovered that underlying the fever that fills the soul of the West there is a restless search for truth. I value that spirit. Let us study our Eastern institutions in that spirit of scientific enquiry and we shall evolve a truer socialism and a truer communism than the world has yet dreamed of. It is surely wrong to presume that Western socialism or communism is the last word on the question of mass poverty.[3]

I do not want to destroy the zamindar, but neither do I feel that the zamindar is inevitable. I expect to convert the zamindar and other capitalists by the non-violent method, and therefore, there is for me nothing like an inevitability of class conflict. For it is an essential part of non-violence to go along the line of least resistance. The moment the cultivators of the soil realize their power, the zamindari evil will be sterilized. What can the poor zamindar do when they say that they will simply not work the land unless they are paid enough to feed and clothe and educate themselves and their children in a decent manner? In reality the toiler is the owner of what he produces. If the toilers intelligently combine, they will become an irresistible power. That is how I do not see the necessity of class conflict. If I thought it inevitable, I should not hesitate to preach it and teach it.[4]

The problem is not to set class against class, but to educate labour to a sense of its dignity. Moneyed men after all form a microscopic minority in the world. They will act on the square, immediately labour realizes its power and yet acts on the square. To inflame labour against moneyed men is to perpetuate class hatred and all the evil consequences flowing form it. The strife is a vicious circle to be avoided at any cost. It is an admission of weakness, a sign of inferiority complex. The moment labour recognizes its own dignity, money will find its rightful place, *i.e.* it will be held in trust for labour. For labour is more than money.[5]

9
STRIKES

Strikes are the order of the day. They are a symptom of the existing unrest. All kinds of vague ideas are floating in the air. A vague hope inspires all, and great will be the disappointment if that vague hope does not take definite shape. The labour world in India, as elsewhere, is at the mercy of those who set up as advisers and guides. The latter are not always scrupulous, and not always wise even when they are scrupulous. The labourers are dissatisfied with their lot. They have every reason for dissatisfaction. They are being taught, and justly, to regard themselves as being chiefly instrumental in enriching their employers. And so it requires little effort to make them lay down their tools. The political situation too is beginning to affect the labourers of India. And there are not wanting labour leaders who consider that strikes may be engineered for political purposes.

In my opinion, it will be a most serious mistake to make use of labour strikes for such a purpose. I don't deny that such strikes can serve political ends. But they do not fall within the plan of non-violent non-co-operation. It does not require much effort of the intellect to perceive that it is a most dangerous thing to make political use of labour until labourers understand the political condition of the country and are prepared to work for the common good. This is hardly to be expected of them all of a sudden and untill they have bettered their own condition so as to enable them to keep body and soul together in a decent manner.[1]

The greatest political contribution that labourers can make

is to improve their own condition, to become better informed, to insist on their rights, and even to demand proper use by their employers of the manufactures in which they have had such an important hand. The proper evolution, therefore, would be for the labourers to raise themselves to the status of part proprietors.

Strikes, therefore, for the present should only take place for the direct betterment of the labourers' lot, and when they have acquired the spirit of patriotism, for the regulation of prices of the manufactures.

The conditions of successful strike are simple. And when they are fulfilled a strike never need fail.

- The cause of the strike must be just.
- There should be practical unanimity among the strikers.
- There should be no violence used against non-strikers.
- Strikers should be able to maintain themselves during the strike period without falling back upon union funds and should therefore occupy themselves in some useful and productive temporary occupation.
- A strike is no remedy when there is enough other labour to replace strikers. In that case in the event of unjust treatment or inadequate wages or the like, resignation is the remedy.
- Successful strikes have taken place even when the above conditions have not been fulfilled, but that merely proves that the employers were weak and had a guilty conscience.[2]

Obviously there should be no strike which is not justifiable on merits. No unjust strike should succeed. All public sympathy must be withheld from such strikes. The public has no means of judging the merits of a strike, unless it is backed by impartial persons enjoying public confidence. Interested men cannot judge the merits of their own case. Hence, there must be an arbitration accepted by the parties or a judicial adjudication....

As a rule, the matter does not come before the public when there is accepted arbitration or adjudication. Cases have, however, happened when haughty employers have ignored awards or misguided employees, conscious of their power to assert themselves, have done likewise and have decided upon forcible extortion.[3]

Strikes for economic betterment should never have a political end as an ulterior motive. Such a mixture never advances the political end and generally brings trouble upon strikers, even when they do not dislocate public life, as in the case of public utility services, such as the postal strike. The Governemt may suffer some inconvenience, but will not come to a stand-still. Rich persons will put up expensive postal services but the vast mass of the poor people will be deprived during such a strike of a convenience of primary importance to which they have become used for generations. Such strikes can only take place when every other legitimate means has been adopted and failed.

It follows from the foregoing that political strikes must be treated on their own merits and must never be mixed up with or related to economic strikes. Political strikes have a definite place in non-violent action. They are never taken up haphazard. They must be open, never led by *goondaism*. They are calculated never to lead to violence.[4]

10

CHOICE BEFORE LABOUR

Two paths are open before India today, either to introduce the Western principle of "Might is Right" or to uphold the Eastern principle that truth alone conquers, that truth knows no mishap, that the strong and the weak have alike a right to secure justice. The choice is to begin with the labouring class. Should the labourers obtain an increment in their wages by violence, even if that be possible? They cannot resort to anything like violence howsoever legitimate may be their claims. To use violence for securing rights may seem an easy path, but it proves to be thorny in the long run. Those who live by the sword die also by sword. The swimmer often dies by drowning. Look at Europe. No one seems to be happy there, for, not one is contended. The labourer does not trust the capitalist and the capitalist has no faith in the labourer. Both have a sort of vigour and strength but even the bulls have it. They fight to the very bitter end. All motion is not progress. We have got no reason to believe that the people of Europe are progressing. Their possession of wealth does not argue the possession of any moral or spiritual qualities. King Duryodhana was a master of untold wealth, but with all that he was a pauper in comparison with Vidura and Sudama. Today the world adores Vidura and Sudama, whereas Duryodhana's name is remembered only as a byword for the evil qualities one should shun.

...In the struggle between capital and labour, it may be generally said that more often than not the capitalists are in the wrong box. But when labour comes fully to realize its strength,

I know it can become more tyrannical than capital. The mill-owners will have to work on the terms dictated by labour if the latter could command intelligence of the former. It is clear, however, that labour will never attain to that intelligence. If it does, labour will cease to be labour and become itself the master. The capitalists do not fight on the strength of money alone. They possess intelligence and tact.

The question before us is this : When the labourers, remaining what they are, develop a certain consciousness, what should be their course? It would be suicidal if the labourers rely upon their numbers or brute-force, *i.e.* violence. By so doing they will do harm to industries in the country. If on the other hand they take their stand on pure justice and suffer in their person to secure it, not only will they always succeed but they will reform their masters, develop industries and both master and men will be as members of one and the same family. A satisfactory solution of the condition of labour must include the following :
- The hours of labour must leave the workmen some hours of leisure;
- They must get facilities for their own education;
- Provision should be made for an adequate supply of milk, clothing and necessary education for their children;
- There should be sanitary dwellings for the workmen;
- They should be in a position to save enough to maintain themselves during their old age.

None of these conditions is satisfied today. For this both the parties are responsible. The masters care only for the service they get. What becomes of the labourer does not concern them. All their endeavours are generally confined to obtaining maximum service with minimum payment. The labourer on the other hand tries to hit upon all tricks whereby he can get maximum pay with minimum work. The result is that although the labourers get an increment there is no improvement in the work turned out. The relations between the two parties are not purified and the labourers do not make proper use of the increment they get.

A third party has sprung up between these two parties. It has become the labourers' friend. There is need for such a party. Only to the extent to which this party has disinterested friendship for the labourers can it befriend them.

A time has come now when attempts will be made to use labour as a pawn in more ways than one. The occasion demands consideration at the hands of those that would take part in politics. What will they choose? Their own interest or the service of labour and the nation? Labour stands in sore need of friends. It cannot proceed without a lead. What sort of men give this lead will decide the condition of labour.

Strikes, cessation of work and *hartal* are wonderful things no doubt, but it is not difficult to abuse them. Workmen ought to organize themselves into strong labour unions, and on no account shall they strike work without the consent of these unions. Strike should not be risked without negotiation with the mill-owners. If the mill-owners resort to arbitration, the principle of *Panchayat* should be accepted. And once the *pancha* are appointed, their decision must be accepted by both the parties alike, whether they like it or not.[1]

It is my universal experience that as a rule labour discharges its obligations more effectively and more conscientiously than the master who has corresponding obligations towards the labourers. It, therefore, becomes necessary for labour to find out how far labour can impose its will on the masters. If we find that we are not adequately paid or housed, how are we to receive enough wages, and good accommodation? Who is to determine the standard of comfort required by the labourers? The best way, no doubt, is that you labourers understand your own rights, understand the method of enforcing your rights and enforce them. But for that you require a little previous training—education.

In my humble opinion labour can always vindicate itself if labour is sufficiently

> If instead of insisting on rights everyone does his duty, there will immediately be the rule of order established among mankind

united and self-sacrificing. No matter how oppressive the capitalists may be, I am convinced that those who are connected with labour and guide the labour movement have themselves no idea of the resources that labour can command and which capital can never command. If labour would only understand and recognize that capital is perfectly helpless without labour, labour will immediately come to its own.[2]

We have unfortunately come under the hypnotic suggestion and the hypnotic influence of capital, so that we have come to believe that capital is all in all on this earth. But a moment's thought would show that labour has at its disposal capital which the capitalists will never possess....There is in English a very potent word, and you have it in French also, all the languages of the world have it—it is "No" and the secret that we have hit upon is that when capital wants labour to say "Yes", labour roars out "No" if it means "No". And immediately labour comes to recognize that it has got the choice before it of saying "Yes", when it wants to say "Yes" and "No", when it wants to say "No", labour is free of capital and capital has to woo labour. And it would not matter in the slightest degree that capital has guns and even poison gas at its disposal. Capital would still be perfectly helpless if labour would assert its dignity by making good its "No". Then labour does not need to retaliate but labour stands defiant receiving the bullets and poison gas and still insists upon its "No". The whole reason why labour so often fails is that instead of sterilizing capital as I have suggested, labour, (I am speaking as a labourer myself) wants to seize that capital and become capitalist itself in the worst sense of the term. And the capitalist, therefore, who is properly entrenched and organized, finding among the labourers also candidates for the same office, makes use of a portion of these to suppress labour. If we really were not under this hypnotic spell, everyone of us, men and women, would recognize this rock-bottom truth without the slightest difficulty.[3]

11

RIGHTS OR DUTIES?

I want to deal with one great evil that is afflicting society today. The capitalist and the zamindar talk of their rights, the labourer on the other hand of his, the prince of his divine right to rule, the ryot of his to resist it. If all simply insist on rights and no duties, there will be utter confusion and chaos.

If instead of insisting on rights everyone does his duty, there will immediately be the rule of order established among mankind. There is no such thing as the divine right of kings to rule and the humble duty of the ryots to pay respectful obedience to their masters. Whilst it is true that these hereditary inequalities must go as being injurious to the well-being of the society, the unabashed assertion of rights of the hitherto down-trodden millions is equally injurious, if not more so to the same well-being. The latter behaviour is probably calculated to injure the millions rather than the few claimants of divine rights. They could but die a brave or cowardly death but those few would not bring in the orderly life of blissful contentment. It is, therefore, necessary to understand the correlation of the rights and duties. I venture to suggest that rights that do not flow directly from duty well performed are not worth having. They will be usurpations, sooner discarded the better. A wretched parent who claims obedience from his children without first doing his duty by them excites nothing but contempt. It is distortion of religious precepts for a dissolute husband to expect compliance in every respect from his dutiful wife. But the children who flout their parent who is ever ready to do his duty towards them would be considered ungrateful and would harm themselves more than their parent. The same can be said about husband and wife. If you apply this simple and universal rule to employers and labourers, landlords and tenants, the princes and their subjects or the Hindus and the Muslims, you will find that the happiest relations can be established in all walks of life without creating disturbances in and dislocation of life and business which you see in India as in other parts of the world. What I call the law of Satyagraha is to be deduced from an appreciation of duties and rights flowing therefrom.

What is the duty of the Hindu towards his Muslim neighbour? His duty is to befriend him as man, to share his joys and sorrows and help him in distress. He will then have the right to expect similar treatment from his Muslim neighbour and will probably get the expected response. Supposing the Hindus are in a majority in a village with a sprinkling of Muslims in their midst, the duty of the majority towards the few Muslim neighbours is increased manifold, so much so that the few will not feel that their religion makes any difference in the behaviour of the Hindus towards them. The Hindus will *then* earn the right, *not* before, that the Muslims will be natural friends with them and in times of danger both the communities will act as one man. But suppose that the few Muslims do not reciprocate the correct behaviour of the many Hindus and show fight in every action, it will be a sign of unmanliness. What is then the duty of the many Hindus? Certainly not to over-power them by the brute strength of the many; that will be usurpation of an unearned right. Their duty will be to check their unmanly behaviour as they would that of their blood brothers. It is unnecessary for me to dilate further upon the illustration. I will close it by saying that the application will be exactly the same if the position is reversed. From what I have said it is easy enough to extend the application with profit to the whole of the present state which has become baffling because people do not apply in practice the doctrine of deriving every right from a prior duty well performed.

The same rule applies to the princes and the ryots. The former's duty is to act as true servants of the people. They will rule not by right granted by some outside authority, never by the right of the sword. They will rule by right of service, of greater wisdom. They will then have the right to collect taxes voluntarily paid and expect certain services equally voluntarily rendered, not for themselves but for the sake of the people under their care. If they fail to perform this simple and primary duty, the ryots not only owe no return duty but the duty devolves on them of resisting the princely usurpation. It may be otherwise said that the ryots earn the right of resisting the usurpation or misrule. But the resistance will become a crime against man in terms of duty if it takes the form of murder, rapine and plunder. Force that performance of duty naturally generates is the non-violent and invincible force that Satyagraha brings into being.[1]

12

THE PROBLEM OF UNEMPLOYMENT

We should be ashamed of resting or having a square meal so long as there is one able-bodied man or woman without work or food.[1]

Imagine a nation working only five hours per day on an average, and this not by choice but by force of

> We should be ashamed of resting or having a square meal so long as there is one able-bodied man or woman without work or food

circumstances, and you have a realistic picture of India. If the reader would visualize the picture, he must dismiss from his mind the busy fuss of the city life or the grinding fatigue of the factory life or the slavery of the plantation. These are but drops in the ocean of Indian humanity. If he would visualize the picture of the Indian skeleton, he must think of the eighty per cent of the population which is working its own fields, and which has practically no occupation for at least four months in the year, and which therefore lives on the borderland of starvation. This is the normal condition. The ever recurring famines make a large addition to this enforced idleness.[2]

The reason why our average life-rate is deplorably low, the reason why we are getting more and more impoverished is that we have neglected our 7,00,000 villages. We have indeed thought of them, but only to the extent of exploiting them. We read thrilling accounts of the 'glory that was Ind', and of the land that was flowing with milk and honey; but today it is a land of starving millions. We are sitting in this fine pandal under a blaze of electric lights, but we do not know that we are burning these lights at the expense of the poor. We have no right to use these lights if we forget that we owe these to them.

There is a difference between the civilization of the East—the civilization of India—and that of the West. It is not generally realized wherein the difference lies. Our geography is different, our history is different, our ways of living are different. Our continent, though vast, is a speck of the globe, but it is the most thickly populated, barring China. Well, now, the economics and civilization of a country where the pressure of population on land is greatest are and must be different from those of a country where the pressure is least. Sparsely populated, America may have need of machinery. India may not need it at all. Where there are millions and millions of units of idle labour, it is no use thinking of labour-saving devices. If someone devised a machine which saved us the trouble of using our hands to eat, eating would cease to be a pleasure, it would become a torture. The reason of our poverty is the extinction of our industries and our consequent unemployment. Some years ago India's agricultural population was said to be 70 per cent. Today it is said to be 90 per cent. It does not mean that 90 per cent are agriculturists, but that, instead of 70 per cent who depended on land, 90 per cent are now driven to depend on land. In other words, whereas there were industries and crafts enough to feed the 20 per cent, some time ago, these are no longer there and the people have thus been thrown on land. They thus steal their living, not because they want to, but because there is no more land.

Not that there is not enough land to feed our 35 crores. It is absurd to say that India is overpopulated and that the surplus population must die. I am sure that if all the land that is available was properly utilized and made to yield up to its capacity, it would surely maintain the whole population. Only we have got to be industrious and to make two blades of grass grow where one grows today.

The remedy is to identify ourselves with the poor villager and to help him make the land yield its plenty, help him produce what we need, and confine ourselves to use what he produces, live as he lives, and persuade him to take to more rational ways of diet and living.

We eat mill-ground flour, and even the poor villager walks with a head-load of half a maund grain to have it ground in the nearest flour mill. Do you know that in spite of the plenty of foodstuffs we produce we import wheat from outside and we eat the 'superfine' flour from Australia? We will not use our hand-ground flour, and the poor villager also foolishly copies us. We thus turn our wealth into waste, nectar into poison. For whole meal is the proper meal. Mill-ground flour is vitaminless flour, mill-ground flour kept for days is not only vitaminless, but poison. But we will not exert ourselves to produce flour which we must eat fresh every day, and will pay for less nutritious things and purchase ill-health in the bargain. This is not any abstruse economic truth, it is a fact which is daily happening before our eyes. The same is the case with rice and *gur* and oil. We will eat rice, polished of its substance, and eat less nutritious sugar and pay more for it than more nutritious *gur*. We have suffered the village oilman to be driven to extinction and we eat adulterated oils. We idolize the cow, but kill her by slow degrees. We eat honey and kill the honey-bee, with the result that honey is such a rare commodity today that it is only available to a 'Mahatma' like me or to those who must have it from the physician as a vehicle for the drugs he prescribes. If we took the trouble of learning scientific and harmless bee-keeping, we should get it cheaper and our children would get out of it all the carbohydrates they need. In all our dietetics we mistake the shadow for the substance, preferring bone-white sugar to rich brown *gur* and pale white bread to rich brown bran-bread.

We are said to be a nation of daily bathers. That we are, to be sure, but we are none the better for it. For we bathe with unclean water, we foul our tanks and rivers with filth and use that water for drinking and bath. We lawyers and degree-holders and doctors will not learn the elementary principles of sanitation and hygiene. We have not yet devised the most economical method of disposal of our evacuations and we turn our open healthy spaces into breeding grounds of disease.

I implore you to throw off your inertia, to bestir yourselves to study these elementary facts and live more rational lives and learn how to turn waste into wealth. I have told you simple truths which we would soon realize and act up to if we threw off the inertia of ages. But we have shunned body-labour to the detriment of our brains, and thus rest content with the irrational ways of diet and living. Let us pull ourselves together and resolve to make our bodies and brains more active.[3]

In one sense the problem of unemployment in our country is not so difficult as in other countries. The mode of life is a great factor. The Western unemployed worker must have warm clothing, boots or shoes and socks like the rest of the people, he must have a warm house and many other things incidental to the cold climate. We do not want all these things. I have indeed wept to see the stark poverty and unemployment in our country, but I must confess our own negligence and ignorance are responsible for it. We do not know the dignity of labour as such. Thus a shoe-maker will not do anything beyond his shoes, he will think all other labour is below his dignity. That wrong notion must go. There is enough employment in India for all who will work with their hands and feet honestly. God has given everyone the capacity to work and earn more than his daily bread and whoever is ready to use that capacity is sure to find work. No labour is too mean for one who wants to earn an honest penny. The only thing is the readiness to use the hands and feet that God has given us.[4]

I hold that a working knowledge of a variety of occupations is to the working class what metal is to the capitalist. A labourer's skill is his capital. Just as the capitalist cannot make his capital fructify without the co-operation of labour, even so the working man cannot make his labour fructify without the co-operation of capital. And, if both labour and capital have the gift of intelligence equally developed in them and have confidence in their capacity to secure a fair deal, each at the hands of the other, they would get to respect and appreciate each other as equal partners in a common enterprise. They need not regard each other as inherently irreconcilable antagonists. But the difficulty is that whilst today capital is organized and seems to be securely entrenched, labour is not. The intelligence of the working man is cramped by his soulless, mechanical occupation which leaves him little scope or chance to develop his mind. It has prevented him from realizing the power and the full dignity of his status. He has been taught to believe that his wages have to be dictated by capitalists instead of his demanding his own terms. Let him only be organized along right lines and have his intelligence quickened, let him learn a variety of occupations, and he will be able to go about with his head erect and never be afraid of being without means of sustenance.[5]

13

DARIDRANARAYAN

Daridranarayan is one of the millions of names by which humanity knows God who is unnameable and unfathomable by human understanding and it means God of the poor, God appearing in the hearts of the poor.[1]

For the poor the economic is the spiritual. You cannot make any other appeal to those starving millions. It will

> *For the poor the economic is the spiritual*

fall flat on them. But you take food to them and they will regard you as their God. They are incapable of any other thought.[2]

With this very hand I have collected soiled pies from them tied tightly in their rags. Talk to them of modern progress. Insult them by taking the name of God before them in vain. They will call you and me fiends if we talk about God to them. They know, if they know God at all, a God of terror, vengeance, a pitiless tyrant.[3]

I am able to restrain myself from committing suicide by starvation because I have faith in India's awakening and her ability to put herself on the way to freedom from this desolating pauperism. Without faith in such a possibility I should cease to take interest in living.[4]

I dare not take before them the message of God. I may as well place before the dog over there the message of God as before those hungry millions who have no lustre in their eyes and whose only God is their bread. I can take before them a message of God only by taking the message of sacred work before them.

It is good enough to talk of God whilst we are sitting here after a nice breakfast and looking forward to a nicer luncheon, but how am I to talk of God to the millions who have to go without two meals a day? To them God can only appear as bread and butter. Well, the peasants of India were getting their bread from their soil. I offered them the spinning wheel in order that they may get butter and if I appear today...in my loin-cloth it is because I come as the sole representative of those half-starved, half-naked dumb millions.[5]

I recognize no God except the God that is to be found in the hearts of the dumb millions. They do not recognize His presence; I do. And I worship the God that is Truth or Truth which is God, through service of these millions.[6]

We are either ignorant or negligent of the divine law by virtue of which man has been given only his daily bread and no more, with the result that there arise inequalities with all the misery attendant upon them. The rich have a superfluous store of things which they do not need and which are, therefore, neglected and wasted; while millions starve and are frozen to death for want of them. If each retained possession only of what he needed, no one would be in want and all would live in contentment. As it is, the rich are discontented no less than the poor. The poor man would become a millionare and the millionaire a multi-millionaire. The poor are often not satisfied when they get just enough to fill their stomachs; but they are clearly entitled to it and society should make it a point to see that they get it. The rich must take an initiative in the matter with a view to a universal diffusion of the spirit of contentment. If only they keep their own property within moderate limits the poor will be easily fed, and will learn the lesson of contentment along with the rich.[7]

> Civilization in the real sense of the term consists not in the multiplication but in the deliberate and voluntary reduction of wants, which promotes real happiness and contentment and increases the capacity for service

Civilization in the real sense of the term consists not in the multiplication but in the deliberate and voluntary reduction of wants, which promotes real happiness and contentment and increases the capacity for service. One can reduce one's wants by perseverance, and the reduction of wants makes for happiness—a healthy body and a peaceful mind.[8]

The golden rule...is resolutely to refuse to have what millions cannot. This ability to refuse will not descend upon us all of a sudden. The first thing is to cultivate the mental attitude that will not have possessions or facilities denied to millions, and the next immediate thing is to re-arrange our lives as fast as possible in accordance with that mentality.[9]

Jesus, Muhammed, Buddha, Nanak, Kabir, Chaitanya, Shankara, Dayanand, Ramakrishna were men who exercised an immense influence over and moulded the character of thousands of men. The world is the richer for their having lived in it. And they were all men who deliberately embraced poverty as their lot.[10]

14

THE GOSPEL OF BREAD LABOUR

The great Nature has intended us to earn our bread in the sweat of our brow. Everyone, therefore, who idles away a single minute becomes to that extent a burden upon his neighbours, and to do so is to commit a breach of the very first lesson of Ahimsa....Ahimsa is nothing if not a well-balanced exquisite consideration for one's neighbour, and an idle man is wanting in that elementary consideration.[1]

The divine law, that man must earn his bread by labouring with his own hands, was first stressed by a Russian writer named T.M. Bondaref. Tolstoy advertised it and gve it wide publicity. In my view the same principle has been set forth in the third chapter of the Gita, where we are told, that he who eats without offering sacrifice eats stolen food. Sacrifice here can only mean bread labour.

Reason too leads to an identical conclusion. How can a man, who does not do body labour, have the right to eat? 'In the sweat of thy brow shalt thou eat thy bread', says the Bible. A millionaire cannot carry on for long, and will soon get tired of his life, if he rolls in his bed all day long, and is even helped to his food.

> If everyone, whether rich or poor, has thus to take exercise in some shape or form, why should it not assume the form of productive, i.e. bread labour?

He, therefore, induces hunger by exercise and helps himself to the food he eats. If everyone, whether rich or poor, has thus to take exercise in some shape or form, why should it not assume the form of productive, *i.e.* bread labour? No one asks the cultivator to take breathing exercise or to work his muscles. And more than nine-tenths of humanity lives by tilling the soil. How much happier, healthier and more peaceful would the world become, if the remaining tenth followed the example of the overwhelming majority, at least to the extent of labouring enough for their food !

There is a world-wide conflict between capital and labour, and the poor envy the rich. If all worked for their bread, distinctions of rank would be obliterated; the rich would still be there, but they would deem themselves only trustees of their property, and would use it mainly in the public interest.

Bread labour is a veritable blessing to one who would observe non-violence, worship Truth and make the observance of *brahmacharya* a natural act. This labour can truly be related to agriculture alone. But at present at any rate, everybody is not in a position to take to it. A person can therefore spin or weave, or take up carpentry or smithery, instead of tilling the soil, always regarding agriculture, however, to be the ideal. Every one must be his own scavenger. Evacuation is as necessary as eating; and the best thing would be for every one to dispose of his own waste. If this is impossible, each family should see to its own scavenging.

I have felt for years, that there must be something radically wrong, where scavenging has been made the concern of a separate class in society. We have no historical record of the man who first assigned the lowest status to this essential sanitary service. Whoever he was, he by no means did us a good. We should, from our very childhood, have the idea impressed upon our minds that we are all scavengers, and the easiest way of doing so is, for every one who has realized this, to commence bread-labour as a scavenger. Scavenging, thus intelligently taken up, will help to a true appreciation of the equality of man.[2]

The true source of rights is duty. If we all discharge our duties, rights will not be far to seek. If leaving duties unperformed we run after rights, they escape us like a will-o'-the-wisp. The more we pursue them, the farther they fly. The same teaching has been embodied by Krishna in the immortal words: 'Action alone is thine. Leave thou the fruit severely alone.' Action is duty: fruit is the right.[3]

Every man has an equal right to the necessaries of life even as birds and beasts have. And since every right carries with it a corresponding duty and the corresponding remedy for resisting any attack upon it, it is merely a matter of finding out the corresponding duties and remedies to vindicate the elementary fundamental equality. The corresponding duty is to labour with my limbs and the corresponding remedy is to non-co-operate with him who deprives me of the fruit of my labour.[4]

> *The true source of rights is duty. If we all discharge our duties, rights will not be far to seek*

If all laboured for their bread and no more, then there would be enough food and enough leisure for all. Then there would be no cry of over-population, no disease and no such misery as we see around. Such labour will be the highest form of sacrifice. Men will no doubt do many other things either through their bodies or through their minds, but all this will be labour of love for the common good. There will then be no rich and no poor, none high and none low, no touchable and no untouchable.

This may be an unattainable ideal. But we need not, therefore, cease to strive for it. Even if, without fulfilling the whole law of sacrifice, that is, the law of our being, we performed physical labour enough for our daily bread, we should go a long way towards the ideal.

If we did so, our wants would be minimized, our food would be simple. We should then eat to live, not live to eat. Let anyone who doubts the accuracy of this proposition try to sweat for his bread, he will derive the greatest relish from the productions of his labour, improve his health, and discover that many things he took were superfluities.[5]

Intelligent bread labour is any day the highest form of social service.

The adjective 'intelligent' has been prefixed to labour in order to show that labour to be social service must have that definite purpose behind it. Otherwise every labourer can be said to render social service. He does in a way, but what is meant here is something much more than that. A person who labours for the general good of all serves society and is worthy of his hire. Therefore, such bread labour is not different from social service.[6]

May not men earn their bread by intellectual labour? No. The needs of the body must be supplied by the body. "Render unto Caesar that which is Caesar's" perhaps applies here well. Mere mental, that is, intellectual labour is for the soul and is its own satisfaction. It should never demand payment. In the ideal state, doctors, lawyers and the like will work solely for the benefit of society, not for self. Obedience to the law of bread labour will bring about a silent revolution in the structure of society. Man's triumph will consist in substituting the struggle for existence by the struggle for mutual service. The law of the brute will be replaced by the law of man.

Return to the villages means a definite, voluntary recognition of the duty of bread labour and all it connotes. But says the critic, "Millions of India's children are today living in the villages and yet they are living a life of semi-starvation." This, alas, is but too true. Fortunately we know that theirs is not voluntary obedience. They would perhaps shirk body labour if they could, and even rush to the nearest city if they could be accommodated in it. Compulsory obedience to a master is a state of slavery, willing obedience to one's father is the glory of sonship. Similarly compulsory obedience to the law of bread labour breeds poverty, disease and discontent. It is a state of slavery. Willing obedience to it must bring contentment and health. And it is health which is real wealth, not pieces of silver and gold. The Village Industries Association is an experiment in willing bread labour.[7]

Beggary

My Ahimsa would not tolerate the idea of giving a free meal to a healthy person who has not worked for it in some honest way, and if I had the power, I would stop every

My Ahimsa would not tolerate the idea of giving a free meal to a healthy person who has not worked for it in some honest way *sadavrata* where free meals are given. It has degraded the nation and it has encouraged laziness, idleness, hypocrisy and even crime. Such misplaced charity adds nothing to the wealth of the country, whether material or spiritual, and gives a false sense of meritoriousness to the donor. How nice and wise it would be if the donor were to open institutions where they would give meals under healthy, clean surroundings to men and women who would work for them. I personally think that the spinning wheel or any of the processes that cotton has to go through will be an ideal occupation. But if they will not have that, they may choose any other work; only the rule should be "No labour, no meal". Every city has its own difficult problem of beggars, a problem for which the moneyed men are responsible. I know that it is easier to fling free meals in the faces of idlers, but much more difficult to organize an institution where honest work has to be done before meals are served. From a pecuniary standpoint, in the initial stages at any rate, the cost of feeding people after taking work from them will be more than the cost of the present free kitchens. But I am convinced that it will be cheaper in the long run, if we do not want to increase in geometrical progression the race of loafers which is fast over-running this land.[8]

I do feel that whilst it is bad to encourage begging, I will not send away a beggar without offering him work and food. If he does not work, I shall let him go without food. Those who are physically disabled like the halt and the maimed have got to be supported by the State. There is, however, a lot of fraud going on under cover of pretended blindness or even genuine blindness. So many blind have become rich because of ill-gotten gains. It would be a good thing if they were taken to an asylum, rather than be exposed to this temptation.[9]

15

SARVODAYA

To observe morality is to attain mastery over our mind and our passions. We notice that the mind is a restless bird; the more it gets the more it wants, and still remains unsatisfied. The more we indulge our passions the more unbridled they become. Our ancestors, therefore, set a limit to our indulgences. They saw that happiness was largely a mental condition. A man is not necessarily happy because he is rich, or unhappy because he is poor. The rich are often seen to be unhappy, the poor to be happy. Millions will always remain poor. Observing all this, our ancestors dissuaded us from luxuries and pleasures. We have managed with the same kind of plough as existed thousands of years ago. We have retained the same kind of cottages that we had in former times and our indigenous education remains the same as before. We have had no system of life-corroding competition. Each followed his own occupation or trade and charged a regulation wage. It was not that we did not know how to invent machinery, but our forefathers knew that, if we set our hearts after such things, we would become slaves and lose our moral fibre. They, therefore, after due deliberation, decided that we should only do what we could with our hands and feet. They saw that our real happiness and health consisted in a proper use of our hands and feet. They further reasoned that large cities were a snare and a uselesss encumbrance and that people would not be happy in them, that there would be gangs of thieves and robbers, prostitution and vice flourishing in them and that poor men would be robbed by rich men. They were, therefore, satisfied with small villages. The saw that kings and their swords were inferior to the sword of ethics, and they therefore, held the sovereigns of the earth to be inferior to the Rishis and the Fakirs. A nation with a constitution like this is fitter to teach others than to learn from others. This nation had courts, lawyers and doctors, but they were all within bounds. Everybody knew that these professions were not particularly superior; moreover, these Vakils and vaids did not rob people; they were considered people's dependents, not their masters. Justice was tolerably fair. The ordinary rule was to avoid courts. There were no touts to lure people into them. This evil, too, was noticeable only in and around capitals. The common people lived independently and followed their agricultural occupation. They enjoyed true Home Rule.[1]

> Realization of the goal is in exact proportion to that of the means. This is a proposition that admits of no exception

A life of service must be one of humility. He who would sacrifice his life for others, has hardly time to reserve for himself a place in the sun. Inertia must not be mistaken for humility, as it has been in Hinduism. True humility means most strenuous and constant endeavour entirely directed to the service of humanity. God is continuously in action without resting for a single moment. If we would serve him or become one with Him, our activity must be as unwearied as His.[2]

No work that is done in His name and dedicated to Him is small. All work when so done assumes equal merit. A scavenger who works in His service shares equal distinction with a king who uses his gifts in His name and as a mere trustee.[3]

A votary of Ahimsa cannot subscribe to the utilitarian formula (of the greatest good of the greatest number). He will strive for the greatest good of all and die in the attempt to realize the idea. he will, therefore, be willing to die, so that the others may live. He will serve himself with the rest, by himself dying. The greatest good of all inevitably includes the good of the greatest number, and therefore, he and the utilitarian will converge in many points in their career, but there does come a time when they must part company, and even work in opposite directions. The utilitarian to be logical will never sacrifice himself. The absolutist will even sacrifice himself.[4]

Service is not possible unless it is rooted in love or Ahimsa. True love is boundless like the ocean and rising and swelling within one spreads itself out and crossing all boundaries and frontiers envelops the whole world. This service is again impossible without bread labour, otherwise described in the Gita as Yajna. It is only when a man or woman has done bodily labour for the sake of service that he or she has the right to live.[5]

Not until we have reduced ourselves to nothingness can we conquer the evil in us. God demands nothing less than complete self-surrender as the price for the only real freedom that is worth having. And when a man thus loses himself, he immediatelv finds himself in the service of all that lives. It becomes his delight and his recreation. He is a new man never weary of spending himself in the service of God's creation.[6]

All our activities should be centred in Truth. Truth should be the very breath of our life. When once this stage in the pilgrim's progress is reached, all other rules of correct living will come without effort, and obedience to them will be instinctive. But without Truth it is impossible to observe any principles or rules in life.[7]

A seeker after Truth, a follower of the Law of Love, cannot hold anything against tomorrow. God never provides for the morrow. He never creates more than what is strictly needed from day to day. If, therefore, we repose faith in His Providence, we should rest assured that He will give us

> *Impure means result in an impure end*

everyday our daily bread, supplying enough that we require.[8]

Ends and Means

They say, 'means are after all means.' I would say, 'means are after all everything.' As the means so the end. There is no wall of separation between the means and the end. Indeed the Creator has given us control (and that too very limited) over means, none over the end. Realization of the goal is in exact proportion to that of the means. This is a proposition that admits of no exception.[9]

Violent means will give violent Swaraj. That would be a menace to the world and India herself.[10]

Impure means result in an impure end. Hence the prince and the peasant will not be equalized by cutting off the prince's head, nor can the process of cutting off equalize the employer and the employed. One cannot reach truth by untruthfulness. Truthful conduct alone can reach truth. Are not non-violence and truth twins? The answer is an emphatic 'no'. Non-violence is embedded in truth and *vice versa*. Hence has it been said that they are faces of the same coin. Either is inseparable from the other. Read the coin either way. The spelling of words will be different. The value is the same. This blessed state is unattainable without perfect purity. Harbour impurity of mind or body and you have untruth and violence in you.

Therefore, only truthful, non-violent and pure-hearted socialists will be able to establish a socialistic society in India and the world.[11]

16

THEORY OF TRUSTEESHIP

Suppose I have come by a fair amount of wealth either by way of legacy, or by means of trade and industry, I must know that all that wealth does not belong to me, what belongs to me is the right to an honourable livelihood, no better than that enjoyed by millions of others. The rest of my wealth belongs to the community and must be used for the welfare of the community. I enunciated this theory when the Socialist theory was placed before the country in respect to the possessions held by zamindars and ruling chiefs. They would do away with these privileged classes. I want them to outgrow their greed and sense of possession, and to come down in spite of their wealth to the level of those who earn their bread by labour. The labourer has to realize that the wealthy man is less owner of his wealth than the labourer is owner of *his* own, *viz.*, the power to work.

The question how many can be real trustees according to this definition is beside the point. If the theory is true, it is immaterial whether many live up to it or only one man lives up to it. The question is of conviction. If you accept the principle of Ahimsa, you have to strive to live up to it, no matter whether you succeed or fail. There is nothing in this theory which can be said to be beyond the grasp of intellect, though you may say it is difficult of practice.[1]

You may say that trusteeship is a legal fiction. But if people meditate over it constantly and try to act up to it, then life on earth would be governed far more by love than it is at present. Absolute trusteeship is an abstraction like Euclid's definition of a point, and is equally unattainable. But if we strive for it, we

Theory of Trusteeship   69

shall be able to go further in realizing a state of equality on earth than by any other method.... It is my firm conviction that if the State suppressed capitalism by violence, it will be caught in the coils of violence itself, and fail to develop non-violence at any time. The State represents violence in a concentrated and organized form. The individual has a soul, but as the state is a soulless machine, it can never be weaned from violence to which it owes its very existence. Hence I prefer the doctrine of trusteeship. The fear is always there that the State may use too much violence against those who differ from it. I would be very happy indeed if the people concerned behaved as trustees; but if they fail, I believe we shall have to deprive them of their possessions through the State with the minimum exercise of violence.... (That is why I said at the Round Table Conference that every vested interest must be subjected to scrutiny, and confiscation ordered where necessary....with or without compensation as the case demanded.) What I would personally prefer would be not a centralization of power in the hands of the State, but an extension of the sense of trusteeship; as in my opinion the violence of private ownership is less injurious than the violence of the State. However, if it is unavoidable, I would support a minimum of State-ownership.[2]

It has become the fashion these days to say that society cannot be organized or run on non-violent lines. I join issue on that point. In a family, when the father slaps his delinquent child, the latter does not think of retaliating. He obeys his father not because of the deterrent effect of the slap but because of the offended love which he senses behind it. That in my opinion is an epitome of the way in which society is or should be governed. What is true of the family must be true of society which is but a larger family.[3]

"तेन त्यक्तेन भुंजीथा:" is a mantra based on uncommon knowledge. It is the surest method to evolve a new order of life of universal benefit in the place of the present one where each one lives for himself without regard to what happens to his neighbour

I hold that non-violence is not merely a personal virtue. It is also a social virtue to be cultivated like the other virtues. Surely society is largely regulated by the expression of non-violence in its mutual dealings. What I ask for is an extension of it on a larger, national and international scale.[4]

My theory of 'trusteeship' is no make-shift, certainly no camouflage. I am confident that it will survive all other theories. It has the sanction of philosophy and religion behind it. That possessors of wealth have not acted up to the theory does not prove its falsity; it proves the weakness of the wealthy. No other theory is compatible with non-violence. In the non-violent method the wrong-doer compasses his own end, if he does not undo the wrong. For, either through non-violent non-co-operation he is made to see the error, or he finds himself completely isolated.[5]

I have no hesitation in endorsing the opinion that generally rich men and for that matter most men are not particular as to the way they make money. In the application of the method of non-violence, one must believe in the possibility of every person, however, depraved, being reformed under humane and skilled treatment. We must appeal to the good in human beings and expect response. Is it not conducive to the wellbeing of society that every member uses all his talents, only not for personal aggrandizement but for the good of all? We do not want to produce a dead equality where every person becomes or is rendered incapable of using his ability to the utmost possible extent. Such a society must ultimately perish. I therefore suggest that my advice that moneyed men may earn their crores (honestly only, of course) but so as to dedicate them to the service of all is perfectly sound. "तेन त्यक्तेन भुंजीथा:" is a *mantra* based on uncommon knowledge. It is the surest method to evolve a new order of life of universal benefit in the place of the present one where each one lives for himself without regard to what happens to his neighbour.[6]

17

NON-VIOLENT ECONOMY

I suggest that we are thieves in a way. If I take anything that I do not need for my own immediate use and keep it, I thieve it from somebody else. It is the fundamental law of Nature, without exception, that Nature produces enough for our wants from day to day; and if only everybody took enough for himself and nothing more, there would be no pauperism in this world, there would be no man dying of starvation. I am no socialist, and I do not want to dispossess those who have got possessions; but I do say that personally those of us who want to see light out of darkness have to follow this rule. I do not want to dispossess anybody; I should then be departing from the rule of non-violence. If somebody else possesses more than I do, let him. But so far as my own life has to be regulated I dare not possess anything which I do not want.

> I must confess that I do not draw a sharp or any distinction between economics and ethics. Economics that hurt the moral well-being of an individual or a nation are immoral and, therefore, sinful

In India we have got many millions of poeple who have to be satisfied with one meal a day, and that meal consisting of *chapati* containing no fat in it and a pinch of salt. You and I have no right to anything that we really have until these many millions are clothed and fed. You and I, who ought to know better, must adjust our wants, and even undergo voluntary privation in order that they may be nursed, fed, and clothed.[1]

I must confess that I do not draw a sharp or any distinction between economics and ethics. Economics that hurt the moral well-being of an individual or a nation are immoral and, therefore, sinful. Thus, the economics that permit one country to prey upon another are immoral. It is sinful to buy and use articles made by sweated labour.[2]

According to me the economic constitution of India and for the matter of that of the world, should be such that no one under it should suffer from want of food and clothing. In other words, everybody should be able to get sufficient work to enable him to make

> *Economic equality is the master key to non-violent independence*

the two ends meet. And this ideal can be universally utilized only if the means of production of the elementary necessaries of life remain in the control of the masses. These should be freely available to all as God's air and water are or ought to be; they should not be made a vehicle of traffic for the exploitation of others. Their monopolization by any country, nation or group of persons would be unjust. The neglect of this simple principle is the cause of the destitution that we witness today not only in this unhappy land but in other parts of the world too.[3]

True economics never militates against the highest ethical standard, just as all true ethics to be worth its name must at the same time be also good economics. An economics that inculcates Mammon worship, and enables the strong to amass wealth at the expense of the weak, is a false and dismal science. It spells death. True economics, on the other hand, stands for social justice, it promotes the good of all equally including the weakest, and is indispensable for decent life.[4]

I want to bring about an equalization of status. The working classes have all these centuries been isolated and relegated to a lower status. They have been *shoodras*, and the word has been interpreted to mean an inferior status. I want to allow no differentiation between the son of a weaver, of an agriculturist and of a schoolmaster.[5]

Economic equality is the master key to non-vilent independence. Working for economic equality means abolishing the eternal conflict between capital and labour. It means the levelling down of the few rich in whose hands is concentrated the bulk of the nation's wealth on the one hand, and a levelling up of the semi-starved naked millions on the other. A non-violent system of government is clearly an impossibility so long as the wide gulf between the rich and the hungry millions persists. The contrast between the palaces of New Delhi and the miserable hovels of the poor, labouring class cannot last one day in a free India in which the poor will enjoy the same power as the richest in the land. A violent and bloody revolution is a certainty one day unless there is a voluntary abdication of riches and the power which riches give and sharing them for the common good. I adhere to my doctrine of trusteeship in spite of the ridicule that has been poured upon it. It is true that it is difficult to reah. So is non-violence difficult to attain. But we made up our minds in 1920 to negotiate that steep ascent.[6]

I suggest that, if India is to evolve along non-violent lines, it will have to decentralize many things. Centralization cannot be sustained and defended without adequate force. Simple homes from which there is nothing to take away require no policing; the palaces of the rich must have strong guards to protect them against dacoity. So must huge factories. Rurally organized India will run less risk of foreign invasion than urbanized India, well equipped with military, naval and air forces.[7]

Today there is gross economic inequality. The basis of socialism is economic equality. There can be no Ramarajya in the present state of iniquitous inequalities in which a few roll in riches and the masses do not get even enough to eat.[8]

18

THE WAY TO EQUAL DISTRIBUTION

The real implication of equal distribution is that each man shall have the wherewithal to supply all his natural needs and no more. For example, if one man has a weak digestion and requires only a quarter of a pound of flour for his bread and another needs a pound, both should be in a position to satisfy their wants. To bring this ideal into being the entire social order has got to be reconstructed. A society based on non-violence cannot nurture any other ideal. We may not perhaps be able to realize the goal, but we must bear it in mind and work unceasingly to near it. To the same extent as we progress towards our goal we shall find contentment and happiness, and to that extent too shall we have contributed towards the bringing into being of a non-violent society.

It is prefectly possible for an individual to adopt this way of life without having to wait for others to do so. And if an individual can observe a certain rule of conduct, it follows that a group of individuals can do likewise. It is necessary for me to emphasize the fact that no one need wait for anyone else in order to adopt a right course. Men generally hesitate to make a beginning if they feel that the objective cannot be had in its entirety. Such an attitude of mind is in reality a bar to progress.

> *The real implication of equal distribution is that each man shall have the wherewithal to supply all his natural needs and no more*

Now let us consider how equal distribution can be brought

about through non-violence. The first step towards it is for him who has made this ideal part of his being to bring about the necessary changes in his personal life. He would reduce his wants to a minimum, bearing in mind the poverty of India. His earnings would be free of dishonesty. The desire for speculation would be renounced. His habitation would be in keeping with the new mode of life. There would be self-restraint exercised in every sphere of life. When he has done all that is possible in his own life, then only will he be in a position to preach this ideal among his associates and neighbours.

Indeed at the root of this doctrine of equal distribution must lie that of the trusteeship of the wealthy for the superfluous wealth possessed by them. For according to the doctrine they may not possess a rupee more than their neighbours. How is this to be brought about? Non-violently? Or should the wealthy be dispossessed of their possessions? To do this we would naturally have to resort to violence. This violent action cannot benefit society. Society will be the poorer, for it will lose the gifts of a man who knows how to accumulate wealth. Therefore the non-violent way is evidently superior. The rich man will be left in possession of his wealth, of which he will use what he reasonably requires for his personal needs and will act as a trustee for the remainder to be used for the society. In this argument honesty on the part of the trustee is assumed.

As soon as a man looks upon himself as a servant of society, earns for its sake, spends for its benefit, then purity enters into his earnings and there is Ahimsa in his venture. Moreover, if men's minds turn towards this way of life, there will come about a peaceful revolution in society, and that without any bitterness.

It may be asked whether history at any time records such a change in human nature. Such changes have certainly taken place in individuals. One may not perhaps be able to point to them in a whole society. But this only means that up till now there has never been an experiment on a large scale in non-violence. Somehow or other the wrong belief has taken possession of us that Ahimsa is pre-eminently a weapon for individuals and its use should, therefore, be limited to that sphere. In fact this is not the case. Ahimsa is definitely an attribute of society. To convince people of this truth is at once my effort and my experiment. In this age of wonders no one will say that a thing or idea is worthless because it is new. To say it is impossible because it is difficult is again not in consonance with the spirit of the age. Things undreamt of are daily being seen, the impossible is ever becoming possible. We are constantly being astonished these days at the amazing discoveries in the field of violence. But I maintain that far more undreamt of and seemingly impossible discoveries will be made in the field of non-violence. The history of religion is full of such examples. To try to root out religion itself from society is a wild goose chase. And were such an attempt to succeed, it would mean the destruction of society. Superstition, evil customs and other imperfections creep in from age to age and mar religion for the time being. They come and go. But religion itself remains, because the existence of the world in a broad sense depends on religion. The ultimate definition of religion may be said to be obedience to the law of God. God and His law are synonymous terms. Therefore God signifies an unchanging and living law. No one has really found Him. But *avatars* and prophets have, by means of their *tapasya*, given to mankind a faint glimpse of the eternal law.

If, however, in spite of the utmost effort, the rich do not become guardians of the poor in the true sense of the term and the latter are more and more crushed and die of hunger, what is to be done? In trying to find the solution to this riddle I have lighted on non-violent non-co-operation and civil disobedience as the right and infallible means. The rich cannot accumulate wealth without the co-operation of the poor in society. Man has been conversant with violence from the beginning, for he has inherited this strength from the animal in his nature. It was only when he rose from the state of a quadruped (animal) to that of a biped (man) that the knowledge of the strength of Ahimsa entered into his soul. This knowledge has grown within him slowly but surely. If this knowledge were to penetrate to and spread amongst the poor, they would become strong and would learn how to free themselves by means of non-violence from the crushing inequalities which have brought them to the verge of starvation[1]

What India needs is not the concentration of capital in a few hands, but its distribution so as to be within easy reach of the 7½ lakhs of villages that make this continent 1900 miles long and 1500 miles broad.[2]

19

INDIA'S RECORD OF NON-VIOLENCE

I have ventured to place before India the ancient law of self-sacrifice. For Satyagraha and its offshoots, non-co-operation and civil resistance are nothing but new names for the law of suffering. The Rishis, who discovered the law of non-violence in the midst of violence, were greater geniuses than Newton. They were themselves greater warriors than Wellington. Having themselves known the use of arms they realized their uselessness, and taught a weary world that its salvation lay not through violence but through non-violence. Non-violence in its dynamic condition means conscious suffering. It does not mean meek submission to the will of the evil doer, but it means pitting of one's whole soul against the will of the tyrant. Working under this law of our being, it is possible for a single individual to defy the whole might of an unjust empire to save his honour, his religion, his soul, and lay the foundation for that empire's fall or its regeneration. And so I am not pleading for India to practise non-violence because it is weak. I want her to practise non-violence being conscious of her strength and power. No training in arms is required for realization of her strength. We seem to need it, because we seem to think that we are but a

> *Non-violence in its dynamic condition means conscious suffering. It does not mean meek submission to the will of the evil doer, but it means pitting of one's whole soul against the will of the tyrant*

lump of flesh. I want India to recognize that she has a soul that cannot perish and that can rise triumphant above every physical weakness and defy the physical combination of a whole world.[1]

That Indians are not a nation of cowards is proved by the personal bravery and daring of her martial races, whether Hindu, Musalman, Sikh or Gurkha. My point is that the spirit of fighting is foreign to India's soil and that probably she has a higher part to play in the evolution of the world. Time alone can show what is to be her destiny.[2]

India's past training for ages, I mean the training of the masses, has been against violence. Human nature in India has advanced so far that the doctrine of non-violence is more natural for the people at large than that of violence.[3]

India has never waged war against any nation. She has put up sometimes ill-organized or half-organized resistance in self-defence pure and simple. She has, therefore, not got to develop the will for peace. She has that in abundance whether she knows it or not. The way she can promote peace is to offer successful resistance to her exploitation by peaceful means. That is to say, she has to achieve her independence... by peaceful means. If she can do this it will be the largest contribution that any single nation will have made towards world peace.[4]

20

THE SARVODAYA STATE

Many have shaken their heads as they have said, 'But you can't teach non-violence to the masses. It is only possible for individuals and that too in rare cases.' That is, in my opinion, a gross self-deception. If mankind was not habitually non-violent, it would have been self-destroyed ages ago. But in the duel between forces of violence and non-violence the latter have always come out victorious in the end. The

> Political power means capacity to regulate national life through national representatives

truth is that we have not had patience enough to wait and apply ourselves whole-heartedly to the spread of non-violence among the people as a means for political ends.[1]

To me political power is not an end but one of the means of enabling people to better their condition in every department of life. Political power means capacity to regulate national life through national representatives. If national life becomes so perfect as to become self-regulated, no representation becomes necessary. There is then a state of enlightened anarchy. In such a State everyone is his own ruler. He rules himself in such a manner that he is never a hindrance to his neighbour. In the ideal State, therefore, there is no political power because there is no State. But the ideal is never fully realized in life. Hence the classical statement of Thoreau that that government is best which governs the least.[2]

I look upon an increase in the power of the State with the greatest fear, because although while apparently doing good by minimizing exploitation, it does the greatest harm to mankind by destroying individuality which lies at the root of all progress.

The State represents violence in a concentrated and organized form. The individual has a soul, but as the State is a soulless machine, it can never be weaned from violence to which it owes its very existence.

What I disapprove of is an organization based on force which a State is. Voluntary organization there must be.[3]

(As to whether in an ideal society, there should be any or no government.) I do not think, we need worry ourselves about this at the moment. If we continue to work for such a society, it will slowly come into being to an extent, such that the people can benefit by it. Euclid's line is one without breadth but no one has so far been able to draw it and never will. All the same it is only by keeping the ideal line in mind that we have made progress in geometry. What is true here is true of every ideal.

> I look upon an increase in the power of the State with the greatest fear, because although while apparently doing good by minimizing exploitation, it does the greatest harm to mankind by destroying individuality which lies at the root of all progress

It must be remembered that nowhere in the world, does a State without government exist. If at all it could ever come into being, it would be in India; for, ours is the only country where the attempt has, at any rate, been made. We have not yet been able to show that bravery to the degree which is necessary and for the attainment of which there is only one way. Those who have faith in the latter, have to demonstrate it. In order to do so, the fear of death has to be completely shed, just as we have shed the fear of prisons.[4]

Police Force

Even in a non-violent State a police force may be necessary. This, I admit, is a sign of my imperfect Ahimsa. I have not the courage to declare that we can carry on without a police force as I have in respect of an army. Of course, I can and do envisage a State where the police will not be necessary; but whether we shall succeed in realizing it, the future alone will show.

The police of my conception will, however, be of a wholly different pattern from the present-day force. Its ranks will be composed of believers in non-violence. They will be servants, not masters, of the people. The people will instinctively render them every help, and through mutual co-operation they will easily deal with the ever-decreasing disturbances. The police force will have some kind of arms, but they will be rarely used, if at all. In fact the policemen will be reformers. Their police work will be confined primarily to robbers and dacoits. Quarrels between labour and capital and strikes will be few and far between in a non-violent State, because the influence of the non-violent majority will be so great as to command the respect of the principal elements in society. Similarly there will be no room for communal disturbances.[5]

21

SATYAGRAHA AND DURAGRAHA

I hold the opinion firmly that civil disobedience is the purest type of constitutional agitation. Of course, it becomes degrading and despicable, if its civil, *i.e.* non-violent character, is a mere camouflage.[1]

Disobedience to be civil must be sincere, respectful, restrained, never defiant, must be based upon some well-understood principle, must not be capricious and above all, must have no ill-will or hatred behind it.[2]

Those only can take up civil disobedience, who believe in willing obedience even to irksome laws imposed by the State so long as they do not hurt their conscience or religion, and are prepared equally willingly to suffer the penalty of civil disobedience. Disobedience to be civil has to be absolutely non-violent, the underlying principle being the winning over of the opponent by suffering, *i.e.* love.[3]

> *Disobedience to be civil must be sincere, respectful, restrained, never defiant, must be based upon some well-understood principle, must not be capricious and above all, must have no ill-will or hatred behind it*

Civil disobedience is the inherent right of a citizen. He dare not give it up without ceasing to be a man. Civil disobedience is never followed by anarchy. Criminal disobedience can lead to it. Every State puts down criminal disobedience by force. It perishes, if it does not. But to put down civil disobedience is to attempt to imprison conscience.[4]

Since Satyagraha is one of the most powerful methods of direct action, a Satyagrahi exhausts all other means before he resorts to Satyagraha. He will, therefore, constantly and continually approach the constituted authority, he will appeal to public opinion, educate public opinion, state his case calmly and coolly before everybody who wants to listen to him, and only after he has exhausted all these avenues will he resort to Satyagraha. But when he has found the impelling call of the inner voice within him and launches out upon Satyagraha he has burnt his boats and there is no receding.[5]

The word Satyagraha is often most loosely used and is made to cover veiled violence. But as the author of the word I may be allowed to say that it excludes every form of violence, veiled or unveiled, and whether in thought, word or deed. It is a breach of Satyagraha to wish ill to an opponent or to say a harsh word to him or of him with the intention of harming him.... Satyagraha is gentle, it never wounds. It must not be the result of anger or malice. It is never fussy, never impatient, never vociferous. It is the direct opposite of compulsion. It was conceived as a complete substitute for violence.[6]

Duragraha

(Following the report of Gandhiji's arrest on his way to the Punjab early in April, 1919, outbreaks of violence took place in Bombay and other places. When he was brought back to Bombay under police escort and released on the 11th April, he caused a message to be read at all meetings that evening, in the course of which he remarked as follows:)

I have not been able to understand the cause of so much excitement and disturbance that followed my detention. It is not Satyagraha. It is worse than *Duragraha*. Those who join Satyagraha demonstrations were bound one and all to refrain at all hazard from violence, not to throw stones or in any way whatever to injure anybody. But in Bombay we have been throwing stones. We have obstructed tram-cars by putting obstacles in the way. This is not Satyagraha. We have demanded the release of about 50 men who had been arrested for deeds of violence. Our duty is chiefly to get ourselves arrested. It is breach of religious duty to endeavour to secure the release of those who have committed deeds of violence. We are not, therefore, justified on any grounds whatever in demanding the release of those who have been arrested.[7]

I have said times without number that Satyagraha admits of no violence, no pillage, no incendiarism; and still in the name of Satyagraha we have burnt buildings, forcibly captured weapons, extorted money, stopped trains, cut off telegraph wires, killed innocent people and plundered shops and private houses. If deeds such as these could save me from the prison-house or the scaffold, I should not like to be so saved.[8]

I can see nothing but catastrophe for India from methods of violence. Workmen would be committing suicide and India would have to suffer indescribable misery if working men were to vent their anger by criminal disobedience of the law of the land....When I began to preach Satyagraha and civil disobedience it was never meant to cover criminal disobedience. My experience teaches me that truth can never be propagated by doing

> Those only can take up civil disobedience, who believe in willing obedience even to irksome laws imposed by the State so long as they do not hurt their conscience or religion, and are prepared equally willingly to suffer the penalty of civil disobedience

violence. Those who believe in the justice of their cause need to possess boundless patience, and those alone are fit to offer civil disobedience who are above committing criminal disobedience or doing violence. A man cannot commit both civil and criminal disobedience at the same time even as he cannot be both temperate and furious at the same time, and just as self-restraint is acquired only after one has been able to master his passions, so is the capacity for civil disobedience acquired after one has disciplined oneself in complete and voluntary obedience of the laws of the land. Again, just as he alone can be said to be proof against temptations who, having been exposed to them, has succeeded in resisting them, so may we be said to have conquered anger when having sufficient cause for it we have succeeded in controlling ourselves.[9]

Some students have revived the ancient form of barbarity in the form of 'sitting *dhurna*'. I call it 'barbarity' for it is a crude way of using coercion. It is also cowardly because one who sits *dhurna* knows that he is not going to be trampled over. It is difficult to call the practice violence, but it is certainly worse. If we fight our opponent, we at least enable him to return the blow. But when we challenge him to walk over us, we, *knowing* that he will not place him in a most awkward and humiliating position. I know that the overzealous students who sat *dhurna* never thought of the barbarity of the deed. But one, who is expected to follow the voice of conscience and stand even single-handed in the face of odds, cannot afford to be thoughtless.... There must be no impatience, no barbarity, no insolence, no undue pressure. If we want to cultivate a true spirit of democracy, we cannot afford to be intolerant. Intolerance betrays want of faith in one's cause.[10]

Indiscriminate resistance to authority must lead to lawlessness and unbridled licence and consequent self-destruction.[11]

The first indispensable condition precedent to any civil disobedience is that there should be surety against any outbreak of violence whether on the part of those who are identified with civil resistance or on the part of the general public. It would be no answer in the case of an outbreak of violence that it was instigated by the State or other agencies hostile to civil resisters. It should be obvious that civil resistance cannot flourish in an atmosphere of violence. This does not mean that the resources of a Satyagrahi have come to an end. Ways other than civil disobedience should be found out.[12]

Fasting in Satyagraha

Fasting is a potent weapon in the Satyagraha armoury. It cannot be taken by every one. Mere physical capacity to take it is no qualification for it. It is of no use without a living faith in God. It should never be a mechanical effort or a mere imitation. It must come from the depth of one's soul. It is, therefore, rare.[13]

There can be no room for selfishness, anger, lack of faith, or impatience in a pure fast... . Infinite patience, firm resolve, single-mindedness of purpose, perfect calm, and no anger must of necessity be there. But since it is impossible for a person to develop all these qualities all at once, no one who has not devoted himself to following the laws of Ahimsa should undertake a Satyagrahi fast.[14]

One general principle, however, I would like to enunciate. A Satyagrahi should fast only as a last resort when all other avenues of redress have failed. There is no room for imitation in fasts. He who has no inner strength should not dream of it, and never with attachment to success....Ridiculous fasts spread like plague and are harmful.[15]

Of course, it is not to be denied that fasts can be really coercive. Such are fasts to attain a selfish object. A fast undertaken to wring money from a person or for fulfilling some such personal end would amount to the exercise of coercion or undue influence. I would unhesitatingly advocate resistance of such undue influence. I have myself successfully resisted it in the fasts that have been undertaken or threatened against me. And if it is argued that the dividing line between a selfish and unselfish end is often very thin, I would urge that a person who regards the end of a fast to be selfish or otherwise base should resolutely refuse to yield to it, even though the refusal may result in the death of the fasting person.

If people will cultivate the habit of disregarding fasts which in their opinion are taken for unworthy ends, such fasts will be robbed of the taint of coercion and undue influence. Like all human institutions, fasting can be both legitimately and illegitimately used.[16]

22
THE TILLERS OF THE SOIL

If Indian society is to make real progress along peaceful lines, there must be a definite recognition on the part of the moneyed class that the ryot possesses the same soul that they do and that their wealth gives them no superiority over the poor. They must regard themselves even as the Japanese nobles did, as trustees holding their wealth for the good of their wards, the ryots. Then they would take no more than a reasonable amount as commission for their labours. At present there is no proportion between the wholly unnecessary pomp and extravagance of the moneyed class and the squalid surroundings and the grinding pauperism of the ryots in whose midst the former are living. A model Zamindar would therefore at once reduce much of the burden the ryot is now bearing, he would come in intimate touch with the ryots and know their wants and inject hope into them in place of the despair which is killing the very life out of them. He will not be satisfied with the ryots' ignorance of the laws of sanitation and hygiene. He will reduce himself to poverty in order that the ryot may have the necessaries of life. He will study the economic condition of the ryots under his care, establish schools in which he will educate his own children side by side with those of ryots. He will purify the village well and the village tank. He will teach the ryot to sweep his roads and clean his latrines by himself doing this necessary labour. He will throw open without reserve his own gardens for the unrestricted use of the ryot. He will use as hospital, school, or the like most of the unnecessary buildings which he keeps for his pleasure. If only the capitalist class will read the signs of the times, revise their notions of God-given right to all they possess, in an incredibly short space of time the seven hundred thousand dung-heaps which today pass muster as villages can be turned into abodes of peace, health and comfort. I am convinced that the capitalist, if he follows the Samurai of Japan, has nothing really to lose and everything to gain. There is no other choice than between voluntary surrender on the part of the capitalist of superfluities and consequent acquisition of the real happiness of all on the one hand, and on the other the impending chaos into which, if the capitalist does not wake up betimes, the awakened but ignorant and famishing millions will plunge the country and which not even the armed force that a powerful Government can bring into play can avert. I have hoped that India will successfully avert the disaster.[1]

> The Kisan or the peasant, whether as a landless labourer or a labouring proprietor, comes first. He is the salt of the earth which rightly belongs or should belong to him, not to the absentee landlord or Zamindar

The Kisan or the peasant, whether as a landless labourer or a labouring proprietor, comes first. He is the salt of the earth which rightly belongs or should belong to him, not to the absentee landlord or Zamindar. But in the non-violent way the labourer cannot forcibly eject the absentee landlord. He has so to work as to make it impossible for the landlord to exploit him. Closest co-operation amongst the peasants is absolutely necessary. To this end, special organizing bodies or committees should be formed where there are none and those already in existence should be reformed where necessary. The Kisans are for the most part illiterate. Both adults and young persons of school-going age should be educated. This applies to men and women. Where they are landless labourers their wages should be brought to a level that would ensure a decent living which should mean balanced food, dwelling houses and clothing, which should satisfy health requirements.[2]

I have no doubt that if we have democratic Swaraj as it must be if the freedom is won through non-violence, the Kisan must hold power in all its phases including political power.[3]

If Swaraj is attained by the effort of the whole people, as it must be under non-violence, the Kisans must come into their own and have the uppermost voice. But if it is not so and there is a sort of a workable compromise between the people and the Government on the basis of a limited franchise, the interests of the tiller of the soil will need close watching. If the legislature proves itself to be incapable of safeguarding Kisans' interests they will, of course, always have the sovereign remedy of civil disobedience and non-co-operation. But...ultimately it is not paper legislation nor brave words or fiery speeches but the power of non-violent organization, discipline and sacrifice that constitutes the real bulwark of the people against injustice or oppression.[4]

23

BACK TO THE VILLAGE

I have believed and repeated times without number that India is to be found not in its few cities but in its 7,00,000 villages. But we town-dwellers have believed that India is to be found in its towns and the villages were created to minister to our needs. We have hardly ever paused to inquire if those poor folk get sufficient to eat and clothe themselves with and whether they have a roof to shelter themselves from sun and rain.[1]

I have found that the town-dweller has generally exploited the villager, in fact he has lived on the poor villager's subsistence. Many a British official has written about the conditions of the people of India. No one has, to my knowledge, said that the Indian villager has enough to keep body and soul together. On the countrary they have admitted that the bulk of the population live on the verge of starvation and ten per cent are semi-starved, and that millions have to rest content with a pinch of dirty salt and chillies and polished rice or parched grain.

You may be sure that if any of us were to be asked to live on that diet, we should not expect to survive it longer than a month or should be afraid of losing our mental faculties. And yet our villagers go through that state from day to day.[2]

Over 75 per cent of the population are agriculturists. But there cannot be much spirit of self-government about us if we take away or allow others to take away from them almost the whole of the result of their labour.[3]

The cities are capable of taking care of themselves. It is the village we have to turn to. We have to disabuse them of their prejudice, their superstitions, their narrow outlook and we can do so in no other manner than that of staying amongst them and sharing their joys and sorrows and spreading education and intelligent information among them.[4]

We have got to be ideal villagers, not the villagers with their queer ideas about sanitation and giving no thought to how they eat and what they eat. Let us not, like most of them, cook anyhow, eat anyhow, live anyhow. Let us show them the ideal diet. Let us not go by mere likes and dislikes, but get at the root of those likes and dislikes.[5]

We must identify ourselves with the villagers who toil under the hot sun beating on their bent backs and see how we would like to drink water from the pool in which the villagers bathe, wash their clothes and pots, in which their cattle drink and roll. Then and not till then shall we truly represent the masses and they will, as surely as I am writing this, respond to every call

We must identify ourselves with the villagers who toil under the hot sun beating on their bent backs and see how we would like to drink water from the pool in which the villagers bathe, wash their clothes and pots, in which their cattle drink and roll. Then and not till then shall we truly represent the masses and they will, as surely as I am writing this, respond to every call.[6]

We have got to show them that they can grow their vegetables, their greens, without much expense, and keep good health. We have also to show that most of the vitamins are lost when they cook the leaves.[7]

We have to teach them how to economize time, health and money. Lionel Curtis described our villages as dung-heaps. We have to turn them into model villages. Our village-folk do not get fresh air though they are surrounded by fresh air; they don't get fresh food though they are surrounded by the freshest foods. I am talking like a missionary in this matter of food, because my mission is to make villages a thing of beauty.[8]

It is profitless to find out whether the villages of India were always what they are today. If they were never better it is a reflection upon the ancient culture in which we take so much pride. But if they were never better, how is it that they have survived centuries of decay which we see going on around us.... The task before every lover of the country is how to prevent this decay or, which is the same thing, how to reconstruct the villages of India so that it may be as easy for anyone to live in them as it is supposed to be in the cities. Indeed, it is the task before every patriot. It may be that the villagers are beyond redemption, that rural civilization has had its day and that the seven hundred thousand villages have to give place to seven hundred well-ordered cities supporting a population not of three hundred millions but thirty. If such is to be India's fate, even that won't come in a day. It must take time to wipe out a number of villages and villagers and transform the remainder into cities and citizens.[9]

The village movement is as much an education of the city people as of the villagers. Workers drawn from cities have to develop village mentality and learn the art of living after the manner of villagers. This does not mean that they have to starve like the villagers. But it does mean that there must be a radical change in the old style of life.[10]

The only way is to sit down in their midst and work away in steadfast faith, as their scavengers, their nurses, their servants, not as their patrons, and to forget all our prejudices and prepossessions. Let us for a moment forget even Swaraj, and certainly forget the 'haves' whose presence oppresses us at every step. They are there. There are many who are dealing with these big problems. Let us tackle the humbler work of the village which is necessary now and would be even after we have reached our goal. Indeed, the village work when it becomes successful will itself bring us nearer the goal.[11]

The village communities should be revived. Indian villages produced and supplied to the Indian towns and cities all their wants. India became impoverished when our cities became foreign markets and began to drain the villages dry by dumping cheap and shoddy goods from foreign lands.[12]

It is only when the cities realize the duty of making an adequate return to the villages for the strength and sustenance which they derive from them, instead of selfishly exploiting them, that a healthy and moral relationship between the two will spring up. And if the city children are to play their part in this great and noble work of social reconstruction, the vocations through which they are to receive their education ought to be directly related to the requirements of the villages.[13]

We have to tackle the triple malady which holds our villages fast in its grip: (*i*) want of corporate sanitation; (*ii*) deficient diet; (*iii*) inertia.... They are not interested in their own welfare. They don't appreciate modern sanitary methods. They don't want to exert themselves beyond scratching their farms or doing such labour as they are used to. These difficulties are real and serious. But they must not baffle us. We must have an unquenchable faith in our mission. We must be patient with the people. We are ourselves novices in village work. We have to deal with a chronic disease. Patience and perseverance, if we have them, overcome mountains of difficulties. We are like nurses who may not leave their patients because they are reported to have an incurable disease.[14]

The moment you talk to them [the Indian peasants] and they begin to speak, you will find wisdom drops from their lips. Behind the crude exterior you will find a deep reservoir of spirituality. I call this culture—you will not find such a thing in the West. You try to engage an European peasant in conversation and you will find that he is uninterested in things spiritual.[15]

In the case of the Indian villager, an age-old culture is hidden under an encrustment of crudeness. Take away the encrustation, remove his chronic poverty and his illiteracy and you have the finest specimen of what a cultured, cultivated, free citizen should be.[16]

24

EVERY VILLAGE A REPUBLIC

My idea of village Swaraj is that it is a complete republic, independent of its neighbours for its own vital wants and yet interdependent for many others in which dependence is necessary. Thus every village's first concern will be to grow its own food crops, and cotton for its cloth. It should have a reserve for its cattle, recreation and playground for adults and children. Then if there is more land available, it will grow *useful* money crops, thus excluding *ganja*, tobacco, opium and the like.

The village will maintain a village theatre, school and public hall. It will have its own waterworks ensuring clean water supply. This can be done through controlled wells or tanks. Education will be compulsory up to the final Basic course. As far as possible every activity will be conducted on the co-operative basis. There will be no castes such as we have today with their graded untouchability.[1]

> *My idea of village Swaraj is that it is a complete republic, independent of its neighbours for its own vital wants and yet interdependent for many others in which dependence is necessary*

Non-violence with its technique of Satyagraha and non-co-operation will be the sanction of the village community. There will be a compulsory service of village guards who will be selected by rotation from the register maintained by the village. The government of the village will be conducted by a

Panchayat of five persons annually elected by the adult villagers, male and female, possessing minimum prescribed qualifications. These will have all the authority and jurisdiction required. Since there will be no system of punishments in the accepted sense, this Panchayat will be the legislature, judiciary and executive combined to operate for its year of office.

Any village can become such a republic today without much interference, even from the present Government whose sole effectual connection with the village is the exaction of the village revenue. I have not examined here the question of the relations with the neighbouring villages and the Centre if any. My purpose is to present an outline of village government. Here is perfect democracy based upon individual freedom. The individual is the architect of his own Government. The law of non-violence rules him and his Government. He and his village are able to defy the might of the world. For the law governing every villager is that he will suffer death in the defence of his and his village's honour.

To model such a village may be the work of a lifetime. Any lover of democracy and village life can take up a village, treat it as his world and sole work, and he will find good results. He begins by being the village scavenger, spinner, watchman, medicineman and school master all at once. If nobody comes near him he will be satisfied with scavenging and spinning.[2]

The villagers should develop such a high degree of skill that articles prepared by them should command a ready market outside. When our villages are fully developed there will be no dearth in them of men with a high degree of skill and artistic talent. There will be village poets, village artists, village architects, linguists and research workers. In short, there will be nothing in life worth having which will not be had in the villages. Today the villages are dung heaps. Tomorrow they will be like tiny gardens of Eden where dwell highly intelligent folk whom no one can deceive or exploit.

The reconstruction of the villages along these lines should begin now. The reconstruction of the villages should not be organized on a temporary but permanent basis.

Craft, art, health and education should all be integrated into one scheme. Nai Talim is a beautiful blend of all the four and covers the whole education of the individual from the time of conception to the moment of death. Therefore, I would not divide village uplift work into water-tight compartments from the very beginning but undertake an activity which will combine all four. Instead of regarding craft and industry as different from education. I will regard the former as the medium for the latter. Nai Talim therefore ought to be integrated into the scheme.[3]

A village unit as conceived by me is as strong as the strongest. My imaginary village consists of 1,000 souls. Such a unit can give a good account of itself, if it is well organized on a basis of self-sufficiency.[4]

An ideal Indian village will be so constructed as to lend itself to perfect sanitation. It will have cottages with sufficient light and ventilation, built of a material obtainable within a radius of five miles of it. The cottages will have courtyards enabling the householders to plant vegetables for domestic use and to house their cattle. The village lanes and streets will be free of all avoidable dust. It will have wells according to its needs and accessible to all. It will have houses of worship for all, also a common meeting place, a village common for grazing its cattle, a co-operative dairy, primary and secondary schools in which industrial education will be the central factor, and it will have village Panchayats for settling disputes. It will produce its own grains, vegetables and fruit, and its own Khadi.[5]

25
PANCHAYAT RAJ

Independence must begin at the bottom. Thus, every village will be a Republic or Panchayat having full powers. It follows, therefore, that every village has to be self-sustained and capable of managing its affairs even to the extent of defending

> *Independence must begin at the bottom*

itself against the whole world. It will be trained and prepared to perish in its attempt to defend itself against any onslaught from without. Thus, ultimately, it is the individual who is the unit. This does not exclude dependence on and willing help from neighbours or from the world. It will be free and voluntary play of mutual forces. Such a society is necessarily highly cultured, in which every man and woman knows what he or she wants and, what is more, knows that no one should want anything that others cannot have with equal labour.

This society must naturally be based on Truth and Non-violence which, in my opinion, are not possible without a living belief in God, meaning a self-existent, all-knowing living forces which inheres every other force known to the world but which depends on none and which will live when all other forces may conceivably perish or cease to act. I am unable to account for my life without belief in this all-embracing living light.

In this structure composed of innumerable villages there will be ever widening, never ascending circles. Life will not be a pyramid with the apex sustained by the bottom. But it will be an oceanic circle whose centre will be the individual always ready to perish for the village, the latter ready to perish for the circle of villages, till at last the whole becomes one life composed of individuals, never aggressive in their arrogance but ever humble, sharing the majesty of the oceanic circle of which they are integral units.

Therefore, the outermost circumference will not wield power to crush the inner circle but give strength to all within and derive its own from the centre. I may be taunted with the retort that this is all Utopian and therefore not worth a single thought. If Euclid's point, though incapable of being drawn by human agency, has an imperishable value, my picture has its own for mankind to live. Let India live for this true picture, though never realizable in its completeness. We must have a proper picture of what we want before we can have something approaching it. If there ever is to be a republic of every village in India, then I claim verity for my picture in which the last in equal to the first, or in other words, none is to be the first and none the last.

> When Panchayat Raj is established, public opinion will do what violence can never do

In this picture every religion has its full and equal place. We are all leaves of a majestic tree whose trunk cannot be shaken off its roots which are deep down in the bowels of the earth. The mightiest of winds cannot move it.

In this there is no room for machines that would displace human labour and that would concentrate power in a few hands. Labour has its unique place in a cultural human family. Every machine that helps every individual has a place. But I must confess that I have never sat down to think out what that machine can be. I have thought of Singer's sewing machine. But even that is perfunctory. I do not need it to fill in my picture.[1]

When Panchayat Raj is established, public opinion will do what violence can never do. The present power of the zamindars, the capitalists and the rajas can hold sway so long as the common people do not realize their own strength. If the people non-co-operate with the evil of zamindari or capitalism, it must die of inanition. In Panchayat Raj only the Panchayat will be obeyed and the Panchayat can only work through the law of their making.[2]

26

VILLAGE INDUSTRIES

Extinction of village industries would complete the ruin of the 7,00,000 villages of India.

I have seen in the daily press criticism of the proposals I have adumbrated. Advice has been given to me that I must look for salvation in the direction of using the powers of nature that the inventive brain of man has brought

> *I would say that if the village perishes India will perish too. India will be no more India*

under subjection. The critics say that water, air, oil and electricity should be fully utilized as they are being utilized in the go-ahead West. They say that control over these hidden powers of nature enables every American to have thirty-three slaves.

Repeat the process in India and I dare say that it will thirty-three times enslave every inhabitant of this land, instead of giving every one thirty-three slaves.

Mechanization is good when the hands are too few for the work intended to be accomplished. It is an evil when there are more hands than required for the work, as is the case in India. I may not use a plough for digging a few square yards of a plot of land. The problem with us is not how to find leisure for the teeming millions inhabiting our villages. The problem is how to utilize their idle hours, which are equal to the working days of six months in the year. Strange as it may appear, every mill generally is a menace to the villagers. I have not worked out the figures, but I am quite safe in saying that every mill-hand does the work of at least ten labourers doing the same work in their villages. In other words, he earns more than he did in his village at the expense of ten fellow-villagers. Thus spinning and weaving mills have deprived the villagers of a substantial means of livelihood. It is no answer in reply to say that they turn out cheaper, better cloth, if they do so at all. For, if they have displaced thousands of workers, the cheapest mill cloth is dearer than the dearest Khadi woven in the villages. Coal is not dear for the coal miner who can use it there and then, nor is Khadi dear for the villager who manufactures his own Khadi. But if the cloth manufactured in mills displaces village hands, rice-mills and flour-mills not only displace thousands of poor women workers, but damage the health of the whole population in the bargain. Where pepole have no objection to taking flesh diet and can afford it, white flour and polished rice may do no harm, but in India, where millions can get no flesh diet even where they have no objection to eating it if they can get it, it is sinful to deprive them of nutritious and vital elements contained in whole wheatmeal and unpolished rice. It is time medical men and others combined to instruct the people on the danger attendant upon the use of white flour and polished rice.

I have drawn attention to some broad, glaring facts to show that the way to take work to the villágers is not through mechanization but that it lies through revival of the industries they have hitherto followed.[1]

The idea behind the village industries scheme is that we should look to the villages for the supply of our daily needs and that, when we find that some needs are not so supplied, we should see whether with a little trouble and organization they cannot be profitably supplied by the

> Industrialization on a mass scale will necessarily lead to passive or active exploitation of the villagers

villagers. In estimating the profit, we should think of the villager, not of ourselves. It may be that in the initial stages we might have to pay a little more than the ordinary price and get an inferior article in the bargain. Things will improve, if we will interest ourselves in the supplier of our needs and insist on his doing better and take the trouble of helping him to do better.[2]

I would say that if the village perishes India will perish too. India will be no more India. Her own mission in the world will get lost. The revival of the village is possible only when it is no more exploited. Industrialization on a mass scale will necessarily lead to passive or active exploitation of the villagers as the problems of competition and marketing come. Therefore we have to concentrate on the village being self-contained, manufacturing mainly for use. Provided this character of the village industry is maintained, there would be no objection to villagers using even the modern machines and tools that they can make and can afford to use. Only they should not be used as a means of exploitation of others.[3]

We have to make a choice between India of the villages that are as ancient as herself and India of the cities which are a creation of foreign domination. Today the cities dominate and drain the villages so that they are crumbling to ruin. My Khadi mentality tells me that cities must subserve villages when that domination goes. Exploiting of villages is itself organized violence. If we want Swaraj to be built on non-violence, we will have to give the villages their proper place.[4]

Khadi

Khadi to me is the symbol of unity of Indian humanity, of its economic freedom and equality and, therefore, ultimately, in the poetic expression of Jawaharlal Nehru, "the livery of India's freedom".

Moreover, Khadi mentality means decentralization of the production and distribution of the necessaries of life. Therefore, the formula so far evolved is, every village to produce all its necessities and a certain percentage in addition for the requirements of the cities.

> *Khadi to me is the symbol of unity of Indian humanity, of its economic freedom and equality*

Heavy industries will need be centralized and nationalized. But they will occupy the least part of the vast national activity which will mainly be in the villages.

Production of Khadi includes cotton growing, picking,

ginning, cleaning, carding, slivering, spinning, sizing, dyeing, preparing the warp and the woof, weaving, and washing. These, with the exception of dyeing, are essential processes. Every one of them can be effectively handled in the villages and is being so handled in many villages throughout India which the A.I.S.A. is covering.

Since the wanton destruction of this central village industry and the allied handicrafts, intelligence and brightness have fled from the villages, leaving them inane, lustreless, and reduced almost to the state of their ill-kept cattle.[5]

Other Village Industries

These stand on a different footing from Khadi. There is not much scope for voluntary labour in them. Each industry will take the labour of only a certain number of hands. These industries come in as a handmaid to Khadi. They cannot exist without Khadi, and Khadi will be robbed of its dignity without them. Village economy cannot be complete without the essential village industries such as hand-grinding, hand-pounding, soap-making, paper-making, match-making, tanning, oil-pressing, etc. Congressmen

> *Khadi mentality means decentralization of the production and distribution of the necessities of life*

can interest themselves in these and, if they are villagers or will settle down in villages, they will give these industries a new life and a new dress. All should make it a point of honour to use only village articles whenever and wherever available. Given the demand there is no doubt that most of our wants can be supplied from our villages. When we have become village-minded, we will not want imitations of the West or machine-made products, but we will develop a true national taste in keeping with the vision of a new India in which pauperism, starvation and idleness will be unknown.[6]

Compost Manure

Given the willing co-operation of the masses of India, this country can not only drive out shortage of food, but can provide India with more than enough. This organic manure ever enriches, never impoverishes the soil. The daily waste, judiciously composted, returns to the soil in the form of golden manure causing a saving of millions of rupees and increasing manifold, the total yield of grains and pulses. In addition, the judicious use of waste keeps the surroundings clean. And cleanliness is not only next to godliness, it promotes health.[7]

Village Tanning

Village tanning is as ancient as India itself. No one can say when tanning became a degraded calling. It could not have been so in ancient times. But we know today that one of the most useful and indispensable industries has consigned probably a million people to hereditary untouchability. An evil day dawned upon this unhappy country when labour began to be despised and therefore neglected. Millions of those who were the salt of the earth, on whose industry this country depended for its very existence, came to be regarded as low classes, and the microscopic leisured few became the privileged classes, with the tragic result that India suffered morally and materially. Which was the greater of the two losses it is difficult, if not impossible, to estimate. But the criminal neglect of the peasants and artisans has reduced us to pauperism, dulness and habitual idleness. With her magnificent climate, lofty mountains, mighty rivers and an extensive seaboard, India has limitless resources, whose full exploitation in her villages should have prevented poverty and disease. But divorce of the intellect from body-labour has made of us perhaps the shortest-lived, most resourceless and most exploited nation on earth. The state of village tanning is, perhaps, the best proof of my indictment.

It is estimated that rupees nine crores worth of raw hide is annually exported from India and much of it is returned to her in the shape of manufactured articles. This means not only a material, but also an intellectual, drain. We miss the training we should receive in tanning and preparing the innumerable articles of leather we need for daily use.

Here is work for the cent-per cent Swadeshi lover and scope for the harnessing of technical skill to the solution of a great problem. It serves the Harijans, it serves the villagers, and it means honourable employment for the middle class intelligentsia who are in search of employment. Add to this the fact that the intelligentsia have a proper opportunity of coming in direct touch with the villagers.[8]

How to Begin

Correspondents have been writing, and friends have been seeing me, to ask me how to begin the village industries work and what to do first.

The obvious answer is, "Begin with yourself and do first that which is easiest for you to do."

This answer, however, does not satisfy the enquirers. Let me, therefore, be more explicit.

Each person can examine all the articles of food, clothing and other things that he used from day to day and replace foreign makes or city makes, by those produced by the villagers in their homes or fields with the simple inexpensive tools they can easily handle or mend. This replacement will be itself an education of great value and a solid beginning. The next step will be opened out to him of itself. For instance, say, the beginner has been hitherto using a tooth-brush made in a Bombay factory. He wants to replace it with a village brush. He is advised to use a *babul* twig. If he has weak teeth or is toothless, he has to crush one end of it, with a rounded stone or hammer, on a hard surface. The other end he slits with a knife and uses the halves as tongue-scrapers. He will find these brushes to be cheaper and much cleaner than the very unhygienic factory made tooth-brush. The city-made tooth-powder he naturally replaces with equal parts of clean, finely-ground wood-charcoal and clean salt. He will replace mill-cloth with village-spun Khadi, and mill-husked rice with hand-husked, unpolished rice, and white sugar with village-made *gur*. These I have taken merely as samples already mentioned in these columns. I have mentioned them again to deal with the difficulties that have been mentioned by those who have been discussing the question with me.[9]

27

WHAT THE GOVERNMENT CAN DO

It is legitimate to ask what Congress Ministers will do for Khaddar and other village industries now that they are in office. Whether a Minister is separately appointed or not, a department for the work is surely necessary. In these times of scarcity of food and clothing, this department can render the greatest help. The Ministers have experts at their disposal through the A.I.S.A. and the A.I.V.I.A. It is possible to clothe today the whole of India in Khadi on the smallest outlay and in the shortest time possible. Each Provincial Government has to tell the villagers that they must manufacture their own Khaddar for their own use. This brings in automatic local production and distribution. And there will undoubtedly be a surplus for the cities at least to a certain extent which, in its turn, will reduce the pressure on the local mills. The latter will then be able to take part in supplying the want of cloth in other parts of the world.

How can this result be brought about?

The Government should notify the villagers that they will be expected to manufacture Khaddar for the needs of their villages within a fixed date after which no cloth will be supplied to them. The Government in their turn will supply the villagers with cotton seed or cotton whenever required, at cost price and the tools of manufacture also at cost, to be recovered in easy instalments payable in, say, five years or more. They will supply them with instructors wherever necessary and undertake to buy surplus stock of Khaddar, provided that the villagers in question have their cloth requirements supplied from their own manufature. This should do away with cloth shortage without fuss and with very little overhead charges.

The villages will be surveyed and a list prepared of things that can be manufactured locally with little or no help and which may be required for village use or for sale outside, such for instance, as *ghani*-pressed oil and cakes, burning oil prepared through *ghanis*, hand-pounded rice, *tadgud*, honey, toys, mats, hand-made-paper, village soap, etc. If enough care is thus taken the villages, most of them as good as dead or dying, will hum with life and exhibit the immense possibilities they have of supplying most of their wants themselves and of the cities and towns of India.

Then there is the limitless cattle wealth of India suffering from criminal neglect. Goseva Sangh, as yet not properly experienced, can still supply valuable aid.

Without the basic training the villagers are being starved for education. This desideratum can be supplied by the Hindustani Talimi Sangh.[1]

28

VILLAGE EXHIBITIONS

If we want and believe that the village should not only survive but also become strong and flourishing, then the village perspective is the only correct view-point. If this is true then in our exhibitions there can be no place for the glamour and pomp of the cities. There should be no necessity for games and other entertainments that belong to the cities. An exhibition should not become a "Tamasha", nor a source of income; it should never become the advertising medium for traders. No sales should be allowed there. Even Khadi and village industry products should not be sold. An exhibition should be a medium of education, should be attractive and it should be such as to infuse in the villager the impulse to take to some industry or the other. It should bring out the glaring defects and drawbacks in the present day village life, and show methods to be adopted to set them right. It should also be able to indicate the extent of achievement in that direction ever since the idea of village uplift was sponsored. It should also teach how to make village life artistic.

Now let us see what an exhibition will be like if it is to confirm to the above conditions.

1. There should be two models of villages—one as is existing today and the other an improved one. The improved village will be clean all throughout. Its houses, its roads, its surroundings and its fields will be all clean. The condition of the cattle should also improve. Books, charts and pictures should be used to show what industries give increased income and how.

2. It must show how to conduct the various village industries, wherefrom to obtain the needed implements, how to make them. The actual working of each industry should be demonstrated. Along with these the following should also find place:

- Ideal village diet
- Comparison between village industry and machine industry
- Model lessons on rearing animals
- Art section
- Model of village latrine
- Farm-yard manure *v.* chemical manure
- Utilization of hides, bones, etc. of animals
- Village music, musical instruments, village dramas
- Village games, village *akhadas* and forms of exercise
- Nai Talim
- Village medicine
- Village maternity home

Subject to the policy enunciated in the beginning, this list may be further expanded. What I have indicated is by way of example only, it should not be taken to be exhaustive. I have not made any mention of the Charkha and other village industries as they are taken for granted. Without them the exhibition will be absolutely useless.[1]

29

THE MUSIC OF THE SPINNING WHEEL

I think of the poor of India every time I draw a thread on the wheel. The poor of India today have lost faith in God, more so than the middle classes or the rich. For a person suffering from the pangs of hunger, and desiring nothing but to fill his belly, his belly is his God. To him anyone who gives him his bread is his Master. Through him he may even see God. To give alms to such persons, who are sound in all their limbs, is to debase oneself and them. What they need is some kind of occupation, and the occupation that will give employment to millions can

> I think of the poor of India every time I draw a thread on the wheel

only be hand-spinning. ....I have described my spinning as a penance or sacrament. And, since I believe that where there is pure and active love for the poor there is God also, I see God in every thread that I draw on the spinning wheel.[1]

I feel convinced that the revival of hand-spinning and hand-weaving will make the largest contribution to the economic and the moral regeneration of India. The millions must have a simple industry to supplement agriculture. Spinning was the cottage industry years ago, and if the millions are to be saved from starvation, they must be enabled to reintroduce spinning in their homes, and every village must repossess its own weaver.[2]

I can only think of spinning as the fittest and most acceptable sacrificial body labour. I cannot imagine anything nobler or more national than that for, say one hour in the day,

The Music of the Spinning Wheel **111**

we should all do the labour that the poor must do, and thus identify ourselves with them and through them with all mankind. I cannot imagine better worship of God than that in His name. I should labour for the poor even as they do. The spinning wheel spells a more equitable distribution of the riches of the earth.[3]

I...claim for the Charkha the honour of being able to solve the problem of economic distress in a most natural, simple, inexpensive and business like manner. The Charkha, therefore, is not only not useless...but it is a useful and indispensable article for every home. It is the symbol of the nation's prosperity and, therefore, freedom. It is a symbol not of commercial war but of commercial peace. It bears not a message of ill-will towards the nations of the earth but of good-will and self-help. It will not need the protection of a navy threatening a world's peace and exploiting its resources, but it needs the religious determination of millions to spin their yarn in their own homes as today they cook their food in their own homes. I may deserve the curse of posterity for many mistakes of omission and commission, but I am confident of earning its blessings for suggesting a revival of the Charkha. I stake my all on it. For every revolution of the wheel spins peace, good-will and love. And with all that, inasmuch as the loss of it brought about India's slavery, its voluntary revival with all its implications must mean India's freedom.[4]

> I...claim for the Charkha the honour of being able to solve the problem of economic distress in a most natural, simple, inexpensive and business-like manner

What is claimed for spinning is that

- it supplies the readiest occupation to those who have leisure and are in want of a few coppers;
- it is known to the thousands;
- it is easily learnt;
- it requires practically no outlay of capital;
- the wheel can be easily and cheaply made. Most of us do not yet know that spinning can be done even with a piece of tile and splinter;

- the people have no repugnance to it;
- it affords immediate relief in times of famine and scarcity;
- it alone can stop the drain of wealth which goes outside India in the purchase of foreign cloth;
- it automatically distributes the millions thus saved among the deserving poor;
- even the smallest success means so much immediate gain to the people;
- it is the most potent instrument of securing co-operation among the people.[5]

'If hand-spinning is all you say, how is it that it has not already been universally adopted?' asks the critic. The question is quite fair. The answer is simple. The message of the wheel has to be carried to a people who have no hope, no initiative left in them, and who would, if left to themselves, starve and die rather than work and live. Such was not the case before, but long neglect has made laziness a habit with them. That laziness can only be removed by the living contact and example of men of character and industry, plying the wheel before them and by gently showing them the way. The second great difficulty is the absence of a ready-market for khaddar. I confess that it cannot for the time being compete with mill cloth. I will not engage in any such killing competition. The capitalist may, for capturing the market, sell his calico for nothing. The manufacturer whose only capital is labour cannot afford to do so. Can there be any competition between the dead artificial rose, however symmetrical it may be, and the living rose whose two petals will not be alike, or can there be any competition between a wax statue of Cromwell and the living one? Khaddar is a living thing. But India has lost her eye for the real art and is, therefore, satisfied with the glossy exterior. Revive the healthy national taste for khaddar and you will find every village a busy hive. As it is, the resources of khaddar organizations are taxed to the utmost, in order to create a market for the article. ....The marvel is that, in spite of heavy odds against it, the movement is making headway.

I have thus summarized the case for the spinning wheel as a supplementary industry as against the handloom. Let there be no confusion of thought. I am not against the handloom. It is a great and thriving industry. It will progress automatically if the spinning wheel succeeds. It is bound to die if the wheel fails.[6]

The spinning wheel represents to me the hope of the masses. The masses lost their freedom, such as it was, with the loss of the Charkha. The Charkha supplemented the agriculture of the villagers and gave it dignity. It was the friend and solace of the

> The Charkha is the symbol of the nation's prosperity and, therefore, freedom

widow. It kept the villagers from idleness. For the Charkha included all the anterior and posterior industries—ginning, carding, warping, sizing, dyeing and weaving. These in their turn kept the village carpenter and the blacksmith busy. The Charkha enabled the seven hundred thousand villages to become self-contained. With the exit of the Charkha went the other village industries, such as the oil press. Nothing took the place of these industries. Therefore the villages were drained of their varied occupations and their creative talent and what little wealth these brought them.

Hence, if the villagers are to come into their own, the most natural thing that suggests itself is the revival of the Charkha and all it means.

This revival cannot take place without an army of selfless Indians of intelligence and patriotism working with a single mind in the villages to spread the message of the Charkha and bring a ray of hope and light into their lustreless eyes. This is a mighty effort at co-operation and adult education of the correct type. It brings about a silent and sure revolution like the silent but sure and life-giving revolution of the Charkha.[7]

30

THE MILL INDUSTRY

Our mills cannot today spin enough for our wants, and if they did, they would not keep dôwn prices unless they were compelled. They are frankly money-makers and will not, therefore, regulate prices according to the needs of the nation. Hand-spinning is, therefore, designed to put millions of rupees in the hands of poor villagers. Every agricultural country requires a supplementary industry to enable the peasants to utilize the spare hours. Such industry for India has always been spinning. Is it a visionary ideal—an attempt to revive an ancient occupation whose destruction has brought on slavery, pauperism and disappearance of the inimitable artistic talent which was once all expressed in the wonderful fabric of India and which was the envy of the world?[1]

The great mill industry may be claimed to be an Indian industry. But in spite of its ability to compete with Japan and Lancashire, it is an industry that exploits the masses and deepens their poverty in exact proportion to its success over Khadi. In the modern craze for industrialization, my presentation has been questioned, if not brushed aside. It has been contended that the growing poverty of the masses, due to the progress of industrialization, is inevitable, and should, therefore, be suffered. The A.I.S.A. has successfully demonstrated the possibility of the villages manufacturing the whole of the cloth requirements of India, simply by employing the leisure hours of the nation in spinning and the anterior processes. The difficulty lies in weaning the nation from the use of mill cloth.[2]

Mill-owners are not philanthropists to go on providing

yarn to the handloom weaver when he enters into effective competition with them.[3]

As soon as the mill-owners can do so profitably, they will certainly stop selling mill yarn and will weave it themselves. They are not philanthropists. They have set mills to make money. They will stop selling their yarn to handloom weavers, if they find weaving it more profitable.[4]

The use of mill-yarn is the principal stranglehold on the handloom industry. In hand-spun yarn lies its only salvation. If the spinning wheel goes, the handloom is bound to follow suit.[5]

I am personally opposed to great trusts and concentration of industries by means of elaborate machinery. If India takes to khaddar and all it means, I do not lose the hope of India taking only as much of the modern machinery as may be considered necessary for the amenities of life and labour-saving devices.[6]

Organization of machinery for the purpose of concentrating wealth and power in the hands of a few and for the exploitation of many I hold to be altogether wrong. Much of the organization of machinery of the present age is of that type. The movement of the spinning wheel is an organized attempt to displace machinery from that state of exclusiveness and exploitation and to place it in its proper state. Under my scheme, therefore, men in charge of machinery will think not of themselves or even of the nation to which they belong but of the whole human race. Thus Lancashire men will cease to use their machinery for exploiting India and other countries but on the contrary they will devise means of enabling India to convert in her own villages her cotton into cloth. Nor will Americans under my scheme seek to enrich themselves by exploiting the other races of the earth through their inventive skill.[7]

> *Hand-spinning is a visionary ideal—an attempt to revive an ancient occupation whose destruction has brought on slavery, pauperism and disappearance of the inimitable artistic talent which was once expressed in the wonderful fabric of India and which was the envy of the world*

31

THE GOSPEL OF SWADESHI

Swadeshi is that spirit in us which restricts us to the use and service of our immediate surroundings to the exclusion of the more remote. Thus, as for religion, in order to satisfy the requirements of the definition, I must restrict myself to my ancestral religion. That is, the use of my immediate religious surrounding. If I find it defective, I should serve it by purging it of its defects. In the domain of politics I should make use of the indigenous institutions and serve them by curing them of their proved defects. In that of economics I should use only things that are produced by my immediate neighbours and serve those industries by making them efficient and complete where they might be found wanting. It is suggested that such Swadeshi, if reduced to practice, will lead to the millennium....

Let us briefly examine the three branches of Swadeshi as sketched above. Hinduism has become a conservative religion and, therefore, a mighty force because of the Swadeshi spirit underlying it. It is the most tolerant because it is non-proselytizing, and it is as capable of expansion today as it has been found to be in the past. It has succeeded not in driving out, as I think it has been erroneously held, but in absorbing Buddhism. By reason of the Swadeshi spirit, a Hindu refuses to change his religion, not necessarily because he considers it to be the bsest, but because he knows that he can complement it by introducing reforms. And what I have said about Hinduism is, I suppose, true of the other great faiths of the world, only it is held that it is specially so in the case of Hinduism. But here comes the point I am labouring to reach. If there is any substance in what I have said, will not the great missionary bodies of India, to whom she owes a deep debt of gratitude for what they have done and are doing, do still better and serve the spirit of Christianity better by dropping the goal of proselytizing while continuing their philanthropic work?

Following out the Swadeshi spirit, I observe the indigenous institutions, and the village Panchayats hold me. India is really a republican country, and it is because it is that, that it has survived every shock hitherto delivered. Princes and potentates, whether they were Indian born or foreigners, have hardly touched the vast masses except for collecting revenue. The latter in their turn seem to have rendered unto Caesar what was Caesar's and for the rest have done much as they have liked. The vast organization of caste answered not only to the religious wants of the community but it answered to its political needs. The villagers managed their internal affairs through the caste system and through it they dealt with any oppression from the ruling power or powers. It is not possible to deny the organizing ability of a nation that was capable of producing from the caste system its wonderful power of organization. One has but to attend the great Kumbha Mela at Hardwar...to know how skilful that organization must have been which, without any seeming effort, was able effectively to cater for more than a million pilgrims. Yet it is the fashion to say that we lack organizing ability. This is true, I fear, to a certain extent, of those who have been nurtured in the new traditions.

> Swadeshi is that spirit in us which restricts us to the use and service of our immediate surroundings to the exclusion of the more remote

We have laboured under a terrible handicap owing to an almost fatal departure from the Swadeshi spirit. We, the educated classes, have received our education through a foreign tongue. We have, therefore, not reacted upon the masses. We want to represent the masses, but we fail. They recognize us not much more than they recognize the English officers. Their hearts are an open book to neither. Their aspirations are not ours. Hence there is a break. And you witness not in reality failure to organize but want of correspondence between the representatives and the represented. If during the last fifty years we had been educated through the vernaculars, our elders and our servants and our neighbours would have partaken of our knowledge; the discoveries of a Bose or a Ray would have been household treasures as are the Ramayan and the Mahabharat. As it is, so far as the masses are concerned, those great discoveries might as well have been made by foreigners. Had instruction in all the branches of learning been given through the vernaculars, I make bold to say that they would have been enriched wonderfully. The question of village sanitation etc. would have been solved long ago. The village Panchayats would be now a living force in a special way, and India would almost be enjoying self-government suited to her requirements, and would have been spared the humiliating spectacle of organized assassination on her sacred soil. It is not too late to mend.

And now for the last division of Swadeshi. Much of the deep poverty of the masses is due to the ruinous departure from Swadeshi in the economic and industrial life. If not one article of commerce had been brought from outside India, she would be today a land flowing with milk and honey. But that was not to be. We were greedy and so was England. The connection between England and India was based clearly upon an error. But she does not remain in India in error. It is her declared policy that India is to be held in trust for her people. If this be true, Lancashire must stand aside. And if the Swadeshi doctrine is a sound doctrine, Lancashire can stand aside without hurt, though it may sustain a shock for the time being. I think of Swadeshi not as a boycott movement undertaken by way of revenge. I conceive it as a religious principle to be followed by all. I am no economist, but I have read some treatises which show that England could easily become a self-sustained country, growing all the produce she needs. This may be an utterly ridiculous proposition, and perhaps the best proof that it cannot be true, is that England is one of the largest importers in the world. But India cannot live for Lancashire or any other country before she is able to live for herself. And she can live for herself only if she produces and is helped to produce everything for her requirements within her own borders. She need not be, she ought not be, drawn into the vortex of mad and ruinous competition which breeds fratricide, jealousy and many other evils. But who is to stop her great millionaires from entering into the world competition? Certainly not legislation. Force of public opinion and proper education, however, can do a great deal in the desired direction. The handloom industry is in a dying condition. I took special care during my wanderings...to see as many weavers as possible, and my heart ached to find how they had lost, how families had retired from this once flourishing and honourable occupation.

If we follow the Swadeshi doctrine, it would be your duty and mine to find out neighbours who can supply our wants and to teach them to supply them where they do not know how to proceed, assuming that there are neighbours who are in want of healthy occupation. Then every villages of India will almost be a self-supporting and self-contained unit, exchanging only such necessary commodities with other villages as are not locally producible. This may all sound nonsensical. Well, India is a country of nonsense. It is nonsensical to parch one's throat with thirst when a kindly Muhammedan is ready to offer pure water to drink. And yet thousands of Hindus would rather die of thirst than drink water from a Muhammedan household. These nonsensical men can also, once they are convinced that their religion demands that they should wear garments manufactured in India only and eat food only grown in India, decline to wear any other clothing or eat any other food.

> *My patriotism is both exclusive and inclusive. It is exclusive in the sense that in all humility I confine my attention to the land of my birth, but is inclusive in the sense that my service is not of a competitive or antagonistic nature*

There is a verse in the *Bhagavadgita* which, freely rendered, means masses follow the classes. It is easy to undo the evil if the thinking portion of the community were to take the Swadeshi vow, even though it may for a time cause considerable inconvenience. I hate legislative interference in any department of life. At best it is the lesser evil. But I would tolerate, welcome—indeed, plead for a stiff protective duty upon foreign goods. Natal, a British colony, protected its sugar by taxing the sugar that came from another British colony, Mauritius. England has sinned against India by forcing free trade upon her. It may have been food for her, but it has been poison for this country.

It has often been urged that India cannot adopt Swadeshi in the economic life at any rate. Those who advance this objection do not look upon Swadeshi as a rule of life. With them it is a mere patriotic effort—not to be made if it involved any self-denial. Swadeshi, as defined here, is a religious discipline to be undergone in utter disregard of the physical discomfort it may cause to individuals. Under its spell the deprivation of a pin or a needle, because these are not manufactured in India, need cause no terror. A Swadeshist will learn to do without hundreds of things which today he considers necessary. Moreover, those who dismiss Swadeshi from their minds by arguing the impossible, forget

> *Even Swadeshi like any other good thing can be ridden to death if it is made a fetish. That is a danger that must be guarded against*

that Swadeshi, after all, is a goal to be reached by steady effort. And we would be making for the goal even if we confined Swadeshi to a given set of articles allowing ourselves as a temporary measure to use such things as might not be procurable in the country.

There now remains for me to consider one more objection that has been raised against Swadeshi. The objectors consider it to be a most selfish doctrine without any warrant in the civilized code of morality. With them to practise Swadeshi is to revert to barbarism. I cannot enter into a detailed analysis of the proposition. But I would urge that Swadeshi is the only doctrine consistent with the law of humility and love. It is arrogance to think of launching out to serve the whole of India when I am hardly able to serve even my own family. It were better to concentrate my effort upon the family and consider that through them I was serving the whole nation and, if you will, the whole of humanity. This is humility and it is love. The motive will determine the quality of the act. I may serve my family regardless of the sufferings I may cause to others. As, for instance, I may accept an employment which enables me to extort money from people. I enrich myself thereby and then satisfy many unlawful demands of the family. Here I am neither serving the family nor the State. Or I may recognize that God has given me hands and feet only to work with for my sustenance and for that of those who may be dependent upon me. I would then at once simplify my life and that of those whom I can directly reach. In this instance I would have served the family without causing injury to anyone else. Supposing that every one followed this mode of life, we should have at once an ideal state. All will not reach that state at the same time. But those of us who, realizing its truth, enforce it in practice, will clearly anticipate and accelerate the coming of that happy day. Under this plan of life, in seeming to serve India to the exclusion of every other country, I do not harm any other country. My patriotism is both exclusive and inclusive. It is exclusive in the sense that in all humility I confine my attention to the land of my birth, but is inclusive in the sense that my service is not of a competitive or antagonistic nature. *Sic utere tuo ut alienum non laedas* is not merely a legal maxim, but it is a grand doctrine of life. It is the key to a proper practice of Ahimsa or love.[1]

Even Swadeshi like any other good thing can be ridden to death if it is made a fetish. That is a danger that must be guarded against. To reject foreign manufactures, merely because they are foreign and to go on wasting national time and money in the promotion in one's country of manufactures for which it is not suited, would be criminal folly and a negation of the Swadeshi spirit. A true votary of Swadeshi will not harbour ill-will towards a foreigner and not be actuated by antagonism towards anybody on the earth. Swadeshi is not a cult of hatred. It is a doctrine of selfless service that has its roots in the purest Ahimsa, *i.e.* love.[2]

32

COW PROTECTION

The central fact of Hinduism is cow protection. Cow protection to me is one of the most wonderful phenomena in human evolution. It takes the human being beyond his species. The cow to me means the entire sub-human world. Man through the cow is enjoined to realize his indentity with all that lives. Why the cow was selected for apotheosis is obvious to me. The cow was in India the best companion. She was the giver of plenty. Not only did she give milk, but she also made agriculture possible. The cow is a poem of pity. One reads pity in the gentle animal. She is the mother to millions of Indian mankind. Protection of the cow means protection of the whole dumb creation of God. The ancient seer, whoever he was, began with the cow. The appeal of the lower order of creation is all the more forcible because it is speechless. Cow protection is the gift of Hinduism to the world. And Hinduism will live so long as there are Hindus to protect the cow....

> Cow protection takes the human being beyond his species. The cow to me means the entire sub-human world. Man through the cow is enjoined to realize his identity with all that which lives

Hindus will be judged not by their *tilaks*, not by the correct chanting of *mantras*, not by their pilgrimages, not by their most punctilious observances of caste rules but by their ability to protect the cow.[1]

Mother cow is in many ways better than the mother who

gave us birth. Our mother gives us milk for a couple of years and then expects us to serve her when we grow up. Mother cow expects from us nothing but grass and grain. Our mother often falls ill and expects service from us. Mother cow rarely falls ill. Hers is an unbroken record of service which does not end with her death. Our mother when she dies means expenses of burial or cremation. Mother cow is as useful dead as when she is alive. We can make use of every part of her body—her flesh, her bones, her intestines, her horns, and her skin. Well, I say this not to disparage the mother who gives us birth, but in order to show you the substantial reasons for my worshipping the cow.[2]

Criminal negligence is the only cause of the miserable condition of our cattle. Our *pinjrapoles*, though they are an answer to our instinct for mercy, are a clumsy demonstration of its execution. Instead of being model dairy-farms and great profitable national institutions, they are merely depots for receiving decrepit cattle. Whilst professing the religion of cow protection, we have enslaved the cow and her progeny, and have become slaves ourselves.[3]

> *Protection of the cow means protection of the whole dumb creation of God*

But let me reiterate...that legislative prohibition is the smallest part of any programme of cow protection. .... People seem to think that when a law is passed against any evil, it will die without any further effort. There never was any grosser self-deception. Legislation is intended and is effective against an ignorant or a small evil-minded minority; but no legislation which is opposed by an intelligent and organized public opinion, or under cover of religion by a fanatical minority, can ever succeed. The more I study the question of cow protection, the stronger the conviction grows upon me, that protection of the cow and her progeny can be attained, only if there is continuous and sustained constructive effort along the lines suggested by me.[4]

Then how can the cow be saved without having to kill her off when she ceases to give the economic quantity of milk or when she becomes otherwise an uneconomic burden? The answer to the question can be summed up as follows:

– By the Hindus performing their duty towards the cow

and her progeny. If they did so, our cattle would be the pride of India and the world. The contrary is the case today.

– By learning the science of cattle-breeding. Today there is perfect anarchy in this work.
– By replacing the present cruel method of castration by the humane method practised in the West.
– By thorough reform of the *pinjarapoles* of India which are today, as a rule, managed ignorantly and without any plan by men who do not know their work.
– When these primary things are done, it will be found that the Muslims will, of their own accord, recognize the necessity, if only for the sake of their Hindu brethren, of not slaughtering cattle for beef or otherwise.

The reader will observe that behind the foregoing requirements lies one thing and that is Ahimsa. If that supreme thing is realized, everything else becomes easy. Where there is Ahimsa. there is infinite patience, inner calm, discrimination, self-sacrifice and true knowledge. Cow protection is not an easy thing. Much money is wasted in its name. Nevertheless, in the absence of Ahimsa the Hindus have become destroyers instead of saviours of the cow. It is even more difficult than the removal of foreign rule from India.

(**Note:** The average quantity of milk that the cow in India yields is said to be roughly 2 lbs. per day, that of New Zealand 14 lbs., of England 15 lbs., of Holland 20 lbs. The index figure for health goes up in proportion to the increase in the yield of milk.)[5]

I am amazed at our partiality for buffalo milk and ghee. Our economics is short-sighted. We took at the immediate gain, but we do not realize that in the last analysis the cow is the more valuable animal. Cow's butter (and ghee) has a naturally yellowish colour which indicates its superiority to buffalo butter (and ghee) in carotene. It has a flavour all its own. Foreign visitors who come to Sevagram go into raptures over the pure cow's milk they get there. Buffalo milk and butter are almost unknown in Europe. It is only in India that one finds a prejudice in favour of buffalo milk and ghee. This has spelt all but extinction of the cow, and that is why I say that, unless we put an exclusive emphasis on the cow, she can not be saved.[6]

33

CO-OPERATIVE CATTLE-FARMING

It is quite impossible for an individual farmer to look after the welfare of his cattle in his own home in a proper and scientific manner. Amongst other causes lack of collective effort has been a principal cause of the deterioration of the cow and hence of cattle in general.

The world today is moving towards the ideal of collective or co-operative effort in every department of life. Much in this line has been and is being accomplished. It has come into our country also, but in such a distorted form that our poor have not been able to reap its benefits. *Pari passu* with the increase in our population land holdings of the average farmer are daily decreasing. Moreover, what the individual possesses is often fragmentary. For such farmers to keep cattle in their homes is a suicidal policy; and yet this is their condition today. Those who give the first place to economics and pay scant attention to religious, ethical or humanitarian considerations proclaim from the house-tops that the farmer is being devoured by his cattle due to the cost of their feed which is out of all proportion to what they yield. They say it is folly not to slaughter wholesale all useless animals.

What then should be done by humanitarians is the question. The answer obviously is to find a way whereby we may not only save the lives of our cattle but also see that they do not become a burden. I am sure that co-operative effort can help us in a large measure.

The following comparison may be helpful:

– Under the collective system no farmer can keep cattle in

his house as he does today. They foul the air, and dirty the surroundings. There is neither intelligence nor humanitarianism in living with animals. Man was not meant to do so. The space taken up by the cattle today would be spared to the farmer and his family, if the collective system were adopted.

- As the number of cattle increases, life becomes impossible to the farmer in his home. Hence he is obliged to sell the calves and kill the male buffaloes or else turn them out to starve and die. This inhumanity would be averted if the care of the cattle were undertaken on a co-operative basis.
- Collective cattle-farming would ensure the supply of veterinary treatment to animals when they are ill. No ordinary farmer can afford this on his own.
- Similarly one selected bull can be easily kept for the need of several cows under the collective system. This is impossible otherwise except for charity.
- Common grazing ground or land for exercising the animals will be easily available under the co-operative system, whereas today generally there is nothing of the kind for individual farmers.
- The expense on fodder will be comparatively far less under the collective system.
- The sale of milk at good prices will be greatly facilitated and there will be no need or temptation for the farmer to adulterate it as he does as an individual.
- It is impossible to carry out tests of the fitness of every head of cattle individually, but this could easily be done for the cattle of a whole village and would thus make it easier to improve the breed.
- The foregoing advantages should be sufficient argument in favour of co-operative cattle-farming. The strongest argument in its favour is that the individualistic system has been the means of making our own condition as well as that of our cattle pitiable. We can only save ourselves and them by making this essential change.

I firmly believe too that we shall not derive the full benefits of agriculture until we take to co-operative farming. Does it not stand to reason that it is far better for a hundred families in a village to cultivate their lands collectively and divide the income therefrom than to divide the land anyhow into a hundred portions? And what applies to land applies equally to cattle.

It is quite another matter that it may be difficult to convert people to adopt this way of life straightaway. The straight and narrow road is always hard to traverse. Every step in the programme of cow service is strewn with thorny problems. But only by surmounting difficulties can we hope to make the path easier. My purpose for the time being is to show the great superiority of collective cattle-farming over the individual effort. I hold further that the latter is wrong and the former only is right. In reality even the individual can only safeguard his independence through co-operation. In cattle-farming the individual effort has led to selfishness and inhumanity, whereas the collective effort can abate both the evils, if it does not remove them altogether.[1]

The excreta of animals and human beings mixed with refuse can be turned into golden manure, itself a valuable commodity. It increases the productivity of the soil which receives it. Preparation of this manure is itself a village industry. But this, like all village industries cannot give tangible results unless the crores of India co-operated in reviving them and thus making India prosperous.[2]

34

VILLAGE SANITATION

Divorce between intelligence and labour has resulted in criminal negligence of the villages. And so, instead of having graceful hamlets dotting the land, we have dung-heaps. The approach to many villages is not a refreshing experience. Often one would like to shut one's eyes and stuff one's nose; such is the surrounding dirt and offending smell. If the majority of Congress-men were derived from our villages, as they

> *Divorce between intelligence and labour has resulted in criminal negligence of the villages*

should be, they should be able to make our villages models of cleanliness in every sense of the word. But they have never considered it their duty to identify themselves with the villagers in their daily lives. A sense of national or social sanitation is not a virtue among us. We may take a kind of a bath, but we do not mind dirtying the well or the tank or the river by whose side or in which we perform ablutions. I regard this defect as a great vice which is responsible for the disgraceful state of our villages and the sacred banks of the sacred rivers and for the diseases that spring from insanitation.[1]

The things to attend to in the villages are cleaning tanks and wells and keeping them clean, getting rid of dung-heaps. If the workers will begin the work themselves, working like paid *bhangis* from day to day and always letting the villagers know that they are expected to join them so as ultimately to do the whole work themselves, they may be sure that they will find that the villagers will sooner or later co-operate.

Lanes and streets have to be cleansed of all the rubbish, which should be classified. There are portions which can be turned into manure, portions which have simply to be buried and portions which can be directly turned into wealth. Every bone picked up is valuable raw material from which useful articles can be made or which can be crushed into rich manure. Rags and waste-paper can be turned into paper, and excreta picked up are golden manure for the village fields. The way to treat the excreta is to mix them, liquid as well as solid, with superficial earth in soil dug no deeper than one foot at the most. In his book on rural hygiene, Dr. Poore says that excreta should be buried in earth no deeper than nine to twelve inches (I am quoting from memory). The author contends that superficial earth is charged with minute life, which, together with light and air which easily penetrate it, turn the excreta into good soft sweet-smelling soil within a week. Any villager can test this for himself. The way to do it is either to have fixed latrines, with earthen or iron buckets, and empty the contents in properly prepared places from day to day, or to perform the function directly on to the ground dug up in squares. The excreta can either be buried in a village common or in individual fields. This can only be done by the co-operation of the villagers. At the worst, an enterprising villager can collect the excreta and turn them into wealth for himself. At present, this rich manure, valued at lakhs of rupees, runs to waste every day, fouls the air and brings disease into the bargain.

Village tanks are promiscuously used for bathing, washing clothes, and drinking and cooking purposes. Many village tanks are also used by cattle. Buffaloes are often to be seen wallowing in them. The wonder is that, in spite of this sinful misuse of village tanks, villages have not been destroyed by epidemics. It is the universal medical evidence that this neglect to ensure purity of the water supply of villages is responsible for many of the diseases suffered by the villagers.

This, it will be admitted, is a gloriously interesting and instructive service, fraught with incalculable benefit to the suffering humanity of India. I hope it is clear from my description of the way in which the problem should be tackled, that, given willing workers who will wield the broom and the shovel with the same ease and pride as the pen and the pencil, the question of expense is almost wholly eliminated. All the outlay that will be required is confined to a broom, a basket, a shovel and a pick-axe, and possibly some disinfectant. Dry ashes are, perhaps, as effective a disinfectant as any that a chemist can supply.[2]

An ideal Indian village will be so constructed as to lend itself to perfect sanitation. It will have cottages with sufficient light and ventilation built of a material obtainable within a radius of five miles of it. The cottages will have courtyards enabling householders to plant vegetables for domestic use and to house their cattle. The village lanes and streets will be free of all avoidable dust. It will have wells according to its needs and accessible to all. It will have houses of worship for all, also a common meeting place, a village common for grazing its cattle, a co-operative dairy, primary and secondary schools in which industrial education will be the central fact, and it will have Panchayats for settling disputes. It will produce its own grains, vegetables and fruit, and its own Khadi. This is roughly my idea of a model village. In the present circumstances its cottages will remain what they are with slight improvements. Given a good zamindar, where there is one, or co-operation among the people, almost the whole of the programme other than model cottages can be worked out at an expenditure within the means of the villagers including the zamindar or zamindars, without Government assistance. With that assistance there is no limit to the possibility of village reconstruction. But my task just now is to discover what the villagers can do to help themselves if they have mutual co-operation and contribute voluntary labour for the common good. I am convinced that they can, under intelligent guidance, double the village income as distinguished from individual income. There are in our villages inexhaustible resources not for commercial purposes in every case but certainly for local purposes in almost every case. The greatest tragedy is the hopeless unwillingness of the villagers to better their lot.

The very first problem the village worker will solve is its sanitation. It is the most neglected of all the problems that baffle workers and that undermine physical well-being and breed disease. If the worker became a voluntary *bhangi*, he would begin by collecting night-soil and turning it into manure and sweeping village streets. He will tell people how and where they should perform daily functions and speak to them on the value of sanitation and the great injury caused by its neglect. The worker will continue to do the work whether the villagers listen to him or no.[3]

35

VILLAGE HEALTH

I hold that where the rules of personal, domestic and public sanitation are strictly observed and due care is taken in the matter of diet and exercise, there should be no occasion for illness or disease. Where there is absolute purity, inner and outer, illness becomes impossible. If the village people could but understand this, they would not need doctors, *hakims* or *vaidyas*.[1]

Nature cure implies an ideal mode of life and that in its turn presupposes ideal living conditions in towns and villages. The name of God is, of course, the hub round which the nature cure system revolves.

Nature cure implies that the treatment should be the cheapest and the simplest possible. The ideal is that such treatment should be carried out in the villages. The villagers should be able to provide the necessary means and equipment. What cannot be had in the villages should be procured. Nature cure does mean a change for the better in one's outlook on life itself. It means regualation of one's life in accordance with the laws of health. It is not a matter of taking the free medicine from the hospital or for fees. A man who takes free

> *Disease springs from a wilful or ignorant breach of the laws of nature. It follows, therefore, that timely return to those laws should mean restoration*

treatment from the hospital accepts charity. The man who accepts nature cure never begs. Self-help enhances self-respect. He takes steps to cure himself by eliminating poisons from the

Village Health   **133**

system and takes precautions against falling ill in the future.

Right diet and balanced diet are necessary. Today our villages are as bankrupt as we are ourselves. To produce enough vegetables, fruits and milk in the villages, is an essential part of the nature cure scheme. Time spent on this should not be considered a waste. It is bound to benefit all the villagers and ultimately the whole of India.[2]

The essence of nature cure is that we learn the principles of hygiene and sanitation and abide by those laws as well as the laws relating to proper nutrition. Thus does every one become his own doctor. The man who eats to live, who is friends with the five powers, earth, water, ether, sun and air and who is a servant of God, the Creator of all these, ought not to fall ill. If he does, he will remain calm relying on God and die in peace, if need be. If there are any medicinal herbs in the fields of his village he may make use of them. Crores live and die like this without a murmur. They have not so much as heard of a doctor, much less seen one face to face. let us become really village-minded. Village children and adults come to us. Let us teach them how to live truly. Doctors aver that 99% of disease springs from insanitation, from eating the wrong food and from under-nourishment. If we can teach this 99% the art of living, we can afford to forget the 1%....They may find a philanthropic doctor.... to look after them. We need not worry about them. Today pure water, good earth, fresh air, are unknown to us. We do not know the inestimable value of ether and the sun. If we make use of these five powers and if we eat the proper and balanced diet, we shall have done the work of ages. For acknowledging this knowledge, we need neither degrees nor crores of money. What we need are a living faith in God, a zeal for service, an acquaintance with the five powers of nature and a knowledge of dietetics. All this can be acquired without wasting time in schools and colleges.[3]

Disease springs from a wilful or ignorant breach of the laws of nature. It follows, therefore, that timely return to those laws should mean restoration. A person who has tried nature beyond endurance, must either suffer the punishment inflicted by nature or in order to avoid it, seek the assistance of the physician or the surgeon as the case may be. Every submission to merited punishment strengthens the mind of man, every avoidance saps it.[4]

I would like to know what the medical men and scientists are doing for the country. One finds them readily going to foreign lands to learn new modes of treating special diseases. I suggest that they should turn their attention towards the seven lakhs of the villages of India. They would immediately discover that all the qualified men and women are required for village service, not after the manner of the West but after the manner of the East. They will then adapt themselves to many indigenous systems. India does not need imported drugs from the West when she has an inexhaustible stock of a variety of drugs grown in the villages themselves. But more than drugs they have to teach the people the right mode of living.[5]

My nature cure is designed solely for villagers and villages. Therefore, there is no place in it for the microscope, X-rays and similar things. Nor is there room in nature cure for medicines, such as quinine, emetin and penicillin. Personal hygiene and healthy living are of primary importance. And these should suffice. If everyone could achieve perfection in this art, there could be no disease. And, while obeying all the laws of Nature in order to cure illness, if it does come, the sovereign remedy ever lies in *Ramanama*. But this cure through *Ramanama* cannot become universal in the twinkling of an eye. To carry conviction to the patient, the physician has to be a living embodiment of the power of *Ramanama*.[6]

36

VILLAGE DIET

Polished *v.* Unpolished Rice

If rice can be pounded in the villages after the old fashion the wages will fill the pockets of the rice pounding sisters and the rice eating millions will get some sustenance from the unpolished rice instead of pure starch which the polished rice provides. Human greed, which takes no count of the health or the wealth of the people who come under its heels, is responsible for the hideous rice-mills one sees in all the rice-producing tracts. If public opinion was strong, it will make rice-mills an impossibility by simply insisting on unpolished rice and appealing to the owners of rice-mills to stop a traffic that undermines the health of a whole nation and robs the poor people of an honest means of livelihood.[1]

Whole-wheat

That branless (wheat) flour is as bad as polished rice is the universal testimony of medical men. Whole-wheat flour ground in one's own *chakki* is any day superior to, and cheaper than, the fine flour to be had in the bazars. It is cheaper because the cost of grinding is saved. Again, in the whole-wheat flour there is no loss of weight. In fine flour there is loss of weight. The richest part of

> The man who eats to live, who is friends with the five powers, earth, water, ether, sun and air and who is a servant of God, the Creator of all these, ought not to fall ill

wheat is contained in its bran. There is a terrible loss of nutrition when the bran of wheat is removed. The villagers and others who eat whole-wheat flour ground in their own *chakkis* save their money and, what is more important, their health. A large part of the millions that flour-mills make will remain in and circulate among the deserving poor when village grinding is revived.[2]

Gur

According to the medical testimony...*gur* is any day superior to refined sugar in food value, and if the villagers cease to make *gur* as they are beginning to do, they will be deprived of an important food adjunct for their children. They may do without *gur* themselves, but their children cannot without undermining their stamina....Retention of *gur* and its use by the people in general means several crores of rupees retained by the villagers.[3]

Green Leaves

Take up any modern text-books on food or vitamins, and you would find in it a strong recommendation to take a few edible green leaves uncooked at every meal. Of course, these should always be well washed half a dozen times to remove all dirt. These leaves are to be had in every village for the trouble of picking. And yet greens are supposed to be only a delicacy of cities.

Villagers in many parts of India live on *dal* and *rice* or *roti*, and plenty of chillies, which harm the system. Since the economic re-organization of villages has been commenced with food reform, it is necessary to find out the simplest and cheapest foods that would enable villagers to regain lost health. The addition of green leaves to their meals will enable villagers to avoid many diseases from which they are now suffering. The villagers' food is deficient in vitamins; many of them can be supplied by fresh green leaves. I had introduced in my diet the leaves of *sarsav, suva,* turnip-tops, carrot-tops, radish-tops and pea-nut leaves. Besides these, it is hardly necessary to state that the radish, turnip and carrot tubers are also known to be edible in their raw state. It is waste of money and 'good' taste to cook these leaves or tubers. The vitamins contained in these vegetables are wholly or partially lost in cooking. I have called cooking these waste of 'good' taste, because the uncooked vegetables have a natural good taste of their own which is destroyed by cooking.[4]

37

THE VILLAGE WORKER

The village work frightens us. We who are town-bred find it trying to take to the village life. Our bodies in many cases do not respond to the hard life. But it is a difficulty which we have to face boldly, even heroically, if our desire is to establish Swaraj for the people, not substitute one class rule by another, which may be even worse. Hitherto the villagers have died in their thousands so that we (town-dwellers) might live. Now we might have to die so that they may live. The difference will be fundamental. The farmer have died unknowingly and involuntarily. Their enforced sacrifice has degraded us. If now we die knowingly and willingly, our sacrifice will ennoble us and the whole nation. Let us not flinch from the necessary sacrifice, if we will live as an independent self-respecting nation.[1]

There is no school equal to a decent home and no teachers equal to honest, virtuous parents. Modern (high school) education is a dead-weight on the villagers. Their children will never be able to get it, and thank God, they will never miss it if they have the training of decent home. If the village worker is not a decent man or woman, capable of conducting a decent home, he or she had better not aspire after the high privilege and honour of becoming a village worker.... What they need is not a knowledge of the three R's but a knowledge of their economic life and how they can better it. They are today working as automatons, without any responsibility whatsoever to their surroundings and without feeling the joy of work.[2]

Villages have suffered long from neglect by those who have

had the benefit of education. They have chosen the city life. The village movement is an attempt to establish healthy contact with the villages by inducing those who are fired with the spirit of service to settle in them and find self-expression in the service of villagers.... Those who have settled in villages in the spirit of service are not dismayed by the difficulties facing them. They knew before they went that they would have to contend against many difficulties including even sullenness on the part of villagers. Only thsoe, therefore, who have faith in themselves and in

> Hitherto the villagers have died in their thousands so that we (town-dwellers) might live. Now we might have to die so that they may live. The difference will be fundamental. The farmer have died unknowingly and involuntarily. Their enforced sacrifice has degraded us. If now we die knowingly and willingly, our sacrifice will ennoble us and the whole nation

their mission will serve the villagers and influence their lives. A true life lived amongst the people is in itself an object-lesson that must produce its own effect upon immediate surroundings. The difficulty with the young man is, perhaps, that he has gone to the village merely to earn a living without the spirit of service behind it. I admit that village life does not offer attractions to those who go there in search of money. Without the incentive of service village life would jar after the novelty has worn out. No young man having gone to a village may abandon the pursuit on the slightest contact with difficulty. Patient effort will show that villagers are not very different from city-dwellers and that they will respond to kindliness and attention. It is no doubt true that one does not have in the villages the opportunity of contact with the great ones of the land. With the growth of village mentality the leaders will find it necessary to tour in the villages and establish a living touch with them. Moreover the companionship of the great and the good is available to all through the works of saints like Chaitanya, Ramakrishna, Tulsidas, Kabir, Nanak, Dadu, Tukaram, Tiruvalluvar, and others too numerous to mention though equally known and pious. The difficulty is to get the mind turned to the reception of permanent values. If it is modern thought—political, social, economical, scientific—that is meant, it is possible to procure literature that will satisfy curiosity. I admit, however, that one does not find such as easily as one finds religious literature. Saints wrote and spoke for the masses. The vogue for translating modren thought to the masses in an acceptable manner has not yet quite set in. But it must come in time. I would, therefore, advise young men...not to give in but persist in their effort and by their presence make the villages more livable and lovable. That they will do by serving the villages in a manner acceptable to the villagers. Everyone can make a beginning by making the villages cleaner by their own labour and removing illiteracy to the extent of their ability. And if their lives are clean, methodical and industrious, there is no doubt that the infection will spread in the villages in which they may be working.[3]

Essential Items of Village Work

If rural reconstruction were not to include rural sanitation, our villages would remain the muck-heaps that they are today. Village sanitation is a vital part of village life and is as difficult as it is important. It needs a heroic effort to eradicate age-long insanitation. The village worker who is ignorant of the science of village sanitation, who is not a successful scavenger, cannot fit himself for village service.

It seems to be generally admitted that without the new or basic education the education of millions of children in India is well-nigh impossible. The village worker has, therefore, to master it, and become a basic education teacher himself.

Adult education will follow in the wake of basic education as a matter of course. Where this new education has taken root, the children themselves become thier parents' teachers. Be that as it may, the village worker has to undertake adult education also.

Woman is described as man's better half. As long as she has not the same rights in law as man, as long as the birth of a girl does not receive the same welcome as that of a boy, so long we should know that India is suffering from partial paralysis. Suppression of woman is a denial of Ahimsa. Every village worker will, therefore, regard every woman as his mother, sister or daughter as the case may be, and look upon her with respect. Only such a worker will command the confidence of the village people.

It is impossible for an unhealthy people to win Swaraj. Therefore we should no longer be guilty of the neglect of the health of our people. Every village worker must have a knowledge of the general principles of health.

Without a common language no nation can come into being. Instead of worrying himself with the controversy about Hindi-Hindustani and Urdu, the village worker will acquire a knowledge of the *rashtrabhasha* which should be such as can be understood by both Hindus and Muslims.

Our infatuation for English has made us unfaithful to provincial languages. If only as penance for this unfaithfulness the village worker should cultivate in the villagers a love of their own speech. He will have equal regard for all the other languages of India, and will learn the language of the part where he may be working, and thus be able to inspire the villagers there with a regard for their own speech.

The whole of this programme will, however, be a structure on sand if it is not built on the solid foundation of economic equality. Economic equality must never be supposed to mean possession of an equal amount of worldly goods by everyone. It does mean, however, that everyone will have a proper house to live in, sufficient and balanced food to eat, and sufficient Khadi with which to cover himself. It also means that the cruel inequality that obtains today will be removed by purely non-violent means.[4]

Requisite Qualifications

(The following are some qualifications prescribed by Gandhiji for Satyagrahis. But as a village worker was according to him also to be a true Satyagrahi, these qualifications may be regarded as applying also to a village worker.)
   – He must have a living faith in God, for He is his only Rock.
   – He must believe in truth and non-violence as his creed and therefore have faith in the inherent goodness of

human nature which he expects to evoke by his truth and love expressed through his suffering.

– He must be leading a chaste life and be ready and willing for the sake of his cause to give up his life and his possessions.
– He must be a habitual Khadi-wearer and spinner. This is essential for India.
– He must be a teetotaller and be free from the use of other intoxicants in order that his reason may be always unclouded and his mind constant.
– He must carry out with a willing heart all the rules of discipline as may be laid down from time to time.

The qualifications are not to be regarded as exhaustive. They are illustrative only.[5]

38

ALL-ROUND VILLAGE SERVICE

A Samagra Gramsevak must know everybody living in the village and render them such service as he can. That does not mean that the worker will be able to do everything single-handed. He will show them the way of helping themselves and procure for them such help and materials as they require. He will train up his own helpers. He will so win over the villagers that they will seek and follow his advice. Supposing I go and settle down in a village with a *ghani*, I won't be an ordinary *ghanchi* earning 15-20 rupees a month. I will be a Mahatma *ghanchi*. I have used the word 'Mahatma' in fun but what I mean to say is that as a *ghanchi* I will become a model for the villagers to follow. I will be a *ghanchi* who knows the Gita and the Quran. I will be learned enough to teach their children. I may not be able to do so for lack of time. The villagers will come to me and ask me : "Please make arrangements for our children's education." I will tell them: "I can find you a teacher but you will have to bear the expenses." And they will be prepared to do so most willingly. I will teach them spinning and when they come and ask me for the services of a weaver, I will find them a weaver on the same terms as I found them a teacher. And the weaver will teach them how to weave their own cloth. I will inculcate in them the importance of hygiene and sanitation and when they come and ask me for a sweeper, I will tell them: "I will be your sweeper and I will train you all in the job." This is my conception of Samagra Gramseva. You may tell me that I will never find a *ghanchi* of this description in this age. Then I will say that we cannot hope to improve our villages in this age. Take the example of a *ghanchi* in Russia. After all the man who runs an oil mill is a *ghanchi*. He has money but his strength does not lie in his money. Real strength lies in knowledge. True knowledge gives a moral standing and moral strength. Everyone seeks the advice of such a man.[1]

Village Factions

Alas for India that parties and factions are to be found in the villages as they are to be found in our cities. And when power politics enter our villages with less thought of the welfare of the villages and more of using them for increasing the parties' own power, this becomes a hindrance to the progress of the villagers rather than a help. I would say that whatever be the consequence, we must make use as much as possible of local help and if we are free from the taint of power politics, we are not likely to go wrong. Let us remember that the English-educated men and women from the cities have criminally neglected the villages of India which are the backbone of the country. The process of remembering our neglect will induce patience. I have never gone to a single village which is devoid of an honest worker. We fail to find him when we are not humble enough to recognize any merit in our villages. Of course, we are to steer clear of local politics and this we shall learn to do when we accept help from all parties and no parties, wherever it is really good.[2]

39

A CALL TO YOUTH

My hope lies in the youth of the country. Such of them as are prey to vice are not vicious by nature. They are helplessly and thoughtlessly drawn to it. They must realize the harm that it has done them and society. They must understand too that nothing but a rigorously disciplined life will save them and the country from utter ruin.[1]

Above all, unless they visualize God and seek His aid in keeping them from temptation, no amount of dry discipline will do them much good. Seeing God face to face is to feel that He is enthroned in our hearts even as a child feels a mother's affection without needing any demonstration.[2]

Young men...claiming...to be the fathers of tomorrow, should be the salt of the nation. If the salt loses its flavour wherewith shall it be salted?[3]

Youth will be emotional all the world over. Hence the utter necessity of preconceived and deliberate *brahmacharya* during the study period, *i.e.* at least 25 years.[4]

> Young men...claiming...to be the fathers of tomorrow, should be the salt of the nation. If the salt loses its flavour wherewith shall it be salted?

Innocent youth is a priceless possession not to be squandered away for the sake of a momentary excitement miscalled pleasure.[5]

Put all your knowledge, learning and scholarship in one scale and truth and purity in the other and the latter will by far outweigh the other. The *miasma* of moral impurity has today spread among our school-going children and like a hidden epidemic is working havoc among them. I therefore appeal to you, boys and girls, to keep your minds and bodies pure. All your scholarship, all your study of the scriptures will be in vain if you fail to translate their teachings into your daily life. I know that some of the teachers too do not lead pure and clean lives. To them I say that even if they impart all the knowledge in the world to their students but inculcate not truth and purity among them, they will have betrayed them and instead of raising them set them on the downward road to perdition. Knowledge without character is a power for evil only, as seen in the instances of so many 'talented thieves' and 'gentlemen rascals' in the world.[6]

I ask you (young men) to go to the villages and bury yourselves there, not as their masters or benefactors, but as their humble servants. Let them know what to do and how to change their modes of living from your daily conduct and way of living. Only feeling will be of no use just like steam which by itself is of no account unless it is kept under proper control— when it becomes a mighty force. I ask you to go forth as messengers of God carrying balm for the wounded soul of India.[7]

As father of, you might say, many boys and girls, you might almost say of thousands of boys and girls, I want to tell you, boys, that after all you hold your destiny in your own hands. I do not care what you learn or what you do not learn in your school, if you will observe two conditions. One condition is that you must be fearlessly truthful against the heaviest odds under every circumstance imaginable. A truthful boy, a brave boy will never think of hurting even a fly. He will defend all the weak boys in his school and help, whether inside school or outside, all those who need his help. A boy who does not observe personal purity of mind and body and action is a boy who should be driven out of any school. A chivalrous boy would always keep his mind pure, his eyes straight and his hands unpolluted. You do not need to go to any school to learn these fundamental maxims of life, and if you will have this triple character with you, you will build on a solid foundation.[8]

We are inheritors of a rural civilization. The vastness of our country, the vastness of the population, the situation and the climate of the country have, in my opinion, destined it for a rural civilization. Its defects are well known, but not one of them is irremediable. To uproot it and substitute for it an urban civilization seems to me an impossibility, unless we are prepared by some drastic means to reduce the population from three hundred million to three or say even thirty. I can therefore suggest remedies on the assumption that we must perpetuate the present rural civilization and endeavour to rid it of its acknowledged defects. This can only be done if the youth of the country will settle down to village life. And if they will do this, they must reconstruct their life and pass every day of their vacation in the villages surrounding their colleges or high schools, and those who have finished their education or are not receiving any should think of settling down in villages.[9]

If the sense of shame that wrongly attaches to physical labour could be got rid of, there is enough work and to spare for young men and women of average intelligence.[10]

No labour is too mean for one who wants to earn an honest penny. The only thing is the readiness to use the hands and feet that God has given us.[11]

40

THE NATION'S HEALTH, HYGIENE AND DIET

It is established beyond doubt that ignorance and neglect of the laws of health and hygiene are responsible for the majority of diseases to which mankind is heir. The very high death rate among us is no doubt due largely to our gnawing poverty, but it could be mitigated if the people were properly educated about their health and hygiene.

Mens sana in corpore sano is perhaps the first law for humanity. A healthy mind in a healthy body is a self-evident truth. There is an inevitable connection between mind and body. If we were in possession of healthy minds, we would shed all violence and, naturally obeying the laws of health, we would have healthy bodies without an effort.

The fundamental laws of health and hygiene are simple and easily learnt. The difficulty is about their observance. Here are some:

Think the purest thoughts and banish all idle and impure thoughts.

Breathe the freshest air day and night.

Establish a balance between bodily labour and mental work.

Stand erect, sit erect, and be neat and clean in every one of your acts, and let these be an expression of your inner condition.

Eat to live for service of fellow-men. Do not live for indulging yourselves. Hence your food must be just enough to keep your mind and body in good order. Man becomes what he eats.

Your water, food and air must be clean, and you will not be satisfied with mere personal cleanliness, but you will infect your surroundings with the same threefold cleanliness that you will desire for yourselves.[1]

Minimum Diet

Use one grain at a time. *Chapati*, rice and pulses, milk, ghee, *gur* and oil are used in ordinary households besides vegetable and fruit. I regard this an unhealthy combination. Those who get animal protein in the shape of milk, cheese, eggs or meat need not use pulses at all, the poor people get only vegetable protein. If the well-to-do give up pulse and oils, they set free these two essentials for the poor who get neither animal protein nor animal fat. Then the grain eaten should not be sloppy. Half the quantity suffices when it is eaten dry and not dripped in gravy. It is well to eat with raw salads such as onion, carrot, radish, salad leaves, tomatoes. An ounce or two of salads serve the purpose of eight ounces of cooked vegetables. *Chapatis* or bread should not be eaten with milk. To begin with, one meal may be raw vegetables and *chapati* or bread, and the other cooked vegetables with milk or curds.

> There is a great deal of truth in the saying that man becomes what he eats. The grosser the food the grosser the body

Sweet dishes should be eliminated altogether. Instead *gur* or sugar in small quantities may be taken with milk or bread or by itself.

Fresh fruit is good to eat, but only a little is necessary to give tone to the system. It is an expensive article, and an over-indulgence by the well-to-do has deprived the poor and the ailing of an article which they need much more than the well-to-do.

Any medical man who has studied the science of dietetics will certify that what I have suggested can do no harm to the body; on the contrary it must conduce to better health.[2]

The unlimited capacity of the plant world to sustain man at his highest is a region yet unexplored by modern medical science which through force of habit pins its faith on the shambles or at least milk and its by-products. It is a duty which awaits discharge by Indian medical men whose tradition is vegetarian. The fast developing researches about vitamins and the possibility of getting the most important of them directly from the sun bids fair to revolutionize many of the accepted theories and beliefs propounded by medical science about food.[3]

It almost seems to me that it is reserved for lay enthusiasts to cut their way through a mountain of difficulties even at the risk of their lives to find the truth. I should be satisfied if scientists would lend their assistance to such humble seekers.[4]

I believe that man has little need to drug himself. 999 cases out of a thousand can be brought round by means of a well-regulated diet, water and earth treatment and similar household remedies.[5]

Instead of using the body as a temple of God we use it as a vehicle for indulgences, and are not ashamed to run to medical men for help in our effort to increase them and abuse the earthly tabernacle.[6]

There is a great deal of truth in the saying that man becomes what he eats. The grosser the food the grosser the body.[7]

I do feel that spiritual progress does demand at some stage that we should cease to kill our fellow creatures for the satisfaction of our bodily wants. The beautiful lines of Goldsmith occur to me as I tell you of my vegetarian fad:

No flocks that range the valley free
To slaughter I condemn,
Taught by the Power that pities me
I learn to pity them.[8]

I do not regard flesh-food as necessary for us at any stage and under any clime in which it is possible for human beings ordinarily to live. I hold flesh-food to be unsuited to our species. We err in copying the lower animal world if we are superior to it. Experience teaches that animal food is unsuited to those who would curb their passions.

But it is wrong to over-estimate the importance of food in the formation of character or in subjugating the flesh. Diet is a powerful factor not to be neglected. But to sum up all religion in terms of diet, as is often done in India, is as wrong as it is to disregard all restraint in regard to diet and to give full reins to one's appetite. Vegetarianism is one of the priceless gifts of Hinduism. It may not be lightly given up. It is necessary, therefore, to correct the error that vegetarianism has made us weak in mind or body or passive or inert in action. The greatest Hindu reformers have been the activest in their generation and they have invariably been vegetarians. Who could show greater activity than say Shankara or Dayananda in their times?[9]

When to Fast

Out of the fulness of my own experience and that of fellow cranks, I say without hesitation, fast (1) if you are constipated, (2) if you are anaemic, (3) if you are feverish, (4) if you have indigestion, (5) if you have a headache, (6) if you are rheumatic, (7) if you are gouty, (8) if you are fretting and fuming, (9) if you are depressed, (10) if you are overjoyed, and you will avoid medical prescriptions and patent medicines.[10]

National Food

I believe that we should be able to accommodate ourselves to the food eaten in the provinces other than our own. I know that this is not so simple a question as it appears. I know southerners who have made a herculean effort to take to Gujarati food and failed. Gujaratis will not take to the southern mode of cooking. Bengal produces dainties which the other provinces will not easily relish. If we would be national instead of provincial, we would have to have an interchange of habits as to food, simplify our tastes and produce healthy dishes all can take with impunity. This means a careful study of the foods taken by different provinces, castes and dinominations. Unfortunately, or fortunately, there are not only different combinations in different provinces, but there are different styles in the same province, among the different communities. It is necessary, therefore, for national workers to study the foods and the methods of preparing them in the various provinces and discover common, simple and cheap dishes which all can take without upsetting the digestive apparatus. In any case, it must be a shame for workers not to know the manners and customs of different provinces and communities....What can and should be aimed at are common dishes for common people. This I know is easily possible if we have the mind. But to make this possible, volunteers will have to learn the art of cooking and for this purpose they will have also to study the values of different foods and evolve common dishes easily and cheaply prepared.[11]

Leprosy

Leper is a word of bad odour. India is perhaps a home of lepers next only to Central Africa. Yet they are as much a part of society as the tallest among us. But the tall absorb our attention though they are least in need of it. The lot of the lepers who are much in need of attention is studied neglect. I am tempted to call it heartless, which it certainly is, in terms of non-violence. It is largely the missionary who, be it said to his credit, bestows care on him. The only institution run by an Indian, as a pure labour of love, is by Shri Manohar Diwan near Wardha. It is working under the inspiration and guidance of Shri Vinoba Bhave. If India is pulsating with new life, there would not be a leper or beggar in India uncared for. What the leper is in India, that we are, if we will but look about us, for the modern civilized world. Examine the condition of our brethren across the ocean and the truth of my remark will be borne home to us.[12]

There are many other contagious diseases like scabies, cholera, plague, even common cold. Leprosy is far less infectious perhaps than these. Why should there be a stigma about leprosy any more than about other infectious diseases? Real leprosy is attached to an unclean mind. To look down upon fellow human beings, to condemn any community or class of men, is a sign of a diseased mind, far worse than physical leprosy. Such men are real lepers of society. He himself did not attach much importance to names. A rose would not lose its fragrance if it was called by any other name.[13]

41

DRINK AND DRUGS

Liquor, as we say, is an invention of the devil. In Islam it is said that when Satan began to beguile men and women he dangled before them the "red water". I have seen in so many cases that liquor has not only robbed men of their money but of their reason, they have for the time being forgotten the distinction between wife and mother, lawful and unlawful. I have seen drunken barristers wallowing in gutters carried home by the police. I have found on two occasions captains of steamers so dead drunk as to be incapable of keeping charge of their boats till they came to their senses. For both flesh-meats and liquor the sovereign rule is "we must not live in order to eat and drink and be merry, but eat and drink in order to make our bodies temples of God and use them for service of man." Liquor may be a medical necessity on occasions; and when life seems to be extinct it may be possible to prolong it with a dose of liquor, but that is about all that can be said for it.[1]

> The drink and the drug evil is in many respects infinitely worse than the evil caused by malaria and the like; for, whilst the latter only injure the body, the former saps both body and soul.

You will not be deceived by the specious argument that India must not be made sober by compulsion, and that those who wish to drink must have facilities provided for them. The State does not cater for the vices of its people. We do not regulate or license houses of ill-fame. We do not provide facilities for thieves to indulge their propensity for thieving. I hold drink to be more damnable than thieving and perhaps even prostitution. Is it not often the parent of both?[2]

Drink is more a disease than a vice. I know scores of men who would gladly leave off drink if they could. I know some who have asked that the temptation might be put away from them. In spite of the temptation having been put away at their instance, I have known them to steal drink. I do not, therefore, think that it was wrong to have removed the temptation. Diseased persons have got to be helped against themselves.[3]

Having identified myself with labour, I know what ruin drink has brought to the homes of labourers given to drink. I know that they will not touch liquor if it was not within easy reach. We have contemporaneous evidence that drinkers themselves are in many cases asking for prohibition.[4]

The drink habit destroys the soul of man and tends to turn him into a beast, incapable of distinguishing between wife, mother and sister. I have seen men who forget this distinction under the influence of liquor.[5]

The drink and the drug evil is in many respects infinitely worse than the evil caused by malaria and the like; for, whilst the latter only injure the body, the former saps both body and soul.[6]

I would rather have India reduced to a state of pauperism than have thousands of drunkards in our midst. I would rather have India without education if that is the price to be paid for making it dry.[7]

Nothing but ruin stares a nation in the face that is a prey to the drink habit. History records that empires have been destroyed through that habit. We have it in India that the great community to which Shri Krishna belonged was ruined by that habit. This monstrous evil was undoubtedly one of the contributory factory in the fall of Rome.[8]

If I was appointed dictator for one hour for all India, the first thing I would do would be to close without compensation all the liquor shops, and compel factory owners to produce humane conditions for their workmen and open refreshment and recreation rooms where these workmen would get innocent drinks and equally innocent amusements.[9]

Toddy

There is a school who favour limited and regulated consumption of alcohol and believe it to be useful. I have not found any weight in their argument. Even if we accept their view for a moment, we have still to face the fact that innumerable human beings cannot be kept under discipline. Therefore, it becomes our duty to prohibit alcoholic drinks even if it were only for the sake of this vast majority.

Parsis have strongly supported the use of toddy. They say that although toddy is an intoxicant it is also a food and even helps to digest other foodstuffs. I have carefully examined this argument and have read a fair amount of literature pertaining to this subject. But I have been a witness of the terrible straits to which toddy reduces the poor and therefore I have come to the conclusion that it can have no place in man's food.

The advantages, attributed to toddy, are all available from other foodstuffs. Toddy is made out of *khajuri* juice. Fresh *khajuri* juice is not an intoxicant. It is known as *nira* in Hindustani and many people have been cured of their constipation as a result of drinking *nira*. I have taken it myself. Though it did not act as a laxative with me, I found that it had the same food value as sugarcane juice. If one drinks a glass of *nira* in the morning instead of tea etc., he should not need anything else for breakfast.

As in the case of sugar-cane juice, palm juice can be boiled to make palm jaggery. *Khajuri* is a variety of palm tree. Several varieties of palm grow spontaneously in our country. All of them yield drinkable juice. As *nira* gets fermented very quickly, it has to be used up immediately and therefore on the spot. Since this condition is difficult to fulfil except to a limited extent, in practice, the best use of *nira* is to convert it into palm jaggery. Palm jaggery can well replace cane-juice jaggery. In fact some people prefer it to the latter. One advantage of palm jaggery over sugar-cane jaggery is that it is less sweet and therefore one can eat more of it...If the palms that are used for making toddy are used for making jaggery, India will never lack sugar and the poor will be able to get good jaggery for very little money.

Palm jaggery can be converted into molasses and refined sugar. But the jaggery is much more useful than refined sugar. The salts present in the jaggery are lost in the process of refining. Just as refined wheat flour and polished rice lose some of their nutritive value because of the loss of the pericarp, refined sugar also loses some of the nutritive value of the jaggery. One may generalize that all foodstuffs are richer if taken in their natural state as far as possible.[10]

Smoking

I have a horror of smoking as of wines. Smoking I consider to be a vice. It deadens one's conscience and is often worse than drink, in that it acts imperceptibly. It is a habit which is difficult to get rid of when once it seizes hold of a person. It is an expensive vice. It fouls the breath, discolours teeth and sometimes even causes cancer. It is an unclean habit.[11]

Smoking is in a way a greater curse than drink, inasmuch as the victim does not realize its evil in time. It is not regarded as a sign of barbarism, it is even acclaimed by the civilized people. I can only say, let those who can, give it up and set the example.[12]

Tobacco has simply worked havoc among mankind. Once caught in its tangle, it is rare to find anyone get out again....Tolstoy has called it the worst of all intoxicants.

In India people use tobacco for smoking, snuffing and also for chewing....Lovers of (or seekers after) health, if they are slaves to any of these evil habits, will resolutely get out of the slavery. Several people are addicted to one, two or all the three of these habits. They do not appear loathsome to them. But if we think over it calmly, there is nothing becoming about blowing off smoke or keeping the mouth stuffed with tobacco and *pan* practically the whole day long or keep on opening the snuff box and take snuff every now and then. All the three are most dirty habits.[13]

42

URBAN SANITATION

The one thing which we can and must learn from the West is the science of municipal sanitation. The people of the West have evolved a science of corporate sanitation and hygiene from which we have much to learn. We must modify western methods of sanitation to suit our requirements.[1]

'Cleanliness is next to godliness.' We can no more gain God's blessing with an unclean body than with an unclean mind. A clean body cannot reside in an unclean city.[2]

> The people of the West have evolved a science of corporate sanitation and hygiene from which we have much to learn

No municipality can cope with insanitation and congestion by the simple process of taxation and paid services. This vital reform is possible only by wholesale and voluntary co-operation of the people both rich and poor.[3]

It is not enough that we clear the villages which are occupied by our Pariah brethren. They are amenable to reason and persuasion. Shall we have to say that the so-called higher classes are not equally amenable to reason and persuasion and to hygienic laws which are indispensable in order to live a city-life? In a village we may do many things with impunity but immediately we transfer ourselves to crowded streets where we have hardly air to breathe, the life becomes changed, and we have to obey another set of laws which immediately come into being. Do we do that? It is no use saddling the muncipality with the responsibilities for the condition in which we find...the central parts of every city in India, and I feel no municipality in the world will be able to over-ride the habits of a class of people handed to them from generation to generation.... I, therefore, suggest that it is a question of sanitary reform in these big cities, which will be a hopeless task if we expect our municipalities to do this unaided by this voluntary work. Far be it from me to absolve the municipalities from their responsibilities.[4]

I consider myself a lover of municipal life. I think that it is a rare privilege for a person to find himself in the position of a municipal councillor but let me note down for you as a man with some experience in public life that one indispensable condition of that privilege is that the municipal councillors dare not approach their office from interested or selfish motives. They must approach their sacred task in a spirit of service. They should pride themselves upon calling themselves scavengers. There is a significant expression for municipal corporation in my mother tongue—*Kachrapatti*, which means literally scavenging department, and a municipality is nothing if it is not a premier scavenging department embracing all spheres of public and social life of a city and if it is not saturated with the spirit of scavenging, scavenging not merely by way of looking after the physical sanitation of a city, but also the internal sanitation of its citizens.[5]

If I were a taxpayer within the jurisdiction of a local board or a municipality, I would refuse to pay a single pie by way of additional taxation and advise others to do likewise unless the money we pay is returned four-fold. Those who enter local boards and municipalities as representatives go there not to seek honour or to indulge in mutual rivalries, but to render a service of love and that does not depend upon money. Ours is a pauper country. If our municipal councillors are imbued with a real spirit of service, they will convert themselves into unpaid sweepers, *bhangis* and road-makers, and take pride in doing so. They will invite their fellow-councillors, who may not have come on the Congress ticket, to join them and if they have faith in themselves and their mission, their example will not fail to evoke response. This means that a municipal councillor has to be a whole-timer. He should have no axe of his own to grind.

The next step would be to map out the entire adult population within the jurisdiction of the municipality or the local board. All should be asked to make their contribution to municipal activities. A regular register should be maintained. Those who are too poor to make any money contribution but are able-bodied and physically fit can be asked to give their free labour.[6]

If night-soil was properly utilized, we would get manure worth lakhs of rupees and also secure immunity from a number of diseases. By our bad habits we spoil our sacred river banks and furnish excellent breeding grounds for flies, with the result that the very flies which through our criminal negligence settle upon uncovered night-soil defile our bodies after we have bathed. A small spade is the means of salvation from a great nuisance. Leaving night-soil, cleaning the nose, or spitting on the road is a sin against God as well as humanity, and betrays a sad want of consideration for others. The man who does not cover his waste deserves a heavy penalty even if he lives in a forest.[7]

43

EVIL WROUGHT BY
THE FOREIGN MEDIUM

To give millions a knowledge of English is to enslave them. The foundation that Macaulay laid of education has enslaved us. I do not suggest that he had any such intention, but that has been the result....Is it not a painful thing that, if I want to go to a court of justice, I must employ the English language as a medium; that, when I become a barrister, I may not speak my mother tongue, and that someone else should have to translate to me from my own language? Is not this absolutely absurd? Is it not a sign of slavery? Am I to blame the English for it or myself? It is we, the English-knowing men, that have enslaved India. The curse of the nation will rest not upon the English but upon us.[1]

The strain of receiving instruction through a foreign medium is intolerable. Our children alone can bear it, but they have to pay for it. They become unfit to bear any other strain. For this reason our graduates are mostly without stamina, weak, devoid of energy, diseased and mere imitators. Originality, research, adventure, ceaseless effort, courage, dauntlessness and such other qualities have become atrophied. We are thus incapacitated for undertaking new enterprises, and we are unable to carry them through if we undertake any. Some who can give proof of such qualities die an untimely death....We the English-educated class are unfit to ascertain the true measure of the harm done by the unnatural system. We should get some idea of it if we realized how little we have reacted upon the masses.

The correspondence that should exist between the school training and the character imbibed with the mother's milk and the training received through her sweet speech is absent when the school training is given through a foreign tongue. However pure may be his motives, he who thus snaps the cord that should bind the school-life and the home-life is an enemy of the nation. We are traitors to our mothers by remaining under such a system. The harm done goes much further. A gulf has been created between the educated classes and the uneducated masses. The latter do not know us. We do not know the former. They consider us to be 'Saheblog'. They are afraid of us. They do not trust us....Fortunately the educated class seems to be waking up from its trance. They experience the difficulty of contact with the masses. How can they infect the masses with their own enthusiasm for the national cause? They cannot do so through English....Owing to the barrier thus created the flow of national life suffers impediment.

The fact is that when English occupies its proper place and the vernaculars receive their due, our minds which are today imprisoned will be set free and our brains though cultivated and trained, and yet being fresh, will not feel the weight of having to learn English as a language. And it is my belief that English thus learnt will be better than our English of today.

When we receive our education through the mother tongue, we should observe a different atmosphere in our homes. At present we are unable to make our wives co-partners with us. They know little of our activity. Our parents do not know what we learn. If we receive instruction through the mother tongue we should easily make our washermen, our barbers, and our *bhangis*, partakers of the high knowledge we might have gained. In England one discusses high politics with barbers while having a shave. We are unable to do so even in our family circle, not because the members of the family or the barbers are ignorant people. Their intellect is as well trained as that of the English barber. We are able to discuss intelligently with them the events of Mahabharat, Ramayana and of our holy places. For the national training flows in that direction. But we are unable to take home what we receive in our schools. We cannot reproduce before the family circle what we have learnt through the English language.

At the present moment the proceedings of our Legislative Councils are conducted in English. In many other institutions the same state of things prevails. We are, therefore, in the position of the miser who buries underground all his riches.... It is brought up as a charge against us that through our thoughtlessness we allow the water that flows from the mountain-tops during the rainy season to go to waste, and similarly treat valuable manure worth lakhs of rupees and get disease in the bargain. In the same manner, being crushed under the weight of having to learn English and through want of far-sightedness, we are unable to give the nation what it should receive at our hands. There is no exaggeration in this statement. It is an expression of the feelings that are raging within me. We shall have to pay dearly for our continuous disregard of the mother tongue. The nation has suffered much by reason of it. It is the first duty of the learned class now to deliver the nation from the agony—*From the presidential address to the Second Gujarat Educational Conference held at Broach on October 20, 1917.*

The greatest service we can render society is to free ourselves and it from the superstitious regard we have learnt to pay to the learning of the English language. It is the medium of instruction in our schools and colleges. It is becoming the *lingua franca* of the country. Our best thoughts are expressed in it....This belief in the necessity of English training has enslaved us. It has unfitted us for true national service. Were it not for force of habit, we could not fail to see that by reason of English being the medium of instruction, our intellect has been segregated, we have been isolated from the masses, the best mind of the nation has become gagged and the masses have not received the benefit of the new ideas we have received. We have been engaged these past sixty years in memorizing strange words and their pronunciation instead of assimilating facts. In the place of building upon the foundation, training received from our parents, we have almost unlearnt it. There is no parallel to this in history. It is a national tragedy. The first and greatest Social Service we can render is to revert to our vernaculars, to restore Hindi to its natural place as the National

> *The foreign medium has caused brain fag, put an undue strain upon the nerves of our children, made them crammers and imitators, unfitted them for original work and thought, and disabled them for filtrating their learning to the family or the masses*

Language and begin carrying on all our provincial proceedings in our respective vernaculars and national proceedings in Hindi. We ought not to rest till our schools and colleges give us instruction through the vernaculars....The day must soon come when our legislatures will debate national affairs in the vernaculars or Hindi as the case may be. Hitherto the masses have been strangers to their proceedings. The vernacular papers have tried to undo the mischief a little. But the task was beyond them. The *Patrika* reserves its biting sarcasm, the *Bengalee* its learning, for ears tuned to English. In this ancient land of cultured thinkers the presence in our midst of a Tagore or a Bose or a Ray ought not to excite wonder. Yet the painful fact is that there are so few of them.—*From the presidential address to the First All India Social Service Conference held at Calcutta on 27th December, 1917.*

It is my considered opinion that English education in the manner it has been given has emasculated the English-educated Indian, it has put a severe strain upon the Indian students' nervous energy, and has made of us imitators. The process of displacing the vernacular has been one of the saddest chapters in the British connection. Rammohan Rai would have been a greater reformer, and Lokmanya Tilak would have been a greater scholar, if they had not to start with the handicap of having to think in English and transmit their thoughts chiefly in English. Their effect on their own people, marvellous as it was, would have been greater if they had been brought up under a less unnatural system. No doubt they both gained from their knowledge of the rich treasures of English literature. But these should have been accessible to them through their own vernaculars. No country can become a nation by producing a race of imitators. Think of what would have happened to the English if they had not an authorized version of the Bible. I do believe that Chaitanya, Kabir, Nanak, Guru Govindsing, Shivaji, and Pratap were greater men than Rammohan Rai and Tilak. I know that comparisons are odious. All are equally great in their own way. But judged by the results, the effect of Rammohan and Tilak on the masses is not so permanent or far-reaching as that of the others more fortunately born. Judged by the obstacles they had to surmount, they were giants, and both would have been greater in achieving results, if they had not been handicapped by the system under which they received their training. I refuse to believe that the Raja and the Lokmanya could not have thought the thoughts they did without a knowledge of the English language. Of all the superstitions that affect India, none is so great as that a knowledge of the English language is necessary for imbibing ideas of liberty, and developing accuracy of thought. It should be remembered that there has been only one system of education before the country for the past fifty years, and only one medium of expression forced on the country. We have, therefore, no data before us as to what we would have been but for the education in the existing schools and colleges. This, however, we do know that India today is poorer than fifty years ago, less able to defend herself, and her children have less stamina. I need not be told that this is due to the defect in the system of Government. The system of education is its most defective part.

It was conceived and born in error, for the English rulers honestly believed the indigenous system to be worse than useless. It has been nurtured in sin, for the tendency has been to dwarf the Indian body, mind and soul.[2]

Reply to Tagore

....English is today studied because of its commercial and so-called political value. Our boys think, and rightly in the present circumstances that without English they cannot get Government service. Girls are taught English as a passport to marriage. I know several instances of women wanting to learn English so that they may be able to talk to Englishmen in English. I know husbands who are sorry that their wives cannot talk to them and their friends in English. I know families in which English is being *made* the mother tongue. Hundreds of youth believe that without a knowledge of English, freedom for India is practically impossible. The canker has so eaten into the society that in many cases, the only meaning of Education is a knowledge of English. All these are for me signs of our slavery and degradation. It is unbearable to me that the vernaculars should be crushed and starved as they have been. I cannot tolerate the idea of parents writing to their children, or husbands writing to their wives, not in their vernaculars but in English. I hope I am as great a believer in free air as the great Poet. I do not want my house to be walled in on all sides and my windows to be stuffed. I want the cultures of all the lands to be blown about my house as freely as possible. But I refuse to be blown off my feet by any. I refuse to live in other people's houses as an interloper, a beggar or a slave. I refuse to put the necessary strain of learning English upon my sisters for the sake of false pride or questionable social advantage. I would have our young men and young women with literary tastes to learn as much English and other world languages as they like, and then expect them to give the benefits of their learning to India and to the world, like a Bose, a Roy or the Poet himself. But I would not have a single Indian to forget, neglect or be ashamed of his mother tongue, or to feel that he or she cannot think or express the best thoughts in his or her own vernacular. Mine is not a religion of the prison-house. It has room for the least among God's creation. But it is proof against insolence, pride of race, religion or colour.[3]

The foreign medium has caused brain fag, put an undue strain upon the nerves of our children, made them crammers and imitators, unfitted them for original work and thought, and disabled them for filtrating their learning to the family or the masses. The foreign medium has made our children practically foreigners in their own land. It is the greatest tragedy of the existing system. The foreign medium has prevented the growth of our vernaculars. If I had the powers of a despot, I would today stop the tuition of our boys and girls through a foreign medium, and require all the teachers and professors on pain of dismissal to introduce the change forthwith. I would not wait for the preparation of text-books. They will follow the change. It is an evil that needs a summary remedy.[4]

But for the fact that the only higher education, the only education worth the name has been received by us through the English medium, there would be no need to prove such a self-evident proposition that the youth of a nation to remain a nation must receive instruction including the highest in its own vernacular or vernaculars. Surely, it is a self-demonstrated proposition that the youth of a nation cannot keep or establish a living contact with the masses unless their knowledge is received and assimilated through a medium understood by the people. Who can calculate the immeasurable loss sustained by the nation owing to thousands of its young men having been obliged to waste years in mastering a foreign language and its idiom of which in their daily life they have the least use and in learning which they had to neglect their own mother tongue and their own literature? There never was a greater superstition than that a particular language can be incapable of expansion or expressing abstruse or scientific ideas. A language is an exact reflection of the character and growth of its speakers.

Among the many evils of foreign rule, this blighting imposition of a foreign medium upon the youth of the country will be counted by history as one of the greatest. It has sapped the energy of the nation, it has shortened the lives of the pupils. It has estranged them from the masses, it has made education unnecessarily expensive. If this process is still persisted in, it bids fair to rob the nation of its soul. The sooner, therefore, educated India shakes itself free from the hypnotic spell of the foreign medium, the better it would be for them and the people.[5]

44

MY OWN EXPERIENCE

Let me give a chapter from my own experience. Up to the age of 12 all the knowledge I gained was through Gujarati, my mother tongue. I knew then something of Arithmetic, History and Geography. Then I entered a High School. For the first three years the mother tongue was still the medium. But the school master's business was to drive English into the pupil's head. Therefore, more than half of our time was given to learning English, and mastering its arbitrary spelling and pronunciation. It was a painful discovery to have to learn a language that was not pronounced as it was written. It was a strange experience to have to learn the spelling by heart. But that is by the way, and irrelevant to my argument. However, for the first three years it was comparatively plain sailing.

> I must not be understood to decry English or its noble literature. But the nobility of its literature cannot avail the Indian nation any more than the temperate climate or the scenery of England can avail her

The pillory began with the fourth year. Everything had to be learnt through English—Geometry, Algebra, Chemistry, Astronomy, History, Geography. The tyranny of English was so great that even Sanskrit or Persian had to be learnt through English, not through the mother tongue. If any boy spoke in the class in Gujarati which he understood, he was punished. It did not matter to the teacher if a boy spoke bad English which he could neither pronounce correctly nor understand fully. Why should the teacher worry?

His own English was by no means without blemish. It could not be otherwise. English was as much a foreign language to him as to his pupils. The result was chaos. We the boys had to learn many things by heart, though we could not understand them fully and often not at all. My head used to reel as the teacher was struggling to make his exposition on Geometry understood by us. I could make neither head nor tail of Geometry till we reached the 13th theorem of the first book of Euclid. And let me confess to the reader that in spite of all my love for the mother tongue, I do not to this day know the Gujarati equivalents of the technical terms of Geometry, Algebra and the like. I know now that what I took four years to learn of Arithmetic, Geometry, Algebra, Chemistry and Astronomy, I should have learnt easily in one year, if I had not to learn them through English but Gujarati. My grasp of the subjects would have been easier and clearer. My Gujarati vocubulary would have been richer. I would have made use of such knowledge in my own home. This English medium created an impassable barrier between me and the members of my family, who had not gone through English schools. My father knew nothing of what I was doing. I could not, even if I had wished it, interest my father in what I was learning. For though he had ample intelligence, he knew not a word of English. I was fast becoming a stranger in my own home. I certainly became a superior person. Even my dress began to undergo imperceptible changes. What happened to me was not an uncommon experience. It was common to the majority.

The first three years in the High School made little addition to my stock of general knowledge. They were a preparation for fitting the boys for teaching them everything through English. High Schools were schools for cultural conquest by the English. The knowledge gained by the three hundred boys of my High School became a circumscribed possession. It was not for transmission to the masses.

A word about literature. We had to learn several books of English prose and English poetry. No doubt all this was nice. But that knowledge has been of no use to me in serving or bringing me in touch with the masses. I am unable to say that if I had not learnt what I did of English prose and poetry, I should have missed a rare treasure. If I had, instead, passed those precious seven years in mastering Gujarati and have learnt Mathematics, Sciences, and Sanskrit and other subjects through Gujarati, I could easily have shared the knowledge so gained with my neighbours. I would have enriched Gujarati, and who can say that I would not have, with my habit of application and my inordinate love for the country and the mother tongue, made a richer and greater contribution to the service of the masses?

I must not be understood to decry English or its noble literature. The columns of the *Harijan* are sufficient evidence of my love of English. But the nobility of its literature cannot avail the Indian nation any more than the temperate climate or the scenery of England can avail her. India has to flourish in her own climate, and scenery, and her own literature, even though all the three may be inferior to the English climate, scenery and literature. We and our children must build on our own heritage. If we borrow from another we impoverish our own. We can never grow on foreign victuals. I want the nation to have the treasures contained in that language, and for that matter the other languages of the world, through its own vernaculars. I do not need to learn Bengali in order to know the beauties of Rabindranath's matchless productions. I get them through good translation. Gujarati boys and girls do not need to learn Russian to appreciate Tolstoy's short stories. They learn them through good translations. It is the boast of Englishmen that the best of the world's literary output is in the hands of that nation in simple English inside of a week of its publication. Why need I learn English to get at the best of what Shakespeare and Milton thought and wrote?

> We and our children must build on our own heritage. If we borrow from another we impoverish our own. We can never grow on foreign victuals

It would be good economy to set apart a class of students whose business would be to learn the best of what is to be learnt in the different languages of the world and give the translation in the vernaculars. Our masters chose the wrong way for us, and habit has made the wrong appear as right.

I find daily proof of the increasing and continuing wrong being done to the millions by our flase de-Indianizing education. These graduates who are my valued associates themselves flounder when they have to give expression to their innermost thoughts. They are strangers in their own homes. Their vocabulary in the mother tongue is so limited that they cannot always finish their speech without having recourse to English words and even sentences. Nor can they exist without English books. They often write to one another in English. I cite the case of my companions to show how deep the evil has gone. For we have made a conscious effort to mend ourselves.

It has been argued that the wastage that occurs in our colleges need not worry us if, out of the collegians, one Jagdish Bose can be produced by them. I should freely subscribe to the argument, if the wastage was unavoidable. I hope I have shown that it was and is even now avoidable. Moreover, the creation of a Bose does not help the argument. For Bose was not a product of the present education. He rose in spite of the terrible handicaps under which he had to labour. And his knowledge became almost intransmissible to the masses. We seem to have come to think that no one can hope to be like a Bose unless he knows English. I cannot conceive a grosser superstition than this. No Japanese feels so helpless as we seem to do.

The medium of instruction should be altered at once and at any cost, the provincial languages being given their rightful place. I would prefer temporary chaos in higher education to the criminal waste that is daily accumulating.

In order to enhance the status and market-value of the provincial languages, I would have the language of the law courts to be the language of the province where the court is situated. The proceedings of the provincial legislatures must be in the language, or even the languages of the province where a province has more than one language within its borders. I suggest to the legislators that they could, by enough application, inside of a month, understand the languages of their provinces. There is nothing to prevent a Tamilian from easily learning the simple grammar and a few hundred words of Telugu, Malayalam, and Kanarese all allied to Tamil. At the centre Hindustani must rule supreme.

In my opinion this is not a question to be decided by academicians. They cannot decide through what language the boys and girls of a place are to be educated. That question is already decided for them in every free country. Nor can they decide the subjects to be taught. That depends upon the wants of the country to which they belong. There is a privilege of enforcing the nation's will in the best manner possible. When this country becomes really free, the question of medium will be settled only one way. The academicians will frame the syllabus and prepare text-books accordingly. And the products of the education of a free India will answer the requirements of the country as today they answer those of the foreign ruler. So long as we the educated classes play with this question, I very much fear we shall not produce the free and healthy India of our dream. We have to grow by strenuous effort out of our bondage, whether it is educational, economical, social or political. The effort itself is three-fourths of the battle.[1]

45

INDIA'S CULTURAL HERITAGE

Nothing can be further from my thought than that we should become exclusive or erect barriers. But I do respectfully contend that an appreciation of other cultures can fitly follow, never precede, an appreciation and assimilation of our own. It is my firm opinion that no culture has treasures so rich as ours has. We have not known it, we have been made even to deprecate its study and depreciate its value. We have

> *No culture can live, if it attempts to be exclusive*

almost ceased to live it. An academic grasp without practice behind it is like an embalmed corpse, perhaps lovely to look at but nothing to inspire or ennoble. My religion forbids me to belittle or disregard other cultures, as it insists under pain of civil suicide upon imbibing and living my own.[1]

It stands for synthesis of the different cultures that have come to stay in India, that have influenced Indian life, and that, in their turn, have themselves been influenced by the spirit of the soil. This synthesis will naturally be of the Swadeshi type, where each culture is assured its legitimate place, and not of the American pattern, where one dominant culture absorbs the rest, and where the aim is not towards harmony, but towards an artificial and forced unity.[2]

The Indian culture of our times is in the making. Many of us are striving to produce a blend of all the cultures which seem today to be in clash with one another. No culture can live, if it attempts to be exclusive. There is no such thing as pure Aryan culture in existence today in India. Whether the Aryans were indigenous to India or were unwelcome intruders, does not interest me much. What does interest me is the fact that my remote ancestors blended with one another with the utmost freedom and we of the present generation are a result of that blend. Whether we are doing any good to the country of our birth and the tiny globe which sustains us or whether we are a burden, the future alone will show.[3]

46

THE NEW EDUCATION

Whatever may be true of other countries, in India at any rate where more than eighty per cent of the population is agricultural and another ten per cent industrial, it is a crime to make education merely literary, and to unfit boys and girls for manual work in after-life. Indeed I hold that as the larger part of our time is devoted to labour for earning our bread, our children must from their infancy be taught the dignity of such labour. Our children should not be so taught as to despise labour. There is no reason why a peasant's son after having gone to school should become useless, as he does become, as an agricultural labourer. It is a sad thing that our schoolboys look upon manual labour with disfavour, if not contempt.[1]

In my opinion, intelligent labour is for the time being the only primary and adult education in this land of starving millions.... Literary education should follow the education of the hand—the one gift that visibly distinguishes man from beast. It is a superstition to think that the fullest development of man is impossible without a knowledge of the art of reading and writing. That knowledge undoubtedly adds grace to life,

> There is no school equal to a decent home and no teachers equal to honest, virtuous parents

but it is in no way indispensable for man's moral, physical, or material growth.[2]

I hold that true education of the intellect can only come through a proper exercise and training of the bodily organs, *e.g.* hands, feet, eyes, ears, nose, etc. In other words, an intelligent use of the bodily organs in a child provides the best and quickest way of developing his intellect. But unless the development of the mind and body goes hand in hand with a corresponding awakening of the soul, the former alone would prove to be a poor lop-sided affair. By spiritual training I mean education of the heart. A proper and all-round development of the mind, therefore, can take place only when it proceeds *pari passu* with the education of the physical and spiritual faculties of the child. They constitute an indivisible whole. According to this theory, therefore, it would be a gross fallacy to suppose that they can be developed piecemeal or independently of one another.[3]

> *Our children must from their infancy be taught the dignity of labour*

The baneful effects of absence of proper co-ordination and harmony among the various faculties of body, mind and soul respectively are obvious. They are all around us; only we have lost perception of them owing to our present perverse associations.[4]

Man is neither mere intellect, nor the gross animal body, nor the heart or soul alone. A proper and harmonious combination of all the three is required for the making of the whole man and constitutes the true economics of education.[5]

By education I mean an all-round drawing out of the best in child and man—body, mind and spirit. Literacy is not the end of education nor even the beginning. It is only one of the means whereby man and woman can be educated. Literacy in itself is no education. I would therefore begin the child's education by teaching it a useful handicraft and enabling it to produce from the moment it begins its training. I hold that the highest development of the mind and the soul is possible under such a system of education. Only every handicraft has to be taught not merely mechanically as is done today but scientifically, *i.e.* the child should know the why and the wherefore of every process.[6]

> *Literacy is not the end of education nor even the beginning. It is only one of the means whereby man and woman can be educated. Literacy in itself is no education*

In my scheme of things the hand will handle tools before it draws or traces the writing. The eyes will read the pictures of letters and words as they will know other things in life, the ears will catch the names and meanings of things and sentences. The whole training will be natural, responsive and, therefore, the quickest and the cheapest in the world.[7]

> I am a firm believer in the principle of free and compulsory Primary Education for India

Manual work will have to be the very centre of the whole thing.... The manual training will not consist in producing articles for a school museum, or toys which have no vlaue. It should produce marketable articles. The children will not do this as children used to do under the whip in the early days of the factories. They will do it because it entertains them and stimulates their intellect.[8]

I am a firm believer in the principle of free and compulsory Primary Education for India. I also hold that we shall realize this only by teaching the children a useful vocation and utilizing it as a means for cultivating their mental, physical and spiritual faculties. It will check the progressive decay of our villages and lay the foundation of a juster social order in which there is no unnatural division between the 'haves' and the 'have-nots' and everybody is assured of a living wage and the rights to freedom.[9]

My plan to impart Primary Education through the medium of village handicrafts like spinning and carding etc. is thus conceived as the spearhead of a silent social revolution fraught with the most far-reaching consequences. It will provide a healthy and moral basis of relationship between the city and the village and thus go a long way towards eradicating some of the worst evils of the present social insecurity and poisoned relationship between the classes.[10]

47

BASIC EDUCATION

This education is meant to transform village children into model villagers. It is principally designed for them. The inspiration for it has come from the villages....Basic education links the children, whether of the cities or the villages, to all that is best and lasting in India. It develops both the body and the mind, and keeps the child rooted to the soil with a glorious vision of the future in the realization of which he or she begins to take his or her share from the very commencement of his or her career in school.[1]

The object of Basic Education is the physical, intellectual and moral development of the children through the medium of a handicraft. But I hold that any scheme which is sound from the educative point of view and is efficiently managed is bound to be sound economically. For instance, we can teach our children to make clay toys that are to be destroyed afterwards. That too will develop their intellect. But it will neglect a very important moral principle, *viz.* that human labour and material should never be used in a wasteful or unproductive way. The emphasis laid on the principle of spending every minute of one's life usefully is the best education for citizenship and incidentally makes Basic Education self-sufficient.[2]

Let us now glance at the fundamentals of Basic Education:
  - All education to be true must be self-supporting, that is to say, in the end it will pay its expenses excepting the capital which will remain intact.
  - In it the cunning of the hand will be utilized even up to the final stage, that is to say, hands of the pupils will be

skilfully working at some industry for some period during the day.

- All education must be imparted through the medium of the provincial language.
- In this there is no room for giving sectional religious training. Fundamental universal ethics will have full scope.
- This education, whether it is confined to children or adults, male or female, will find its way to the homes of the pupils.
- Since millions of students receiving this education will consider themselves as of the whole of India, they must learn an inter-provincial language. This common inter-provincial speech can only be Hindustani written in Nagari or Urdu script. Therefore, pupils have to master both the scripts.[3]

The introduction of manual training will serve a double purpose in a poor country like ours. It will pay for the education of our children and teach them an occupation on which they can fall back in after-life, if they choose, for earning a living. Such a system must make our children self-reliant. Nothing will demoralize the nation so much as that we should learn to despise labour.[4]

48

HIGHER EDUCATION

I would revolutionize college education and relate it to national necessities. There would be degrees for mechanical and other engineers. They would be attached to the different industries which should pay for the training of the graduates they need. Thus the Tatas would be expected to run a college for training engineers under the supervision of the State, the mill associations would run among them a college for training graduates whom they need.

Similarly for the other industries that may be named. Commerce will have its college. There remain arts, medicine and agriculture. Several private arts colleges are today self-supporting. The State would, therefore, cease to run its own. Medical colleges would be attached to certified hospitals. As they are popular among moneyed men they may be expected by voluntary contributions to support medical colleges. And agricultural colleges to be worthy of the name must be self-supporting. I have a painful experience of some agricultural graduates. Their knowledge is superficial. They lack practical experience. But if they had their apprenticeship on farms which are self-sustained and answer the requirements of the country, they would not have to gain experience after getting their degrees and at the expense of their employers.[1]

The State Universities should be purely examining bodies, self-supporting through the fees charged for examinations.

Universities will look after the whole of the field of education and will prepare and approve courses of studies in the various departments of education. No private school should be run without the previous sanction of the respective Universities. University charters should be given liberally to any body of persons of proved worth and integrity, it being always understood that the Universities will not cost the State anything except that it will bear the cost of running a Central Education Department.[2]

New Universities

There seems to be a mania for establishing new universities in the provinces. Gujarat wants one for Gujarati, Maharashtra for Marathi, Carnatic for Kannad, Orissa for Oriya, Assam for Assami and what not. I do believe that there should be such universities if these rich provincial languages and the people who speak them are to attain their full height.

At the same time I fear that we betray ourselves into undue haste in accomplishing the object. The first step should be linguistic political redistribution of provinces. Their separate administration will naturally lead to the establishment of universities where there are none.

There should be a proper background for new universities. They should have feeders in the shape of schools and colleges which will impart instruction through the medium of their respective provincial languages. Then only can there be a proper milieu. University is at the top. A majestic top can only be sustained if there is a sound foundation.

Though we are politically free, we are hardly free from the subtle domination of the West. I have nothing to say to that school of politicians who believe that knolwedge can only come from the West. Nor do I subscribe to the belief that

> Mass illiteracy is India's sin and shame and must be liquidated. Of course, the literacy campaign must not begin and end with a knowledge of the alphabet. It must go hand in hand with the spread of useful knowledge

nothing good can come out of the West. I do fear, however, that we are unable as yet to come to a correct decision in the matter. It is to be hoped that no one contends that because we seem to be politically free from foreign domination, the mere fact gives us freedom from the more subtle influence of the foreign language and foreign thought. Is it not wisodm, does not duty to the country dictate, that before we embark on new universities we should stop and fill our own lungs first with the ozone of our newly got freedom? A university never needs a pile of majestic buildings and treasures of gold and silver. What it does need most of all is the intelligent backing of public opinion. It should have a large reservoir of teachers to draw upon. Its founders should be far-seeing.

In my opinion it is not for a democratic State to find money for founding universities. If the people want them they will supply the funds. Universities so founded will adorn the country which they represent. Where administration is in foreign hands, whatever comes to the people comes from top and thus they become more and more dependent. Where it is broad-based on popular will, everything goes from bottom upward and hence it lasts. It is good-looking and strengthens the people. In such a democratic scheme money invested in the promotion of learning gives a tenfold return to the people even as a seed sown in good soil returns a luxuriant crop. Universities founded under foreign domination have run in the reverse direction. Any other result was perhaps impossible. Therefore, there is every reason for being cautious about founding new universities till India has digested the newly-acquired freedom.[3]

Adult Education

If I had charge of adult education, I should begin with opening the minds of the adult pupils to the greatness and vastness of their country. The villager's India is contained in his village. If he goes to another village, he talks of his own village as his home. Hindustan is for him a geographical term. We have no notion of the ignorance prevailing in the villages. The villagers know nothing of foreign rule and its evils....They do not know how to get rid of it. They do not know that the foreigner's presence is due to their own weaknesses and their ignorance of the power they possess to rid themselves of the foreign rule. My adult education means, therefore, first, true political education of the adult by word of mouth....Side by side with the education by the mouth will be the literary education. This is itself a speciality. Many methods are being tried in order to shorten the period of education.[4]

Mass illiteracy is India's sin and shame and must be liquidated. Of course, the literacy campaign must not begin and end with a knowledge of the alphabet. It must go hand in hand with the spread of useful knowledge. The dry knowledge of the three R's is not even now, it can never be, a permanent part of the villagers' life. They must have knowledge given to them which they must use daily. It must not be thrust upon them. They should have the appetite for it. What they have today is something they neither want nor appreciate. Give the villagers village arithmetic, village geography, village history, and the literary knowledge that they must use daily, *i.e.* reading and writing letters, etc. They will treasure such knowledge and pass on to the other stages. They have no use for books which give them nothing of daily use.[5]

Religious Education

....there is no doubt that the vast majority of students who pass through the Government educational institutions are devoid of any religious instruction....I know also that there is a school of thought which believes in only secular instruction being given in public schools. I know also that in a country like India, where there are most religions of the world represented and where there are so many denominations in the same religion, there must be difficulty about making provision for religious instruction. But if Inida is not to declare spiritual bankruptcy, religious instruction of its youth must be held to be at least as necessary as secular instruction. It is true, that knowledge of religious books is no equivalent of that of religion. But if we cannot have religion we must be satisfied with providing our boys and girls with what is next best. And whether there is such instruction given in the schools or not, grown up students must cultivate the art of self-help about matters religious as about other. They may start their own class just as they have their debating and now spinners' clubs.[6]

I do not believe that the state can concern itself or cope with religious education. I believe that religious education must be

> *Real education has to draw out the best from the boys and girls to be educated. This can never be done by packing ill-assorted and unwanted information into the heads of the pupils. It becomes a dead weight crushing all originality in them and turning them into mere automata*

the sole concern of religious associations. Do not mix up religion and ethics. I believe that fundamental ethics is common to all religions. Teaching of fundamental ethics is undoubtedly a function of the State. By religion I have not in mind fundamental ethics but what goes by the name of denominationalism. We have suffered enough from State-aided religion and a State Church. A society or a group, which depends partly or wholly on State aid for the existence of its religion, does not deserve, or, better still, does not have any religion worth the name.[7]

A curriculum of religious instruction should include a study of the tenets of faiths other than one's own. For this purpose the students should be trained to cultivate the habit of understanding and appreciating the doctrines of various great religions of the world in a spirit of reverence and broad-minded tolerance. This if properly done would help to give them a spiritual assurance and a better appreciation of their own religion....There is one rule, however, which should always be kept in mind while studying all great religions and that is, that one should study them only through the writings of known votaries of the respective religions.[8]

Text-books

There seems to me to be no doubt that in the public schools the books used, especially for children, are for the most part useless when they are not harmful. That many of them are cleverly written cannot be denied. They might even be the best for the people and the environment for which they are written. But they are not written for Indian boys and girls, not for the Indian environment. When they are so written, they are generally undigested imitations hardly answering the wants of the scholar.

I have, therefore, come to the conclusion that books are required more for the teachers than for the taught. And every teacher, if he is to do full justice to his pupils, will have to prepare the daily lesson from the material available to him. This, too, he will have to suit to the special requirements of his class. Real education has to draw out the best from the boys and girls to be educated. This can never be done by packing ill-assorted and unwanted information into the heads of the pupils. It becomes a dead weight crushing all originality in them and turning them into mere automata.[9]

Teachers

I believe in the ancient idea of teachers teaching for the love of it and receiving the barest maintenance. The Roman Catholics have retained that idea and they are responsible for some of the best educational institutions in the world. The Rishis of old did even better. They made their pupils members of their families, but in those days that class of teaching which they imparted was not intended for the masses. They simply brought up a race of real teachers of mankind in India. The masses got their training in their homes and in their hereditary occupations. It was a good enough ideal for those times. Circumstances have now changed. There is a general insistent demand for literary training. The masses claim the same attention as the classes. How far it is possible and beneficial to mankind generally cannot be discussed here. There is nothing inherently wrong in the desire for learning. If it is directed in a healthy channel it can only do good. Without, therefore, stopping to devise means for avoiding the inevitable, we must make the best possible use of it. Thousands of teachers cannot be had for the asking, not will they live by begging. They must have a salary guaranteed and we shall require quite an army of teachers; their remuneration cannot be in proportion to the intrinsic worth of their calling, but it will have to be in proportion to the capacity of the nation for payment. We may expect a steady rise as we realize the relative merits of the different callings. The rise must be painfully slow. There must therefore arise a class of men and women in India who will from patriotic motives choose teaching as a profession, irrespective of the material gain that it may bring them. Then the nation will not underrate the calling of the teacher. On the contrary, it will give the first place in its affection to these self-sacrificing men and women. And so we come to this that as our Swaraj is possible largely by our own efforts, so is the teachers' rise possible mainly by their own effort. They must bravely and patiently cut their way through to success.[10]

Self-supporting Education

The suggestion has often been made... that in order to make education compulsory, or even available to every boy and girl wishing to receive education, our schools and colleges should become almost, if not wholly, self-supporting, not through donations or State aid or fees exacted from students, but through remunerative work done by the students themselves. This can only be done by making industrial training compulsory. Apart from the necessity which is daily being more and more recognized of students having an industrial training side by side with literary training, there is in this country the additional necessity of pursuing industrial training in order to make education directly self-supporting. This can only be done when our students begin to recognize the dignity of labour and when the convention is established of regarding ignorance of manual occupation a mark of disgrace. In America, which is the richest country in the world and where, therefore, perhaps there is the least need for making education self-supporting, it is the most usual thing for students to pay their way wholly or partially.... If America has to model her schools and colleges so as to enable students to earn their scholastic expenses, how much more necessary it must be for our schools and colleges? Is it not far better that we find work for poor students than that we pauperize them by providing free studentships? It is impossible to exaggerate the harm we do to Indian youth by filling their minds with the false notion that it is ungentlemanly to labour with one's hands and feet for one's livelihood or schooling. The harm done is both moral and material, indeed much more moral than material. A freeship lies and should lie like a load upon a conscientious lad's mind throughout his whole life. No one likes to be reminded in after life that he had to depend upon charity for his education. Contrarily where is the person who will not recall with pride those days if he had the good fortune to have had them when he worked in a carpentry-shop or the like for the sake of educating himself—mind, body and soul?[11]

49

ASHRAM IDEAL OF EDUCATION

[The following translation by Shri V. G. Desai of some of the notes on the Ashram ideal of education written by Mahatma Gandhi in Gujarati appeared in the issues of *Harijan* of 15th July and 5th August, 1950.]

I have my own perhaps peculiar views on education which have not been accepted by my colleagues in full, and here they are:

- Young boys and girls should have co-education till they are eight years of age.
- Their education should mainly consist in manual training under the supervision of an educationist.
- The special aptitudes of each child should be recognized in determining the kind of work he (or she) should do.
- The reasons for every process should be explained when the process is being carried on.
- General knowledge should be imparted to each child as he begins to understand things. Learning to read or write shoud come later.
- The child should first be taught to draw simple geometrical figures, and when he has learnt to draw these with ease, he should be taught to write the alphabet. If this is done, he will write a good hand from the very first.
- Reading should come before writing. The letters should be treated as pictures to be recognized and later on to be copied.
- A child taught on these lines will have acquired

considerable knowledge according to his capacity by the time he is eight.

- Nothing should be taught to a child by force.
- He should be interested in everything taught to him.
- Education should appear to the child like play. Play is an essential part of education.
- All education should be imparted through the mother tongue.
- The child should be taught Hindi-Urdu as the national language, before he learns letters.
- Religious education is indispensable and the child should get it by watching the teacher's conduct and by hearing him talk about it.
- Nine to sixteen constitutes the second stage in the child's education.
- It is desirable that boys and girls should have co-education during the second stage also as far as possible.
- Hindu children should now be taught Sanskrit and Muslim children Arabic.
- Manual training should be continued during the second stage. Literary education should be allotted more time as is necessary.
- The boys during this stage should be taught their parents' avocation in such a way that they will by their own choice obtain their livelihood by practising the hereditary craft. This does not apply to the girls.
- During this stage the child should acquire a general knowledge of world history and geography, botany, astronomy, arithmetic, geometry, and algebra.
- Each child should now be taught to sew and to cook.
- Sixteen to twenty-five is the third stage, during which every young person should have an education according to his or her wishes and circumstances.

One who has appreciated the value of studies is a student all his life

- During the second stage (9-16) education should be self-supporting; that is, the child, all the time that he is learning, is working upon some industry, the proceeds

of which will meet the expenditure of the school.
- Production starts from the very beginning, but during the first stage it does not still catch up with the expenditure.
- Teachers should be paid not very high salaries but only a living wage. They should be inspired by a spirit of service. It is a despicable thing to take any Tom, Dick or Harry as a teacher in the primary stage. All teachers should be men of character.
- Big and expensive buildings are not necessary for educational institutions.
- English should be taught only as one of several languages. As Hindi is the national language, English is to be used in dealing with other nations and international commerce.

Women's Education

As for women's education I am not sure whether it should be different from men's and when it should begin. But I am strongly of opinion that women should have the same facilities as men and even special facilities where necessary.

There should be night schools for illiterate adults. But I do not think that they must be taught the three R's; they must be helped to acquire general knowledge through lectures etc., and if they wish, we should arrange to teach them the three R's also.

Experiments in the Ashram have convinced us of one thing, *viz.* that industry in general and spinning in particular should have pride of place in education, which must be largely self-supporting as well as related to and tending to the betterment of rural life.

> A man's real teacher is himself

Real education begins after a child has left school. One who has appreciated the vlaue of studies is a student all his life. His knowledge must increase from day to day while he is discharging his duty in a conscientious manner.

The superstition that no education is possible without a teacher is an obstacle in the path of educational progress. A man's real teacher is himself. And now-a-days there is ample apparatus available for self-education. A diligent person can easily acquire knowledge about many things by himself and obtain the assistance of a teacher when one is needed. Experience is the biggest of all schools. Quite a number of crafts cannot be learnt at school but only in the workshop. Knowledge of these acquired at school is often only parrot-like. Knowledge of the other subjects can be acquired with the help of books. Therefore, what adults need is not so much a school as a thirst for knowledge, diligence and self-confidence.

The education of children is primarily a duty to be discharged by the parents. Therefore, the creation of a vital educational atmosphere is more important than the foundation of innumerable schools. When once this atmosphere has been established on a firm footing, the schools will come in due course.

This is the Ashram ideal of education which has been achieved to some extent, as every department for Ashram activity is a veritable school.

50

NATIONAL LANGUAGE AND SCRIPT

If we are to make good our claim as one nation, we must have several things in common. We have a common culture running through a variety of creeds and sub-creeds. We have common disabilities. I am endeavouring to show that a common material for our dress is not only desirable but necessary. We need also a common language not in supersession of the vernaculars, but in addition to them. It is generally agreed that that medium should be Hindustani—a resultant of Hindi and Urdu, neither highly Sanskritized, nor highly Persianized or Arabianized. The greatest obstacle in the way are the numerous scripts we have for the vernaculars. If it is possible to adopt a common script, we should remove a great hindrance in the way of realizing the dream, which at present it is, of having a common language.

A variety of scripts is an obstacle in more ways than one. It constitutes an effectual barrier against the acquisition of knowledge. The Aryan languages have so much in common that, if a great deal of time had not to be wasted in mastering the different scripts, we should all know several languages without much difficulty; for instance, most people who have a little knowledge of Sanskrit would have no difficulty in understanding the matchless creation of

> *We need also a common language not in supersession of the vernaculars, but in additon to them*

Rabindranath Tagore, if it was all printed in Devanagari script. But the Bengali script is a notice to the non-Bengalis—"hands off". Conversely, if the Bengalis knew the Devanagari script, they would at once be able to enjoy the marvellous beauty and spirituality of Tulsidas and a host of other Hindustani writers.... A common script for all India is a distant ideal. A common script for all those who speak the Indo-Sanskrit languages, including the Southern stock, is a practical ideal, if we but shed our provincialisms. There is little virtue, for instance, in a Gujarati clinging to the Gujarati script. Provincial patriotism is good where it feeds the larger stream of all-India patriotism, as the latter is good to the extent that it serves the still larger end of the universe. But a provincial patriotism that says "India is nothing, Gujarat is all", is wickedness.... That the Devanagari should be the common script, I suppose, does not need any demonstration—the deciding factor being that it is the script known to the largest part of India.... A spirit that is so exclusive and narrow as to want every form of speech to be perpetuated and developed, is anti-national and anti-universal. All undeveloped and unwritten dialects should, in my humble opinion, be sacrificed and merged in the great Hindustani stream. It would be a sacrifice only to be nobler, not a suicide. If we are to have a common language for cultured India, we must arrest the growth of any process of disintegration or multiplication of languages and scripts. We must promote a common language.... If I could have my way, I would make the learning of Devanagari script and Urdu script, in addition to the established provincial script, compulsory in all the provinces and I would print in Devanagari chief books in the different vernaculars with a literal translation in Hindustani.[1]

Let us now consider the question of a national language. If English is to become our national language then it must be made a compulsory subject in our schools. Let us first consider whether English can become our national language.

Some of our learned men, who are also good patriots, contend that even to raise the question betrays ignorance. In their opinion it already occupies that place.

On a superficial consideration, this view appears correct. Looking at the educated section of our society, one is likely to gain the impression that in the absence of English, all our work would come to a stop. But deeper reflection will show that English cannot and ought not to become our national language.

Let us see what should be the requirements of a national language:

- It should be easy to learn for Government officials.
- It should be capable of serving as a medium of religious, economic and political intercourse throughout India.
- It should be the speech of the majority of the inhabitants of India.
- It should be easy to learn for the whole of the country.
- In choosing this language considerations of temporary or passing interest should not count.

English does not fulfil any of these requirements.

The first ought to have been placed last, but I have purposely given it the first place, because it seems as though English fulfilled it. Closer examination will, however, show that even at the present moment it is not for the officials an easy language to learn or to handle. The constitution under which we are being ruled envisages that the number of English officials will progressively decrease until finally only the Viceroy and a few more will be left here. The majority of the people in Government services are even today Indians and their number will increase as time goes on. I think no one will deny that. For them English is more difficult than any other language.

> *Our love of the masses must be skin-deep, if we will not take the trouble of spending over learning Hindustani as many months as the years we spend over learning English*

As regards the second requirement: Religious intercourse through English is an impossibility unless our people throughout the land begin to speak English. Spread of English among the masses to this extent is clearly impossible.

English simply cannot satisfy the third requirement, because the majority in India do not speak it.

The fourth also cannot be met by English because it is not an easy language to learn for the whole of India.

Considering the fifth we see that the status which English enjoys today is temporary. The fact is that in India the need for

English in national affairs will be, it at all, very little. It will certainly be required for imperial affairs. It will remain the language of diplomacy between different States within the Empire. But that is a different matter. English will be necessary for that purpose. We do not hate English. All that we want is not to allow it to go beyond its proper limits. And because English will remain the imperial language we will compel our Malaviyajis, our Shastris and our Banerjees to learn it and expect them to enhance the glory of our country wherever they go. But English cannot become the national language of India. To give it that place will be like introducing Esperanto into the country. To think that English can become our national language is a sign of weakness and betrays ignorance.

Then which is the language which fulfills all the five requirements? We shall have to admit that it is Hindi.

No other language can compete with Hindi in satisfying these five requirements. Next to Hindi comes Bengali. But the Bengalis themselves make use of Hindi outside Bengal. The Hindi-speaking man speaks Hindi wherever he goes and no one feels surprized at this. The Hindi-speaking Hindu preachers and the Urdu-speaking Maulvis make their religious speeches throughout India in Hindi and Urdu, and even the illiterate masses understand them. Even an unlettered Gujarati, when he goes to the North attempts to speak a few Hindi words. But the Northern *bhaiya* who works as gate-keeper to the Bombay *seth* declines to speak in Gujarati and it is the *seth*, his employer, who is obliged to speak to him in broken Hindi. I have heard Hindi spoken even in far off Southern provinces. It is not correct to say that in Madras one cannot do without English. I have successfully used Hindi there for all my work. In the trains I have heard Madrasi passengers speaking to other passengers in Hindi. Besides, the Muslims of Madras know enough Hindi to use it sufficiently well. It has to be noted that Muslims throughout India speak Urdu and they are found in large numbers in every province.

Thus Hindi has already established itself as the national language of India. We have been using it as such for a long time. The birth of Urdu itself is due to this fact.

Muslim kings could not make Persian or Arabic the

national language. They accepted the Hindi grammar; only they used more Persian words in their speech and employed the Urdu script for writing. But they could not carry on intercourse with the masses through a foreign tongue. Similar is the case with the English rulers. Those who have any knowledge of how they deal with the *sipahees* in the army know that for this purpose they have coined Hindi or Urdu terms.

Thus we see that Hindi alone can become the national language. No doubt it presents some difficulty to the educated classes of Madras. But for Maharashtrians, Gujaratis, Sindhis and Bengalis it should be very easy. In a few months they can acquire enough command of Hindi to be able to use it for national purposes. It is not so easy for Tamilians.

Tamil and the other languages of the South belong to the Dravidian group. Their structure and grammar are different from those of Sanskrit. The only thing common between these two groups is their Sanskrit vocabulary.

But the difficulty is confined to the present educated classes only. We have a right to appeal to their patriotic spirit and expect them to put forth special effort to learn Hindi.

If Hindi attains to its due status, then it will be introduced in every school in Madras and Madras will thus be in a position to cultivate acquaintance with other provinces. English has failed to reach the masses. But Hindi will do so in no time. The Telugu people have already started moving in this direction.

Our love of the masses must be skin-deep, if we will not take the trouble of spending over learning Hindustani as many months as the years we spend over learning English.[2]

51

PROVINCIAL LANGUAGES

Our love of the English language in preference to our own mother tongue has caused a deep chasm between the educated and politically-minded classes and the masses. The languages of India have suffered impoverishment. We flounder when we make the vain attempt to express abstruse thought in the mother tongue. There are no equivalents for scientific terms. The result has been disastrous. The masses remain cut off from the modern mind. We are too near our own times correctly to measure the disservice caused to India by this neglect of its great languages. It is easy enough to understand that, unless we undo the mischief, the mass mind must remain imprisoned. The masses can make no solid contribution to the construction of Swaraj. It is inherent in Swaraj based on non-violence that every individual makes his own direct contribution to the independence movement. The masses cannot do this fully unless they understand every step with all its implications. This is impossible unless every step is explained in their own languages.[1]

I must cling to my mother tongue as to my mother's breast, in spite of its shortcomings. It alone can give me the life-giving milk. I love the English tongue in its own place, but I am its inveterate opponent, if it usurps a place which does not belong to it. English is today admittedly the world language. I would therefore accord it a place as a second, optional language, not in the school but in the university course. That can only be for the select few—not for the millions. Today when we have not the means to introduce even free compulsory primary education, how can we make provision for teaching English? Russia has achieved all her scientific progress without English. It is our mental slavery that makes us feel that we cannot do without English. I can never subscribe to that defeatist creed.[2]

Unless the Governments and their Secretariats take care, the English language is likely to usurp the place of Hindustani. This must do infinite harm to the millions of India who would never be able to uderstand English. Surely it must be quite easy for the Provincial Governments to have a staff which would carry on all transactions in the provincial languages and the inter-provincial language, which, in my opinion, can only be Hindustani written in Nagari or Urdu script.

Every day lost in making this necessary change is so much cultural loss to the nation. The first and foremost thing is to revive the rich provincial languages with which India is blessed. It is nothing short of mental sluggishness to plead that in our courts, in our schools and even in the Secretariats, some time, probably a few years, must lapse before the change is made. No doubt a little difficulty will be felt in multi-lingual provinces, as in Bombay and Madras, until redistribution of provinces takes place on the linguistic basis. Provincial Governments can devise a method in order to enable the people in those Provinces to feel that they have come into their own. Nor need the Provinces wait for the Union for solving the question, whether for inter-provincial speech it shall be Hindustani written in either Nagari or Urdu script or mere Hindi written in Nagari. This should not detain them in making the desired reform. It is a wholly unnecessary controversy likely to be the door through which English may enter to the eternal disgrace of India. If the first step, that is, revival of provincial speech in all public departments takes place immediately, that of inter-provincial speech will follow in quick succession. The Provinces will have to deal with the Centre. They dare not do so in English, if the Centre is wise enough quickly to realize that they must not tax the nation culturally for the sake of a handful of Indians who are too lazy to pick up the speech which can be easily common to the whole of India without offending any party or section. My plea is for banishing English as a cultural usurper as we successfully banished the political rule of the English usurper. The rich English language will ever retain its natural place as the international speech of commerce and diplomacy.[3]

Place of Sanskrit

I am of opinion that Sanskrit cannot be dispensed with in matters religious. The translation, no matter however accurate, cannot replace the original *mantras* which have an import of their own. Besides it would be detracting from the solemnity of the *mantras* which have been repeated in Sanskrit for centuries, to repeat them today in the vernaculars. But I am clear that each *mantra* and every rite should be accurately interpreted and explained to the person repeating the *mantra* or participating in the rite. A Hindu's education must be regarded as inadequate without a knowledge of the rudiments of Sanskrit. Hinduism would be extinct without Sanskrit learning and Sanskrit scholarship being cultivated on an adequate scale. We have made the language difficult by the present system of education, it is not really so. But even if it is difficult, practice of religion is still more so. He, therefore, who would practise religion must regard as comparatively easy all the steps to it, however difficult they may appear to be.[4]

52

HINDI IN THE SOUTH*

I have the greatest faith in the Dravidians some day taking up Hindi study seriously. If an eighth of the industry that they put in mastering English were to be devoted to learning Hindi, instead of the rest of India remaining a sealed book to them, they will be one with us as never before. I know that some would say the argument cuts both ways. The Dravidians being in a minority, national economy suggests that they should learn the common language of the rest of India than that the rest should learn Tamil, Telugu, Kanarese and Malayalam in order to be able to converse with Dravidian India. It is for that reason that Hindi-propaganda work of an intense type has been going on in the Madras presidency.

Let no Dravidian think that learning Hindi is at all difficult. A little time taken from the recreation hour daily and in a systematic manner will enable an average man to learn Hindi in one year. I would venture to suggest too that large municipalities might now introduce Hindi as an optional language to be learnt in the municipal schools. I can say from experience that Dravidian children take to Hindi in a remarkably easy manner. Little does anyone know that almost all the Tamils and the Telugus living in South Africa can carry on an intelligent conversation in Hindi. I venture to hope therefore that the young men of Madras will show their appreciation of Marwadi generosity by availing themselves of the facility afforded to them of learning Hindi without payment.[1]

Bengal and Madras are the two Provinces that are cut off from the rest of India for want of a knowledge of Hindustani on their part. Bengal, because of its prejudice against learning any other language of India, and Madras, because of the difficulty of the

---

The following figures, based on 1951 census, are taken from the Report of the Official Language Commission, p. 468:

(In thousands)

States	Population	Literates	Literates in English (S.L.C. or equivalent)	Percentage of col. 4 to col. 3	Percentage of col. 4 to col. 2
1	2	3	4	5	6
Bombay	35,956	8,829	458	5.19	1.27
Punjab	12,641	2,039	325	15.93	2.56
West Bengal	24,810	6,088	597	9.81	2.41
Ajmer	693	139	18	13.11	2.63
South India (i.e. Madras, Mysore Travancore-Cochin and Coorg)	75,600	17,234	876	5.08	1.15
Madras (after separation of Andhra)	35,735	7,800	400	5.13	1.12
Andhra	20,508	3,108	165	5.32	0.81
Mysore (including Bellary Talukas)	9,849	1,956	136	6.94	1.38

LITERACY IN HINDI

The following figures pertaining to the spread of literacy in Hindi are from the report of the Dakshina Bharat Hindi Prachar Sabha, Madras, for the period 1918-1955:

(In lakhs)

	Population	Literates	Literates in Hindi
Andhra	203.2	30.4	8.02
Tamil Nadu	277.7	51.8	8.98
Kerala	140.1	72.8	14.22
Karnataka	228.4	48.7	9.87
Telangana	80.0	13.3	1.36
Madras City	14.2	4.3	1.75

Dravidians about picking up Hindustani. An average Bengali can really learn Hindustani in two months if he gave it three hours per day and a Dravidian in six months at the same rate. Neither a Bengali nor a Dravidian can hope to achieve the same result with English in the same time. A knowledge of English opens up intercourse only with the comparatively few English-knowing Indians, whereas a possible knowledge of Hindustani enables us to hold intercourse with the largest number of our countrymen.... I appreciate the difficulty with the Dravidians, but nothing is difficult before their industrious love for the motherland.[2]

English is the language of international commerce, it is the language of diplomacy, and it contains many a rich literary treasure, it gives us an introduction to Western thought and culture. For a few of us, therefore, a knowledge of English is necessary. They can carry on the departments of national commerce and international diplomacy, and for giving to the nation the best of Western literature, thought, and science. That would be the legitimate use of English, whereas today English has usurped the dearest place in our hearts and dethroned our mother tongues. It is an unnatural place due to our unequal relations with Englishmen. The highest development of the Indian mind msut be possible without a knowledge of English. It is doing violence to the manhood and specially the womanhood of India to encourage our boys and girls to think that an entry into the best society is impossible without a knowledge of English. It is too humiliating a thought to be bearable. To get rid of the infatuation for English is one of the essentials of Swaraj.[3]

If we were not living in artificial conditions, the people living in the South will not consider the learning of Hindi as a strain on them, much less a superfluity. It is surely more necessary for them to learn Hindi than for the Hindi-speaking population to learn the Southern languages. There are two speaking and understanding Hindi against one speaking the Southern languages in all India. There must be for all India a common language of inter-provincial contact *in addition to, not in the place of*, the provincial language or languages. It can be Hindi-Hindustani.

Some who altogether dismiss the masses from their minds

would regard English not merely as an altenative but the only possible medium. This proposition would be unthinkable but for the hypnotic influence of foreign domination. For the masses of the South who must take an ever-growing part in national affairs, what can be easier—learning Hindi which has many words in common with their languages and which at once gives them access practically to the whole of the North or to learn English, a wholly foreign tongue spoken only by a select few?

The choice really depends upon one's conception of Swaraj. If it is to be of and for only the English-knowing Indians, English is undoubtedly the common medium. If it is to be for and of the starving millions, of the illiterate millions, of the illiterate women, of the suppressed 'untouchables', Hindi is the only possible common language.[4]

Though I consider these Southern languages to be daughters of Sanskrit they are different from Hindi, Ooria, Bengali, Assamese, Punjabi, Sindhi, Marathi and Gujarati. Their grammar is totally different from Hindi. In describing them as the daughters of Sanskrit, I only mean that they have a large number of Sanskrit words in their vocabulary and when they are in difficulty, they go to Sanskrit as to a mother—they seek her help and receive from her in the form of new words their requisite nourishment. They might have been indpendent in the olden days, but now they are enriching themselves with words taken from Sanskrit. There are many other reasons also why they should be regarded as the daughters of Sanskrit. But we may not go into them here.

I have always held that in no case whatsoever do we want to injure, much less suppress or destroy, the provincial languages. We want only that all should learn Hindi as a common medium for inter-provincial intercourse. This does not mean that we have any undue partiality for Hindi. We regard Hindi as our national language. It is fit to be adopted as such. That language alone can become the national language which is easy to learn. To our knowledge there has been no opposition to this view serious enough to take notice of.

If Hindi takes the place of English, I for one would be pleased. But we know well the importance of the English language. Knowledge of English is necessary to us for the acquisition of modern knowledge, for the study of modern literature, for knowledge of the world, for intercourse with the present rulers and such other purposes. As things are, we have to learn English even if we do not wish to. English is an international language.

But English can never become our national language. True, it seems to dominate the scene today. In spite of all efforts to resist its hold on us, it continues to occupy a large place in the conduct of our national affairs. But this should not lead us to entertain the illusion that it is going to become our national language.

We can easily find proof for this from our experience in any province. Take for instance Bengal or South India where we find the influence of English to be the largest. Should we want anything done in these parts by the people, we cannot have it done through English, though at the moment we may also not be able to do it through Hindi. With the help of a few words of Hindi, however, we may succeed in expressing our meaning at least to some extent; but through English not even this much.

Of course, it may be accepted that hitherto no language has been able to establish itself as the national language. English is the official language. That is natural under the prevailing circumstances. But I consider it quite impossible for it to go beyond this. If we want to make India one nation, whether one believes it or not, Hindi alone can be the national language for the simple reason that no other language can hope to have the advantages enjoyed by Hindi. With some slight variations Hindi-Hindustani is the language spoken by about twenty-two crores of people, both Hindus and Muslims.

Therefore the most proper and under the circumstances the only possible thing would be to use the language of the province in the province, to use Hindi for all-India purposes and to use English for inter-national purposes. While the Hindi-speaking people may be counted in crores, the number of those who speak English can never be increased to more than a few lakhs. Even the attempt to do so would be unjust to the people.

There is nothing wrong in making a knowledge of Hindustani compulsory, if we are sincere in our declarations that Hindustani is or is to be the Rashtrabhasha or the common medium of expression. Latin was and probably still is compulsory in English schools. The study did not interfere with the study of English. On the contrary English was enriched by a knowledge of the noble language. The cry of "mother tongue in danger" is either ignorant or hypocritical. And where it is sincere it speaks little for the patriotism of those who will grudge our children an hour per day for Hindustani. We must break through the provincial crust if we are to reach the core of all-India nationalism. Is India one country and one nation or many countries and many nations?[5]

53
A CODE FOR STUDENTS

- Students must not take part in party politics. They are students, searchers, not politicians.
- They may not resort to political strikes. They must have their heroes but their devotion to them is to be shown by copying the best in their heroes, not by going on strikes if their heroes are imprisoned or die or are even sent to the gallows. If their grief is unbearable and if all the students feel equally, schools or colleges may be closed on such occasions with the consent of their principals. If the principals will not listen, it is open to the students to leave their institutions in a becoming manner till the managers repent and recall them. On no account may they use coercion against dissentients or against the authorities. They must have the confidence that if they are united and dignified in their conduct they are sure to win.
- They must all do sacrificial spinning in a scientific manner. Their tools shall be always neat, clean and in good order and condition. If possible, they will learn to make them themselves. Their yarn will naturally be of the highest quality. They will study the literature about spinning with all its economic, social, moral and political implications.
- They will be Khadi users all through and use village products to the exclusion of all analogous things, foreign or machine made.
- They may not impose 'Bande Mataram' or the National

Flag on others. They may wear National Flag buttons on their own persons but not force others to do the same.

- They can enforce the message of the Tricolour Flag in their own persons and harbour neither communalism nor untouchability in their hearts. They will cultivate real friendship with students of other faiths and with Harijans as if they were their own kith and kin.
- They will make it a point to give first aid to their injured neighbours and do scavenging and cleaning in the neighbouring villages and instruct village children and adults.
- They will all learn the national language, Hindustani, in its present double dress—two forms of speech and two scripts—so that they may feel at home whether Hindi or Urdu is spoken and Nagari or Urdu script is written.
- They will translate into their own mother tongue everything new they may learn and transmit it in their weekly rounds to the surrounding villages.
- They will do nothing in secret. They will be above-board in all their dealings, they will lead a pure life of self-restraint, shed all fear and be always ready to protect their weak fellow-students and be ready to quell riots by non-violent conduct at the risk of their lives. And when the final heat of the struggle comes they will leave their institutions and, if need be, sacrifice themselves for the freedom of their country.

> *The base imitation of the West, the ability to speak and write polished English, will not add one brick to the temple of freedom*

- They will be scrupulously correct and chivalrous in their behaviour towards their girl fellow-students.

For working out the programme I have sketched for them, the students must find time. I know that they waste a great deal of time in idleness. By strict economy they can save hours. But I do not want to put an undue strain upon any student. I would, therefore, advise patriotic students to lose one year, not at a stretch, but spread it over their whole study. They will find that one year so given will not be a waste of time. The effort

A Code for Students 207

will add to their equipment, mental, moral and physical, and they will have made even during their studies a substantial contribution to the freedom movement.[1]

The base imitation of the West, the ability to speak and write polished English, will not add one brick to the temple of freedom. The student world which is receiving an education far too expensive for starving India, an education which only a microscopic minority can ever hope to receive, is expected to qualify itself for it by giving its life-blood to the nation. Students must become pioneers in conservative reform, conserving all that is good in the nation and fearlessly ridding society of the innumerable abuses that have crept into it.

Students have to react upon the dumb millions. They have to learn to think not in terms of a province, or a town, or a class, or a caste, but in terms of a continent and of the millions who include untouchables, drunkards, hooligans and even prostitutes, for whose existence in our midst every one of us is responsible. Students in olden times were called *brahmacharis*, that is those who walked with and in the fear of God. They were honoured by kings and elders. They were a voluntary charge on the nation, and in return they gave to the nation a hundredfold strong souls, strong brains, strong arms. Students in the modern world, wherever they are to be found among fallen nations, are considered to be their hope, and have become the self-sacrificing leaders of reforms in every department. Not that we have no such examples in India; but they are far too few. What I plead for is that students' conferences should stand for this kind of work befitting the status of *brahmacharis*.[2]

The students should devote the whole of their vacation to village service. To this end, instead of taking their walks along beaten paths, they should walk to the villages within easy reach of their institutions and study the condition of the village folk and befriend them. This habit will bring them in contact with the villagers who, when the students actually go to stay in their midst, will, by reason of the previous occasional contact, receive them as friends rather than as strangers to be looked upon with suspicion. During the long vacations the students will stay in the villages and offer to conduct classes for adults and to teach the rules of sanitation to the villagers and to attend to the ordinary cases of illness. They will also introduce the spinning-wheel amongst them and teach them the use of every spare minute. In order that this may be done students and teachers will have to revise their ideas of the uses of vacation. Often do thoughtless teachers prescribe lessons to be done during the vacation. This, in my opinion, is in any case a vicious habit. Vacation is just the period when students' minds should be free from the routine work and be left free for self-help and original development. The village work I have mentioned is easily the best form of recreation and light instruction. It is obviously the best preparation for dedication to exclusive village service after finishing the studies.[3]

Put your talents in the service of the country instead of converting them to money. If you are a medical man, there is disease enough in India to need all your medical skill. If you are a lawyer, there are differences and quarrels enough in India. Instead of fomenting more trouble, patch up those quarrels and litigation. If you are an engineer, build model houses suited to the means and needs of your people and yet full of health and fresh air. There is nothing that you have learnt which cannot be turned to account.[4]

Students and Politics

Students should have the greatest freedom of expression and of opinion. They may openly sympathize with any political party they like. But in my opinion they may not have freedom of action whilst they are studying. A student cannot be an active politician and pursue his studies at the same time.[5]

Students cannot afford to have party politics. They hear all parties, as they read all sorts of books, but their business is to assimilate the truth of all and reject the balance.

Power politics should be unknown to the student world. Immediately they dabble in that class of work, they cease to be students and will, therefore, fail to serve the country in its crisis.[6]

54

REGENERATION OF INDIAN WOMEN

Woman has been suppressed under custom and law for which man was responsible and in the shaping of which she had no hand. In a plan of life based on non-violence, woman has as much right to shape her own destiny as man has to shape his. But as every right in a non-violent society proceeds from the previous performance of a duty, if follows that rules of social conduct must be framed by mutual co-operation and consultation. They can never be imposed from outside. Men have not realized this truth in its fulness in their behaviour towards women. They have considered themselves to be lords and masters of women instead of considering them as their friends and co-workers. Women are in the position somewhat of the slave of old who did not know that he could or ever had to be free. And when freedom came, for the moment he felt helpless. Women have been taught to regard themselves as slaves of men. It is up to Congressmen to see that they enable them to realize their full status and play their part as equals of men.

This revolution is easy, if the mind is made up. Let Congressmen begin with their own homes. Wives should not be dolls and objects of indulgence, but should be treated as honoured comrades in common service. To this end those who have not received a liberal education should receive such instruction as is possible from their husbands. The same observation applies, with the necessary changes, to mothers and daughters.

It is hardly necessary to point out that I have given a one-sided picture of the helpless state of India's women. I am quite conscious of the fact that in the villages generally they hold their own with their men folk and in some respects even rule them. But to the impartial outsider the legal and customary status of woman is bad enough throughout and demands radical alteration.[1]

Legislation has been mostly the handiwork of men; and man has not always been fair and discriminating in performing that self-appointed task. The largest part of our effort, in promoting the regeneration of women, should be directed towards removing those blemishes which are represented in our Shastras as the necessary and ingrained characteristics of women. Who will attempt this and how? In my humble opinion, in order to make the attempt we will have to produce women, pure, firm and self-controlled as Sita, Damayanti and Draupadi. If we do produce them, such modern sisters will have the same authority as the Shastras. We will feel ashamed of the stray reflections on them in our Smritis, and will soon forget them. Such revolutions have occurred in Hinduism in the past, and will still take place in the future, leading to the stability of our faith.[2]

> *I am uncompromising in the matter of women's rights. In my opinion she should labour under no legal disability not suffered by men. I should treat the daughters and sons on a footing of pefect equality*

Woman is the companion of man, gifted with equal mental capacities. She has the right to participate in every minute detail in the activities of man and she has an equal right of freedom and liberty with him. She is entitled to a supreme place in her own sphere of activity as man is in his. This ought to be the natural condition of things and not as a result only of learning to read and write. By sheer force of a vicious custom, even the most ignorant and worthless men have been enjoying a superiority over women which they do not deserve and ought not to have. Many of our movements stop half way because of the conditions of our women. Much of our work done does not yield appropriate results; our lot is like that of the penny-wise and pound-foolish trader who does not employ enough capital in his business.[3]

Equality of Sexes

I am uncompromising in the matter of women's rights. In my opinion she should labour under no legal disability not suffered by men. I should treat the daughters and sons on a footing of perfect equality.[4]

Equality of sexes does not mean equality of occupations. There may be no legal bar against a woman hunting or wielding a lance. But she instinctively recoils from a function that belongs to man. Nature has created sexes as complements of each other. Their functions are defined as are their forms.[5]

Marriage

A large part of the miseries of today can be avoided, if we look at the relations between the sexes in a healthy and pure light, and regard ourselves as trustees for the moral welfare of the future generations.[6]

Marriage is a natural thing in life, and to consider it derogatory in any sense is wrong.... The ideal is to look upon marriage as a sacrament, and therefore, to lead a life of self-restraint in the married state.[7]

The Purdah

Chastity is not a hot-house growth. It cannot be protected by the surrounding wall of the *purdah*. It must grow from within, and to be worth anything it must be capable of withstanding every unsought temptation.[8]

> *Why is there all this morbid anxiety about female purity? Have women any say in the matter of male purity? We hear nothing of women's anxiety about men's chastity*

And why is there all this morbid anxiety about female purity? Have women any say in the matter of male purity? We hear nothing of women's anxiety about men's chastity. Why should men arrogate to themselves the right to regulate female purity? It cannot be superimposed from without. It is a matter of evolution from within and therefore of individual self-effort.[9]

The Dowry System

The system has to go. Marriage must cease to be a matter of arrangement made by the parents for money. The system is intimately connected with caste. So long as the choice is retricted to a few hundred young men or young women of a particular caste, the system will persist no matter what is said against it. The girls or boys or their parents will have to break the bonds of caste if the evil is to be eradicated. All this means education of a character that will revolutionize the mentality of the youth of the nation.[10]

Any young man who makes dowry a condition of marriage discredits his education and his country and dishonours womanhood. There are many youth movements in the country. I wish that these movements would deal with questions of this character. Such associations often become self-adulation societies, instead of becoming, as they should be, bodies representing solid reform from within.... A strong public opinion should be created in condemnation of the degrading practice of dowry and young men who soil their fingers with such ill-gotten gold should be excommunicated from society. Parents of girls should cease to be dazzled by English degrees and should not hesitate to travel outside their little castes and provinces to secure true, gallant young men for their daughters.[11]

Widow Re-marriage

Voluntary widowhood consciously adopted by a woman who has felt the affection of a partner adds grace and dignity to life, sanctifies the home and uplifts religion itself. Widowhood imposed by religion or custom is an unbearable yoke and defiles the home by secret vice and degrades religion.

If we would be pure, if we would save Hinduism, we must rid ourselves of this poison of enforced widowhood. The reform must begin by those who have girl widows taking courage in both their hands and seeing that the child widows in their charge are duly and well married—not remarried. They were never really married.[12]

Divorce

Marriage confirms the right of union between two partners to the exclusion of all the others when in their joint opinion they consider such union to be desirable, but it confers no right upon one partner to demand obedience of the other to one's wish for union. What should be done when one partner on moral or other grounds cannot conform to the wishes of the other is a separate question. Personally, if divorce was the only alternative, I should not hesitate to accept it, rather than interrupt my moral progress,—assuming that I want to restrain myself on purely moral grounds.[13]

For me, the married state is as much a state of discipline as any other. Life is duty, a probation. Married life is intended to promote mutual good, both here and hereafter. It is meant also to serve humanity. When one partner breaks the law of discipline, the right accrues to the other of breaking the bond. The breach here is moral and not physical. It precludes divorce. The wife or the husband separates but to serve the end for which they have united. Hinduism regards each as absolute equal of the other. No doubt a different practice has grown up, no one knows since when. But so have many other evils crept into it. This, however, I do know that Hinduism leaves the individual absolutely free to do what he or she likes for the sake of self-realization, for which and which alone he or she is born.[14]

Woman's Honour

I have always held that it is physically impossible to violate a woman against her will. The outrage takes place only when she gives way to fear or does not realize her moral strength. If she cannot meet the assailant's physical might, her purity will give her the strength to die before he succeeds in violating her. Take the case of Sita. Physically she was a weakling before Ravana, but her purity was more than a match even for his giant might. He tried to win her with all kinds of allurements but could not carnally touch her without her consent. On the other hand, if a woman depends on her own physical strength or upon a weapon she possesses, she is sure to be discomfited whenever her strength is exhausted.[15]

When a woman is assaulted she may not stop to think in terms of *himsa* or *ahimsa*. Her primary duty is self-protection. She is at liberty to employ every method or means that come to her mind in order to defend her honour. God has given her nails and teeth. She must use them with all her strength and, if need be, die in the effort. The man or woman who has shed all fear of death will be able not only to protect himself or herself but others also through laying down his life.[16]

Prostitution

Prostitution is as old as the world, but I wonder if it was ever a regular feature of town life as it is today. In any case the time must come when humanity will rise against the curse and make prostitution a thing of the past, as it has got rid of many evil customs, however time-honoured they might have been.[17]

55

WOMEN'S EDUCATION

I have pointed out from time to time that there is no justification for men to deprive women or to deny them equal rights on the ground of their illiteracy; but education is essential for enabling women to uphold these natural rights, to improve them and to spread them; again, the true knowledge of self is unattainable by the millions who are without such education.

Man and woman are of equal rank but they are not identical. They are a peerless pair being supplementary to one another; each helps the other, so that without the one the existence of the other cannot be conceived, and therefore it follows as a necessary corollary from these facts that anything that will impair the status of either of them will involve the equal ruin of them both. In framing any scheme of women's education this cardinal truth must be constantly kept in mind. Man is supreme in the outward activities of a married pair and, therefore, it is in the fitness of things that he should have a greater knowledge thereof. On the other hand, home life is entirely the sphere of woman and, therefore, in domestic affairs, in the upbringing and education of children, women ought to have more knowledge. Not that knowledge should be divided into watertight compartments, or that some branches of knowledge should be closed to any one; but unless courses of instruction are based on a discriminating appreciation of these basic principles, the fullest life of man and woman cannot be developed.

I have come to the conclusion that in the ordinary course of our lives neither our men nor our women need necessarily have any knowledge of English. True, English is necessary for making a living and for active association in our political movements. I do not believe in women working for a living or undertaking commercial enterprises. The few women who may require or desire to have English education, can very easily have their way by joining the schools for men. To introduce English education in schools meant for women could only lead to prolongation of our helplessness. I have often read and heard people saying that the rich treasures of English literature should be opened alike to men and women. I submit in all humility that there is some misapprehension in assuming such an attitude. No one intends to close these treasures against women while keeping them open for men.

There is none on earth to prevent you from studying the literature of the world if you have literary tastes. But when courses of education have been framed with the needs of a particular society in view, you cannot supply the requirements of the few who have cultivated a literary taste. In asking our men and women to spend less time in the study of English than they are doing now, my object is not to deprive them of the pleasure which they are likely to derive from it, but I hold that the same pleasure can be obtained at less cost and trouble if we follow a more natural method. The world is full of many a gem of priceless beauty, but then these gems are not all of English setting. Other languages can well boast of productions of similar excellence; all these should be made available for our common people and that can only be done if our learned men will undertake to translate them for us in our own languages.[1]

I believe in the proper education of women. But I do believe that woman will not make her contribution to the world by mimicking or running a race with man. She can run the race, but she will not rise to the great heights she is capable of by mimicking man. She has to be complement of man.[2]

Co-education

I cannot definitely state as yet whether it will be successful or not. It does not seem to have succeeded in the West. I tried it myself years ago when I even made boys and girls sleep in the same verandah with no partition between them, Mrs. Gandhi and myself sharing the verandah with them. I must say it brought undesirable results.

....Co-education is still in its experimental stage and we cannot definitely say one way or the other as to its results. I think we should begin with the family first. There boys and girls should grow together freely and naturally. The co-education will come of itself.[3]

If you keep co-education in your schools, but not in your training-schools, the children will think there is something wrong somewhere. I should allow my children to run the risk. We shall have to rid ourselves one day of this sex mentality. We should not seek for examples from the West. Even in training-schools, if the teachers are intelligent, pure and filled with the spirit of Nai Talim, there is no danger. Supposing if some accidents do take place, we should not be frightened by them. They would take place anywhere. Although I speak boldly, I am not unaware of the attendant risks.[4]

56
BIRTH-CONTROL

There can be no two opinions about the necessity of birth-control. But the only method handed down from ages past is self-control or *brahmacharya*. It is an infallible sovereign remedy doing good to those who practise it.

And medical men will earn the gratitude of mankind, if instead of devising artificial means of birth-control they will find out the means of self-control.

> *Artificial methods are like putting a premium upon vice*

Artificial methods are like putting a premium upon vice. They make man and woman reckless. And respectability that is being given to the methods must hasten the dissolution of the restraints that public opinion puts upon one. Adoption of artificial methods must result in imbecility and nervous prostration. The remedy will be found to be worse than the disease.

It is wrong and immoral to seek to escape the cosequences of one's acts. It is good for a person who overeats to have an ache and a fast. It is bad for him to indulge his appetite and then escape the consequence by taking tonics or other medicine. It is still worse for a person to indulge in his animal passions and escape the consequences of his acts. Nature is relentless and will have full revenge for any such violation of her laws. Moral results can only be produced by moral restraints. All other restraints defeat the very purpose for which they are intended.[1]

The practice of preventing progeny, by means of artificial

methods, is not a new thing. In the past such methods were practised secretly and they were crude. Modern society has given them a respectable place and made improvements. They have been given a philanthropic garb. The advocates of contraceptives say that sexual desire is a natural instinct—some call it a blessing. They therefore say that it is not desirable to suppress the desire even if it were possible. Birth-control by means of self-restraint is, in their opinion, difficult to practise. If a substitute for self-restraint is not prescribed, the health of innumerable women is bound to suffer through frequent pregnancies.

> *Moral results can only be produced by moral restraints. All other restraints defeat the very purpose for which they are intended*

They add that if births are not regulated, over-population will ensue; individual families will be pauperized and their children will be ill-fed, ill-clothed and ill-educated. Therefore, they argue, it is the duty of scientists to devise harmless and effective methods of birth-control.

This argument has failed to convince me. The use of contraceptives is likely to produce evils of which we have no conception. But the worst danger is that the use of contraceptives bids fair to kill the desire for self-restraint. In my opinion it is too heavy a price to pay for any possible immediate gain.... Self-deception is the greatest stumbling block. Instead of controlling mind, the fountain of all animal desire, men and women involve themselves in the vain endeavour to avoid the physical act. If there is a determination to control the thought and the action, victory is sure to follow. Man must understand that woman is his companion and helpmate in life and not a means of satisfying his carnal desire. There must be a clear perception that the purpose of human creation was wholly different from that of the satisfaction of animal wants.[2]

I know what havoc secret vice has played among school boys and girls. The introduction of contraceptives under the name of science and the *imprimatur* of known leaders of society have intensified the complication and made the task of reformers who work for purity of social life, well-nigh impossible for the moment. I betray no confidence when I inform the reader that there are unmarried girls of impressionable age studying in schools and colleges who study birth-control literature and magazines with avidity and even possess contraceptives. It is impossible to confine their use to married women. Marriage loses its sanctity when its purpose and highest use is conceived to be the satisfaction of the animal passion without contemplating the natural result of such satisfaction.

I have no doubt that those learned men and women who are carrying on propaganda with missionary zeal in favour of the use of contraceptives, are doing irreparable harm to the youth of the country under the false belief that they will be saving thereby, the poor women who may be obliged to bear children against their will. Those who need to limit their children will not be easily reached by them. Our poor women have not the knowledge or the training that the women of the West have. Surely the propaganda is not being carried on behalf of the middle class women, for they do not need the knowledge, at any rate so much as the poor classes do.

The greatest harm, however, done by that propaganda lies in its rejection of the old ideal and substitution in its place of one which, if carried out, must spell the moral and physical extinction of the race. The horror with which ancient literature has regarded the fruitless use of the vital fluid was not a superstition born of ignorance. What shall we say of a husbandman who will sow the finest seed in his possession on stony ground or of the owner of a field who will receive, in his field rich with fine soil, good seed under conditions that will make it impossible for it to grow? God has blessed man with seed that has the highest potency and woman with a field richer than the richest earth to be found anywhere on this globe. Surely it is criminal folly for man to allow his most precious possession to run to waste. He must guard it with a care greater than he will bestow upon the richest pearls in his possession. And so is a woman guilty of criminal folly who will receive the seed in her life-producing field with the deliberate intention of letting it run to waste. Both he and she will be judged guilty of the misuse of the talents given to them and they will be dispossessed of what they have been given. Sex urge is a fine and noble thing. There is nothing to be ashamed of it. But it is meant only for the act of creation. Any other use of it is a sin against God and humanity. Contraceptives of a kind there were before and there will be hereafter; but the use of them was formerly regarded as sinful. It was reserved for our generation to glorify vice by calling it virtue. The greatest disservice protagonists of contraceptives are rendering to the youth of India is to fill their minds with what appears to me to be wrong ideology. Let the young men and women of India who hold her destiny in their hands beware of this false god and guard the treasure with which God has blessed them and use it, if they wish, for the only purpose for which it is intended.[3]

I do not believe that woman is prey to sexual desire to the same extent as man. It is easier for her than for man to exercise self-restraint. I hold that the right education in this country is to teach woman the art of saying *no* even to her husband, to teach her that it is no part of her duty to become a mere tool or a doll in her husband's hands. She has rights as well as duties. .... The first thing is to free her from mental slavery, to teach her sacredness of her body, and to teach her dignity of national service and the service of humanity. It is not fair to assume that India's women are beyond redemption, and that they have therefore to be simply taught the use of contraceptives for the sake of preventing births and preserving such health as they may be in possession of.

Let not the sisters who are rightly indignant over the miseries of women who are called upon to bear children, whether they will or no, be impatient. Not even the propaganda in favour of contraceptives is going to promote the desired end overnight. Every method is a matter of education. My plea is for the right type.[4]

Sterilization

I consider it inhuman to impose sterilization law on the poeple. But in cases of individuals with chronic diseases, it is desirable to have them sterilized if they are agreeable to it. Sterilization is a sort of contraceptive and though I am against the use of contraceptives in case of women, I do not mind voluntary sterilization in case of man since he is the aggressor.[5]

Bogey of Over-population

If it is contended that birth-control is necessary for the nation because of over-population, I dispute the proposition. It has never been proved. In my opinion, by a proper land-system, better agriculture and a supplementary industry, this country is capable of supporting twice as many people as there are today.[6]

This little globe of ours is not a toy of yesterday. It has not suffered from the weight of over-population through its age of countless millions. How can it be that the truth has suddenly dawned upon some people that it is in danger of perishing of shortage of food unless birth rate is checked through the use of contraceptives?

The bogey of increasing birth rate is not a new thing. It has been often trotted out. Increase in population is not and ought not to be regarded as a calamity to be avoided. Its regulation or restriction by artificial methods is a calamity of the first grade whether we know it or not. It is bound to degrade the race, if it becomes universal, which, thank God, it is never likely to be. Pestilence, wars and famines are cursed antidotes against cursed lust which is responsible for unwanted children. If we would avoid this threefold curse we would avoid too the curse of unwanted children by the sovereign remedy of self-control.... Let me say propagation of the race rabbitwise must undoubtedly be stopped; but not so as to bring greater evils in its train. It should be stopped by methods which in themselves ennoble the race. In other words, it is all a matter of proper education which would embrace every department of life; and dealing with one curse will take in its orbit all the others. A way is not to be avoided because it is upward and therefore uphill. Man's upward progress necessarily means ever increasing difficulty, which is to be welcomed.[7]

57

SEX EDUCATION

What place has...instruction in sexual science in our educational system, or has it any place there at all? Sexual science is of two kinds—that which is used for controlling or overcoming the sexual passion, and that which is used to stimulate and feed it. Instruction in the former is as necessary a part of a child's education as the latter is harmful and dangerous and fit therefore only to be shunned. All great religions have rightly regarded *kama* as the arch-enemy of man, anger or hatred coming only in the second place. According to the Gita, the latter is an offspring of the former. The Gita, of course, uses the word *kama* in its wider sense of desire. But the same holds good of the narrow sense in which it is used here.

> The sex education that I stand for, must have for its object the conquest and sublimation of the sex passion. Such education should automatically serve to bring home to children, the essential distinction between man and brute

This, however, still leaves unanswered the question, *i.e.* whether it is desirable to impart to young pupils a knowledge about the use and function of generative organs. It seems to me that it is necessary to impart such knowledge to a certain extent. At present they are often left to pick up such knowledge anyhow with the result that they are misled into abusive practices. We cannot properly control or conquer the sexual passion by turning a blind eye to it. I am, therefore, strongly in favour of teaching young boys and girls, the significance and right use of their generative organs. And in my own way I have tried to impart this knowledge to young children of both sexes for whose training I was responsible.

But the sex education that I stand for, must have for its object the conquest and sublimation of the sex passion. Such education should automatically serve to bring home to children, the essential distinction between man and brute, to make them realize that it is man's special privilege and pride to be gifted with the faculties of head and heart both; that he is thinking no less than a feeling animal, as the very derivation of the word मनुष्य shows, and to renounce the sovereignty of reason over the blind instincts is, therefore, to renounce a man's estate. In man, reason quickens and guides the feeling. In brute, the soul lies ever dormant. To awaken the heart is to awaken the dormant soul, to awaken reason, and to inculcate discrimination between good and evil.

Who should teach this true science of sex? Clearly, he who has attained mastery over his passions. To teach astronomy and kindered sciences we have teachers who have gone through course of training in them and are masters of their art. Even so must we have as teachers of sexual science, *i.e.* the science of sex-control, those who have studied it and have acquired mastery over self. Even a lofty utterance, that has not the backing of sincerity and experience, will be inert and lifeless, and will utterly fail to penetrate and quicken the hearts of men, while the speech that springs from self-realization and genuine experience is always fruitful.

Today our entire environment—our reading, our thinking, our social behaviour—is generally calculated to subserve and cater for the sex-urge. To break through its coils is no easy task. But it is a task worthy of our highest endeavour. Even if there are a handful of teachers endowed with practical experince, who accept the ideal of attaining self-control as the highest duty of man, and are fired by a genuine and undying faith in their mission, and are sleeplessly vigilant and active, their labour will light the path of the children...., save the unwary from falling into the mire of sexuality, and rescue those who might be already engulfed in it.[1]

58

CHILDREN

Children inherit the qualities of the parents, no less than their physical features. Environment does play an important part, but the original capital on which a child starts life is inherited from its ancestors. I have always seen children successfully surmounting the effects of evil inheritance. That is due to purity being an inherent attribute of the soul.[1]

> *The real property that a parent can transmit to all equally is his or her character and educational facilities*

The real property that a parent can transmit to all equally is his or her character and educational facilities. ....Parents should seek to make their sons and daughters self-reliant, well able to earn an honest livelihood by the sweat of the brow.[2]

I believe implicity that the child is not born mischievous in the bad sense of the term. If parents would behave themselves whilst the child is growing, before it is born and after, it is a well-known fact that the child would instinctively obey the law of Truth and the law of Love.... And believe me, from my experience of hundreds—I was going to say thousands—of children, I know that they have perhaps a finer sense of honour than you or I have. The greatest lessons of life, if we would but stoop and humble ourselves, we would learn not from grown-up learned men, but from the so-called ignorant children. Jesus never uttered a loftier or a grander truth than when he said that wisdom cometh out of the mouth of babes. I believe it. I have noticed it in my own experience that if we would approach babes in humility and innocence, we would learn wisdom from them. I have learned this one lesson—that what is impossible with man is child's play with God and if we have faith in that Divinity which persides on the detiny of the meanest of His creation, I have no doubt that all things are possible and in that final hope, I believe and pass my time and endeavour to obey His will. If we are to reach real peace in this world and if we are to carry on a real war against war, we shall have to begin with children; and if they will grow up in their natural innocence, we won't have to struggle, we won't have to pass fruitless, idle resolutions, but we shall go from love to love and peace to peace, until at last all the corners of the world are covered with that peace and love for which, consciously or unconsciously, the whole world is hungering.[3]

59

COMMUNAL UNITY

Everybody is agreed about the necessity of this (communal) unity. But everybody does not know that unity does not mean political unity which may be imposed. It means an unbreakable heart unity. The first thing essential for achieving such unity is for every Congressman,

> Unity does not mean political unity which may be imposed. It means an unbreakable heart unity

whatever his religion may be, to represent in his own person Hindu, Muslim, Christian, Zoroastrian, Jew, etc., shortly, every one of the millions of the inhabitants of Hindustan. In order to realize this, every Congressman will cultivate personal friendship with persons representing faiths other than his own. He should have the same regard for the other faiths as he has for his own.[1]

Hindus and Musalmans, Christians, Sikhs and Parsis must not settle their differences by resort to violence.... Hindus and Musalmans prate about no compulsion in religion. What is it but compulsion if Hindus will kill a Musalman for saving a cow? It is like wanting to convert a Musalman to Hiduism by force. And similarly what is it but compulsion, if Musalmans seek to prevent by force Hindus from playing music before mosques? Virtue lies in being absorbed in one's prayers in the presence of din and noise. We shall both be voted irreligious savages by posterity if we continue to make a futile attempt to compel one another to respect our religious wishes.

If Hindu-Muslim unity is endangered because an Arya Samaj preacher or a Musalman preacher preaches his faith in obedience to a call from within, that unity is only skin-deep. Why should we be ruffled by such movements? Only they must be genuine. If the Malkanas wanted to return to the Hindu fold they had a perfect right to do so whenever they liked. But no propaganda can be allowed which reviles other religions. For, that would be negation of toleration. The best way of dealing with such propaganda is publicly to condemn it. Every movement attempts to put on the cloak of respectability. As soon as the public tear the cloak down, it dies for want of respectability.

> No propaganda can be allowed which reviles other religions. For, that would be negation of toleration

It is now time to examine the treatment of two constant causes of friction.

The first is cow slaughter. Though I regard cow protection as the central fact of Hinduism, central because it is common to classes as well as masses, I have never been able to understand the antipathy towards the Musalmans on that score. We say nothing about the slaughter that daily takes place on behalf of Englishmen. Our anger becomes red-hot when a Musalman slaughters a cow. All the riots that have taken place in the name of the cow have been an insane waste of effort. They have not saved a single cow, but they have on the contrary stiffened the backs of the Musalmans and resulted in more slaughter.... Cow protection should commence with ourselves. In no part of the world perhaps are cattle worse treated than in India. I have wept to see Hindu drivers goading their jaded oxen with the iron points of their cruel sticks. The half-starved condition of the majority of our cattle is a disgrace to us. The cows find their necks under the butcher's knife because Hindus sell them. The only effective and honourable way is to befriend the Musalmans and leave it to their honour to save the cow. Cow protection societies must turn their attention to the feeding of cattle, prevention of cruelty, preservation of the fast disappearing pasture lands, improving the breed of cattle, buying from poor shepherds and turning *pinjrapols* into model self-supporting dairies. Hindus do sin against God and man when they omit to do any of the things I have described above.

They commit no sin, if they cannot prevent cow slaughter at the hands of Musalmans, and they do sin grievously when in order to save the cow, they quarrel with the Musalmans.

The question of music before mosques, and now even *arati* in Hindu temples, has occupied my prayerful attention. This is a sore point with the Musalmans as cow slaughter is with the Hindus. And just as Hindus cannot compel Musalmans to refrain from killing cows, so can Musalmans not compel Hindus to stop music or *arati* at the point of the sword. They must trust the good sense of the Hindus. As a Hindu, I would certainly advise the Hindus, without any bargaining spirit, to consult the sentiment of their Musalman neighbours and wherever they can, accommodate them. I have heard that in some places, Hindus purposely and with the deliberate intention of irritating Musalmans, perform *arati* just when the Musalman prayers commence. This is an insensate and unfriendly act. Friendship presupposes the utmost attention to the feelings of a friend. It never requires consideration. But Musalmans should never expect to stop Hindu music by force. To yield to the threat or actual use of violence is a surrender of one's self-respect and religious conviction. But a person, who never will yield to threat, would always minimize and, if possible, even avoid occasions for causing irritation.

I am convinced that the masses do not want to fight, if the leaders do not. If, therefore, the leaders agree that mutual rows should be, as in all advanced countries, erased out of our public life as being barbarous and irreligious, I have no doubt that the masses will quickly follow them.

Were Hindus and Musalmans and Sikhs always at war with one another when there was no British rule, when there was no English face seen here? We have chapter and verse given to us by Hindu historians and by Musalman historians to say that we were living in comparative peace even then. And Hindus and Musalmans in the villages are not even today quarrelling. In those days they were not known to quarrel at all.... This quarrel is not old.... I dare say, it is coeval with the British advent, and immediately this relationship, the unfortunate, artificial, unnatural relationship between Great Britain and India is transformed into a natural relationship, when it becomes, if it does become, a voluntary partnership to be given up, to be dissolved at the will of either party, when it becomes

> I am convinced that the masses do not want to fight, if the leaders do not

that, you will find that Hindus, Musalmans, Sikhs, Europeans, Anglo-Indians, Christians, Untouchables, will all live together as one man.[2]

I have not a shadow of doubt that the iceberg of communal differences will melt under the warmth of the sun of freedom.[3]

60

VARNASHRAMA DHARMA

I believe that every man is born in the world with certain natural tendencies. Every person is born with certain definite limitations which he cannot overcome. From a careful observation of those limitations the law of Varna was deduced. It establishes certain spheres of action for certain people with certain tendencies. This avoided all unworthy competition. Whilst recognizing limitations the law of Varna admitted of no distinctions of high and low; on the one hand it guaranteed to each the fruits of his labours, and on the other it prevented him from pressing upon his neighbours. This great law has been degraded and fallen into disrepute. But my conviction is that an ideal social order will only be evolved when the implications of this law are fully understood and given effect to.[1]

> *We are all absolutely equal. But equality is of souls and not bodies. Hence, it is a mental state. We need to think of, and to assert, equality because we see great inequalities in the physical world*

Varnashrama Dharma defines man's mission on this earth. He is not born day after day to explore avenues for amassing riches and to explore different means of livelihood; on the contrary man is born in order that he may utilize every atom of his energy for the purpose of knowing his Maker. It restricts him, therefore, for the purpose of holding body and soul together, to the occupation of his forefathers. That and nothing more or nothing less is Varnashrama Dharma.[2]

India of My Dreams

I consider the four divisions alone to be fundamental, natural, and essential. The innumerable subcastes are sometimes a convenience, often a hindrance. The sooner there is fusion the better.[3]

Today Brahmanas and Kshatriyas, Vaishyas and Shudras are mere labels. There is utter confusion of Varna as I understand it and I wish that all the Hindus will voluntarily call themselves Shudras. That is the only way to demonstrate the truth of

> *Untouchability is the product, therefore, not of the caste system, but of the distinction of high and low that has crept into Hinduism and is corroding it*

Brahmanism and to revive Varnadharma in its true state.[4]

Caste

I have frequently said that I do not believe in caste in the modern sense. It is an excrescence and a handicap on progress. Nor, do I believe in inequalities between human beings. We are all absolutely equal. But equality is of souls and not bodies. Hence, it is a mental state. We need to think of, and to assert, equality because we see great inequalities in the physical world. We have to realize equality in the midst of this apparent external inequality. Assumption of superiority by any person over any other is a sin against God and man. Thus caste, in so far as it connotes distinctions in status, is an evil. I do, however, believe in Varna which is based on hereditary occupations. Varnas are four to mark four universal occupations,— imparting knowledge, defending the defenceless, carrying on agriculture and commerce, and performing service through physical labour. These occupations are common to all mankind, but Hinduism, having recognized them as the law of our being, has made use of it in regulating social relations and conduct. Gravitation affects us all, whether one knows its existence or not. But scientists who knew the law have made it yield results that have startled the world. Even so, has Hinduism startled the world by its discovery and application of the law of Varna. When Hindus were seized with inertia, abuse of Varna resulted in innumerable castes, with unnecessary and harmful restrictions as to inter-marriage and inter-dining. The law of

Varna has nothing to do with these restrictions. People of different Varnas may inter-marry and interdine. These restrictions may be necessary in the interest of chastity and hygiene. But a Brahmana who marries a Shudra girl, or *vice versa*, commits no offence against the law of Varna.[5]

It is as wrong to destroy caste because of the out-caste, as it would be to destroy a body because of an ugly growth in it or of a crop because of the weeds. The outcasteness, in the sense we understand it, has therefore to be destroyed altogether. It is an excess to be removed, if the whole system is not to perish. Untouchability is the product, therefore, not of the caste system, but of the distinction of high and low that has crept into Hinduism and is corroding it. The attack on untouchability is thus an atack upon this 'high-and-low'-ness. The moment untouchability goes, the caste system itself will be purified, that is to say, according to my dream, it will resolve itself into the true Varnadharma, the four divisions of society, each complementary of the other and none inferior or superior to any other, each as necessary for the whole body of Hinduism as any other.[6]

From the economic point of view, its value was once very great. It ensured hereditary skill; it limited competition. It was the best remedy against pauperism. And it had all the advantages of trade guilds. Although it did not foster adventure or invention there, it is not known to have come in the way either.

Historically speaking, caste may be regarded as man's experiment or social adjustment in the laboratory of Indian society. If we can prove it to be a success, it can be offered to the world as a leaven and as the best remedy against heartless competition and social disintegration born of avarice and greed.[7]

Inter-marriage and Inter-dining

Though there is in Varnashrama no prohibition against inter-marriage and inter-dining, there can be no compulsion. It must be left to the unfettered choice of the individual as to where he or she will marry or dine.[8]

61

THE CURSE OF UNTOUCHABILITY

There is an ineffaceable blot that Hinduism today carries with it. I have declined to believe that it has been handed down to us from immemorial times. I think that this miserable, wretched, enslaving spirit of 'untouchableness' must have come to us when we were at our lowest ebb. This evil has stuck to us and still remains with us. It is, to my mind, a curse that has come to us, and as long as that curse remains with us, so long, I think, we are bound to consider that every affliction in this sacred land is a proper punishment for the indelible crime that we are committing.[1]

> *Untouchability as it is practised in Hinduism today is, in my opinion, a sin against God and man and is, therefore, like a poison slowly eating into the very vitals of Hinduism. In my opinion, it has no sanction whatsoever in the Hindu Shastras taken as a whole*

Untouchability as it is practised in Hinduism today is, in my opinion, a sin against God and man and is, therefore, like a poison slowly eating into the very vitals of Hinduism. In my opinion, it has no sanction whatsoever in the Hindu Shastras taken as a whole. Untouchability of a healthy kind is undoubtedly to be found in the Shastras and it is universal in all religions. It is a rule of sanitation. That will exist to the end of time; but untouchability as we are observing today in India is a hideous thing and wears various forms in various provinces, even in districts. It has degraded both the untouchables and the touchables. It has stunted the growth of nearly 40 million human beings. They are denied even the ordinary amenities of life. The sooner, therefore, it is ended, the better for Hinduism, the better for India, and perhaps better for mankind in general.[2]

> I have felt for years, that there must be something radically wrong, where scavenging has been made the concern of a separate class in society

Swaraj is a meaningless term, if we desire to keep a fifth of India under perpetual subjection, and deliberately deny to them the fruits of national culture. We are seeking the aid of God in this great purifying movement, but we deny to the most deserving among His creatures the rights of humanity. Inhuman ourselves, we may not plead before the Throne for deliverance from the inhumanity of others.[3]

That untouchability is an old institution, nobody has ever denied. But if it is an evil, it cannot be defended on the ground of its antiquity. If the untouchables are the outcastes of the Aryan society, so much the worse for that society. And if the Aryans at some stage in their progress regarded a certain class of people as outcastes by way of punishment, there is no reason why that punishment should descend upon their progeny irrespective of the causes for which their ancestors were punished. That there is untouchability even amongst untouchables merely demonstrates that the evil cannot be confined and that its deadening effect is all-pervading. The existence of untouchability amongst untouchables is an additional reason for cultured Hindu society to rid itself of the curse with the quickest despatch. If the untouchables are so because they kill animals and because they have to do with flesh, blood, bones and night-soil, every nurse and every doctor should become an untouchable and so should Christians and Musalmans and all so-called high-class Hindus who kill animals for food or sacrifice. The argument that because slaughter-houses, toddy-shops, and houses of ill-fame are or should be isolated, untouchables should likewise be isolated betrays gross prejudice. Slaughter-houses and toddy-shops are and should be isolated. But neither butchers nor publicans are isolated.[4]

Placed as we are in the midst of trials and temptations from within, and touched and polluted as we are by all the most untouchable and the vilest thought currents, let us not, in our arrogance, exaggerate the influence of contact with people whom we often ignorantly

> *In its inception, untouchability was a rule of sanitation and still is in all parts of the world outside India. That is to say, an unclean person or thing is untouchable but immediately his or its uncleanliness is shed, he or it is no longer untouchable*

and more often arrogantly consider to be our inferiors. Before the Throne of the Almighty we shall be judged, not by what we have eaten nor by whom we have been touched but by whom we have served and how. Inasmuch as we serve a single human being in distress, we shall find favour in the sight of God. ... We dare not use abstinence from certain foods as a cover for fraud, hypocrisy and worse vices. We dare not refuse to serve a fallen or a dirty brother lest his contact should injure our spiritual growth.[5]

Scavengers

I have felt for years, that there must be something radically wrong, where scavenging has been made the concern of a separate class in society. We have no historical record of the man, who first assigned the lowest status to this essential sanitary service. Whoever he was, he by no means did us a good. We should, from our very childhood, have the idea impressed upon our minds that we are all scavengers, and the easiest way of doing so is, for every one who has realized this, to commence bread labour as a scavenger. Scavenging, thus intelligently taken up, will help one to a true appreciation of the equality of man.[6]

In its inception, untouchability was a rule of sanitation and still is in all parts of the world outside India. That is to say, an unclean person or thing is untouchable but immediately his or its uncleanliness is shed, he or it is no longer untouchable. Therefore, persons who are to attend to scavenging, whether a paid *bhangi* or an unpaid mother, they are unclean until they have washed themselves clean of their unclean work. If instead of being regarded as untouchable for ever, the *bhangi* was treated as a brother and was given an opportunity and even made to become clean after performing an unclean service for society he should be as acceptable as any other member of that society.[7]

62

RELIGIOUS TOLERANCE IN INDIA

Hinduism

I have found it to be the most tolerant of all religious known to me. Its freedom from dogma makes a forcible appeal to me inasmuch as it gives the votary the largest scope for self-expression. Not being an exclusive religion, it enables the followers of that faith not merely to respect all the other religions, but it also enables them to admire and assimilate whatever may be good in the other faiths. Non-violence is common to all religions, but it has found the highest expression and application in Hinduism (I do not regard Jainism or Buddhism as separate from Hinduism). Hinduism believes in the oneness not of merely all human life but in the oneness of all that lives. Its worship of the cow is, in my opinion, its unique contribution to the evolution of humanitarianism. It is a practical application of the belief in the oneness and, therefore, sacredness, of all life. The great belief in transmigration is a direct consequence of that belief. Finally the discovery of the law of Varnashrama is a magnificent result of the ceaseless search for truth.[1]

Buddhism

It is my fixed opinion that Buddhism or rather the teaching of Buddha found its full fruition in India and it could not be otherwise, for Gautama was himself a Hindu of Hindus. He was saturated with the best that was in Hinduism, and he gave life to some of the teachings that were buried in the Vedas and which were overgrown with weeds.... Buddha never rejected

Hinduism, but he broadened its base. He gave it a new life and a new interpretation.[2]

He undoubtedly rejected the notion that a being called God was actuated by malice, could repent of his actions, and like the kings of the earth could possibly be open to temptations and bribes and could possibly have favourites. His whole soul rose in mighty indignation against the belief that a being called God required for his satisfaction the living blood of animals in order that he might be pleased—animals who were His own creation. He, therefore, reinstated God in the right place and dethroned the usurper who for the time being seemed to occupy that White Throne. He emphasized and redeclared the eternal and unalterable existence of the moral government of this universe. He unhesitatingly said that the law was God Himself.[3]

Christianity

I cannot ascribe exclusive divinity to Jesus. He is as divine as Krishna or Rama or Muhammad or Zoroaster. Similarly I do not regard every word of the Bible as the inspired word of God even as I do not regard every word of the Vedas or the Koran as inspired. The sum total of each of these books is certainly inspired, but I miss that inspiration in many of the things taken individually. The Bible is as much a book of religion with me as the Gita and the Koran.[4]

> I am both an idolater and an iconoclast in what I conceive to be the true sense of the terms. I value the spirit behind idol-worship

It is my firm opinion that Europe today represents not the spirit of God or Christianity but the spirit of Satan. And Satan's successes are the greatest when he appears with the name of God on his lips. Europe is today only nominally Christian. It is really worshipping Mammon. 'It is easier for a camel to pass through the eye of a needle than for a rich man to enter the Kingdom.' Thus really spoke Jesus Christ. His so-called followers measure their moral progress by their material possessions.[5]

Islam

I do regard Islam to be a religion of peace in the same sense as Christianity, Buddhism and Hinduism are. No doubt there are differences in degrees, but the object of these religions is peace.[6]

Islam's distinctive contribution to India's national culture is its unadulterated belief in the oneness of God and a practical application of the truth of the brotherhood of man for those who are nominally within its fold. I call these two distinctive contributions. For in Hinduism the spirit of brotherhood has become too much philosophized. Similarly though philosophical Hinduism has no other god but God, it cannot be denied that practical Hinduism is not so emphatically uncompromising as Islam.[7]

I do not expect India of my dream to develop one religion, *i.e.*, to be wholly Hindu, or wholly Christian, or wholly Musalman, but I want it to be wholly tolerant, with its religions working side by side with one another.[8]

> *I am an iconoclast in the sense that I break down the subtle form of idolatry in the shape of fanaticism that refuses to see any virtue in any other form of worshipping the Deity save one's own*

Idolatry

We are all idolaters. We all want temples, churches, mosques and synagogues for our spiritual development, and to strengthen our faith in God. Some want images of stone or metal, others an altar or a book or even a picture, to inspire feelings of devotion towards God.[9]

Temples or mosques or churches...I make no distinction between these different abodes of God. They are what faith has made them. They are an answer to man's craving somehow to reach the Unseen.[10]

I am both an idolater and an iconoclast in what I conceive to be the true sense of the terms. I value the spirit behind idol-worship. It plays a most important part in the uplift of the human race. And I would like to possess the ability to defend with my life the thousands of holy temples which sanctify this land of ours.... I am an iconoclast in the sense that I break down the subtle form of idolatry in the shape of fanaticism that refuses to see any virtue in any other form of worshipping the Deity save one's own. This form of idolatry is more deadly for being more fine and evasive than the tangible and gross form of worship that identifies the deity with a little bit of a stone or a golden image.[11]

We worship an image when we visit a temple or a mosque with a feeling of sanctity or reverence. Nor do I see any harm in all this. On the contrary, endowed as man is with a finite, limited understanding, he can hardly do otherwise. Even so far from seeing anything inherently evil or harmful in tree-worship, I find in it a thing instinct with a deep pathos and poetic beauty. It symbolizes true reverence for the entire vegetable kingdom, which with its endless panorama of beautiful shapes and forms, declares to us as it were with a million tongues the greatness and glory of God. Without vegetation our planet would not be able to support life even for a moment. In such a country especially, therefore, in which there is a scarcity of trees, tree-worship assumes a profound economic significance.[12]

63

PROSELYTIZATION

My Hindu instinct tells me that all religions are more or less true. All religions proceed from the same God but all are imperfect because they have come down to us through imperfect human instrumentality. The real *Shuddhi* movement should consist in each one trying to arrive at perfection in his or her own faith. In such a plan character would be the only test. What is the use of crossing from one compartment to another, if it does not mean a moral rise?

> All religions proceed from the same God but all are imperfect because they have come down to us through imperfect human instrumentality

What is the meaning of my trying to convert to the service of God (for that must be the implication of *Shuddhi* or *Tabligh*) when those who are in my fold are every day denying God by their actions? "Physician, heal thyself" is more true in matters religious than mundane.[1]

I am against the modern method of proselytizing. Years' experience of proselytizing both in South Africa and India has convinced me that it has not raised the general moral tone of the converts who have imbibed the superficialities of European civilization, and have missed the teaching of Jesus. I must be understood to refer to the general tendency and not to brilliant exceptions. The indirect contribution, on the other hand, of Christian missionary effort is great. It has stimulated Hindu and Musalman religious research. It has forced us to put our own houses in order. The great educational and curative institutions of Christian missions I also count, amongst indirect results, because they have been established, not for their own sakes, but as an aid to proselytizing.[2]

I hold that proselytizing under the cloak of humanitarian work is, to say the least, unhealthy. It is most certainly resented by the people here. Religion after all is a deeply personal matter, it touches the heart. Why should I change my religion because a doctor who professes Christianity as his religion has cured me of some disease or why should the doctor expect or suggest such a change whilst I am under his influence? Is not medical relief its own reward and satisfaction? Or why should I whilst I am in a missionary educational institution have Christian teaching thrust upon me? In my opinion these are not uplifting and give rise to suspicion if not even secret hostility. The methods of conversion must be like Caesar's wife above suspicion. Faith is not imparted like secular subjects. It is given through the language of the heart. If a man has a living faith in him, it spreads its aroma like the rose its scent. Because of its invisibility, the extent of its influence is far wider than that of the visible beauty of the colour of the petals.

I am, then, not against conversion. But I am against the modern methods of it. Conversion nowadays has become a matter of business, like any other. I remember having read a missionary report saying how much it cost per head to convert and then presenting a budget for 'the next harvest'.

Yes, I do maintain that India's great faiths are all-sufficing for her. Apart from Christianity and Judaism, Hinduism and its offshoots, Islam and Zoroastrianism are living faiths. No one faith is perfect. All faiths are equally dear to their respective votaries. What is wanted, therefore, is a living friendly contact among the followers of the great religions of the world and not a clash among them in the fruitless attempt on the part of each community to show the superiority of its faith over the rest. Through such friendly contact it will be possible for us all to rid our respective faiths of shortcomings and excrescences.

It follows from what I have said above that India is in no need of conversion of the kind I have in mind. Conversion in the sense of self-purification, self-realization is the crying need of the times. That, however, is not what is ever meant by proselytizing. To those who would convert India, might it not be said, 'Physician, heal thyself'?[3]

Why should a Christian want to convert a Hindu to Christianity and *vice versa*? Why should he not be satisfied if the Hindu is a good or godly man? If the morals of a man are a matter of no concern, the form of worship in a particular manner in a church, a mosque or a temple is an empty formula; it may even be a hindrance to individual or soical growth, and insistence on a particular form or repetition of a credo may be a potent cause of violent quarrels leading to bloodshed and ending in utter disbelief in Religion, *i.e.* God Himself.[4]

64

PROBLEMS OF ADMINISTRATION

I am afraid that for years to come India would be engaged in passing legislation in order to raise the down-trodden, the fallen, from the mire into which they have been sunk by the capitalists, by the landlords, by the so-called higher classes, and then, subsequently and scientifically, by the British rulers. If we are to lift these people from the mire, then it would be the bounden duty of the National Government of India, in order to set its house in order, continually to give preference to these people and even free them from the burdens under which they are being crushed. And, if the landlords, zamindars, moneyed men and those who are today enjoying privileges—I do not care whether they are Europeans or Indians—if they find that they are discriminated against, I shall sympathize with them, but I will not be able to help them, even if I could possibly do so, because I would seek their assistance in that process, and without their assistance it would not be possible to raise these people out of the mire.

It will, therefore, be a battle between the haves and the have-nots: and if that is what is feared, I am afraid the National Government will not be able to come into being if all the classes hold the pistol at the head of the dumb millions and say: 'You shall not have a Government of your own unless you guarantee our possessions and our rights.'[1]

Governors

....Much as I would like to spare every pice of the public treasury, it would be bad economy to do away with provincial

246 *India of My Dreams*

Governors and regard Chief Ministers as a perfect equivalent. Whilst I would resent much power of interference to be given to Governors, I do not think that they should be mere figure-heads. They should have enough power enabling them to influence ministerial policy for the better. In their detached position they would be able to see things in their proper perspective and thus prevent mistakes by their Cabinets. Theirs must be an all-pervasive moral influence in their provinces.[2]

Ministers

If the Congress wants to continue as a people's organization, the Ministers cannot live as *sahib log* nor use for private work facilities provided by Government for official duties.[3]

Nepotism

This office-holding is a step towards either greater prestige or its total loss. If it is not to be a total loss, the ministers and the legislators have to be watchful of their own personal and public conduct. They have to be, like Caesar's wife, above suspicion in everything. They may not make private gains either for themselves or for their relatives or friends. If the relatives or friends get any appointment, it must be only because they are the best among the candidates, and their market value is always greater than what they get under the Government. The ministers and the legislators of the Congress ticket have to be fearless in the performance of their duty. They must always be ready to risk the loss of their seats or offices. Offices and seats in the legislatures have no merit outside their ability to raise the prestige and power of the Congress. And since both depend wholly upon the possession of morals, both public and private, any moral lapse means a blow to the Congress.[4]

Taxes

A popular ministry is responsible to the legislatures and cannot do anything without their consent. Every elected member in a popular legislature is responsible to his voters. Therefore, the voter who represents the public should ponder well before embarking on any criticism of the government of his creation. Moreover, one bad habit of the people should be borne in mind. They do not like any tax whatsoever. Where there is good government, the tax-prayer gets full return for his money as, for example, the water tax in cities. No tax-payer could get water on his own for the same payment. But even so, and in spite of the fact that the tax is levied by the popular will, tax-payers always resent even paying such taxes. It is, of course, true that one cannot prove the benefit of all taxes as easily as the one I have cited as an example. But as society grows in size and complexity and the field of service also grows, it is difficult to explain to the individual tax-payer, how he gets his return for any particular tax. This much, however, is clear that taxes as a whole should stand for the general benefit of society. If this were not so, the argument that the taxes were levied by popular will would not hold.[5]

Crime and Its Punishment

In independent India of the non-violent type, there will be crime but no criminals. They will not be punished. Crime is a disease like any other malady and is a product of the prevalent social system. Therefore, all crime including murder will be treated as a disease. Whether such an India will ever come into being is another question.[6]

What should our jails be like in free India? All criminals should be treated as patients and the jails should be hospitals admitting this class of patients for treatment and cure. No one commits crime for the fun of it. It is a sign of a diseased mind. The causes of a particular disease should be investigated and removed. They need not have palatial buildings when their jails become hospitals. No country can afford that, much less can a poor country like India. But the outlook of the jail staff should be that of physicians and nurses in a hospital. The prisoners should feel that the officials are their friends. They are there to help them to regain their mental health and not to harass them in any way. The popular governments have to issue necessary orders, but meanwhile the jail staff can do not a little to humanize their administration. What is the duty of the prisoners?... They should behave as ideal prisoners. They should avoid breach of jail discipline. They should put their heart and soul into whatever work is entrusted to them. For instance, the prisoners' food is cooked by themselves. They should clean the rice, *dal* or whatever cereal is used so that there are no stones and grit or weevils in them. Whatever complaints the prisoners might have should be brought to the notice of the authorities in a becoming manner. They should so behave in their little community as to become better men when they leave the jail than when they entered it.[7]

Adult Suffrage

I am wedded to adult suffrage....Adult suffrage is necessary for more reasons than one, and one of the decisive reasons to me is that it enables me to satisfy all the reasonable aspirations, not only of the Musalmans, but also of the so-called untouchables, of Christians, of labourers and all kinds of classes. I cannot possibly bear the idea that a man who has got character but no wealth or literacy should have no vote, or that a man who works honestly by the sweat of his brow day in and day out should not have the vote for the crime of being a poor man.[8]

Death Duties

In this of all countries in the world possession of inordinate wealth by individuals should be held as a crime against Indian humanity. Therefore the maximum limit of taxation of riches beyond a certain margin can never be reached. In England, I understand, they have already gone as far as 70 per cent of the earnings beyond a prescribed figure. There is no reason why India should not go to a much higher figure. Why should there not be death duties? Those sons of millionaires who are of age and yet inherit their parents' wealth, are losers for the very inheritance. The nation thus becomes a double loser. For the inheritance should rightly belong to the nation. And the nation loses again in that the full faculties of the heirs are not drawn out, being crushed under the load of riches.[9]

Reform by Legislation

People seem to think, that when a law is passed against any evil, it will die without any further effort. There never was a greater self-deception. Legislation is intended and is effective against an ignorant or a small evil-minded minority; but no legislation which is opposed by an intelligent and organized public opinion, or under cover of religion by a fanatical majority, can ever succeed.[10]

The first thing is to avoid the slightest shadow of compulsion or untruth. No reform worth the name has yet, in my humble opinion, been achieved by compulsion. For whilst compulsion may lead to apparent success, it gives rise to so many other evils which are worse than the original evil itself.[11]

Trials by Jury

Trials by jury often result, all over the world, in defeating justice. But people everywhere gladly submit to the drawback for the sake of the more important result of the cultivation of an independent spirit among people and the justifiable sentiment of being judged by one's own peers.[12]

I am unconvinced of the advantages of jury trials over those by judges....We must not slavishly copy all that is English. In matters where absolute impartiality, calmness and ability to sift evidence and understand human nature are required, we may not replace trained judges by untrained men brought together by chance. What we must aim at is an incorruptible, impartial and able judiciary right from the bottom.[13]

Law Courts

If we were not under the spell of lawyers and law-courts, and if there were no touts to tempt us into the quagmire of the courts and to appeal to our basest passions we would be leading a much happier life than we do. Let those who frequent the law-courts—the best of them—bear witness to the fact that the atmosphere about them is foetid. Perjured witnesses are ranged on either side, ready to sell their very souls for money or for friendship's sake.[14]

The first thing which you must always bear in mind, if you would spiritualize the practice of law, is not to make your profession subservient to the interests of your purse, as is unfortunately but too often the case at present, but to use your profession for the service of your country. There are instances of eminent lawyers in all countries who led a life of self-sacrifice, who devoted their brilliant legal talents entirely to the service of their country, although it meant almost pauperism to them.....You can follow Ruskin's precept given in his book *Unto This Last*. 'Why should a lawyer charge fifteen pounds for his work', he asks, 'whilst a carpenter for instance hardly gets as many shillings for his work?' The fees charged by lawyers are unconscionable everywhere. In England, in South Africa, almost everywhere I have found that in the practice of their profession lawyers are consciously or unconsciously led into untruth for the sake of their clients. An eminent lawyer has gone so far as to say that it may even be the duty of a lawyer to defend a client whom he knows to be guilty. There I disagree. The duty of a lawyer is always to place before the judges, and to help them to arrive at, the truth, never to prove the guilty as innocent.[15]

Communal Representation

Independent India cannot afford to have communal representation and yet it must placate all communities, if the rule of independence is not based on coercion of minorities.[16]

Military Expenditure

Our statesmen have for over two generations declaimed against the heavy expenditure on armaments under the British regime, but now that freedom from political serfdom has come, our military expenditure has increased and still threatens to increase and of this we are proud ! There is not a voice raised against it in our legislative chambers. In spite, however, of the madness and the vain imitation of the tinsel of the West, the hope lingers in me and many others that India shall survive this death dance and occupy the moral height that should belong to her after the training, however imperfect, in non-violence for an unbroken period of thirty-two years since 1915.[17]

Navy

I do not know of the navy but I do know that the army of India of the future will not consist of hirelings to be utilized for keeping India under subjection and for depriving other nations of their liberty, but it would be largely cut down, will consist largely of volunteers and will be utilized for policing India.[18]

65

REORGANIZATION OF PROVINCES

The Congress has already adopted the principle (of redistribution of the provinces on a linguistic basis)and has declared its intention to give effect to it constitutionally as soon as they come into power, as such redistribution would be conducive to the cultural advancement of the country. But such redistribution should not militate against the organic unity of India. Autonomy does not and should not mean disruption or that hereafter provinces could go the way they chose, independent of one another and of the Centre. If each province began to look upon itself as a separate, sovereign unit, India's independence would lose its meaning and with it would vanish the freedom of the various units as well.

> *Such redistribution should not militate against the organic unity of India. Autonomy does not and should not mean disruption or that provinces can go the way they choose, independent of one another and of the Centre*

The character of India's independence as conceived by the Congress is based on village autonomy. But all the villages are to derive vitality from the Centre, as the latter in its turn derived all power and authority from the former. It would be fatal if it led to fatal provincialism, mutual bickerings and rivalries...between Tamil and Andhra for instance, Bombay and Karnataka and so on. The redistribution of provinces on a linguistic basis is necessary if provincial languages are to grow to their full height.

Hindustani is to be the lingua franca—*Rashtra Bhasha*—of India, but it cannot take the place of the provincial tongues. It cannot be the medium of instruction in the provinces... much less English. Its function is to make them realize their organic relationship with India. The world outside does not know them as Gujaratis, Maharashtrians, Tamilians etc., but only as Indians. We must, therefore, resolutely discourage all fissiparous tendencies and feel and behave as Indians. Subject to this paramount consideration, a linguistic re-distribution of provinces should give an impetus to education and trade.

(Gandhiji hoped that) they would not need a Boundary Commission to delimit the frontiers on the new basis. That is the foreign way which they have discarded. The best thing would be for themselves to determine the boundaries on the new basis by mutual agreement and consent and place the same before their Prime Minister for his final sanction. That would be true independence. To go to a third party in the shape of Boundary Commission for a settlement would be negation of independence. They must evolve interdependence and mutual help.[1]

I entirely endorse the suggestion...that what is proper to be done should not be delayed without just cause, and that what is improper should not be conceded under any circumstances whatsoever. There can be no compromise with evil and since linguistic redistribution is desirable from almost every point of view, all delay in carrying out the project should be avoided.

But the reluctance to enforce linguistic redistribution is perhaps justifiable in the present depressing atmosphere. The exclusive spirit is ever uppermost. Everyone thinks of himself and his family. No one thinks of the whole of India. The centripetal force is undoubtedly there, but it is not vocal and never boisterous: whereas the centrifugal is on the surface and in its very nature makes the loudest noise, demanding the attention of all. It manifests itself most in matters communal. This has given rise to fear in other fields. The history of the the quarrel between Orissa and Andhra, Orissa and Bihar and Orissa and Bengal is fresh in our minds. The whole of it has not died out even now.... Now, when we have freedom, we seem not to know what to do with it. It is almost mistaken for suicidal anarchy. Even zealous reformers would postpone controversial issues to a more hopeful time when, in the interests of the country, the virtue of give and take would be freely recognized and all sectional interest would be subordinate to the one interest of the good of India, which will include the good of all. Therefore, those who, like me, want constructive suggestions to come into play at this very moment, have to work to bring about a healthy atmosphere promoting concord in the place of discord, peace in the place of strife, progress in the place of retrogression and life in the place of death. That happy day will be most manifest when the communal strife has died out.[2]

It seems to me that if the provinces are all to make equal progress in all directions, the services should be largely confined to the inhabitants of the province concerned for the sake of India as a whole. No province and no tribe or clan can be kept backward if India is to stand erect before the world. It will never do so through its arms of which the world is sick. It must shine through its innate culture expressed in every citizen's life and in the socialism I have recently described....That means elimination of all force for the sake of popularizing one's doctrines or schemes. A thing which is truly popular rarely, if ever, requires force save that of public opinion to make itself acceptable to all. Therefore, the ugly scenes of violence by individuals witnessed in Bihar and Orissa and Assam should never have been. Popular governments are functioning to redress any irregularity or encroachment by persons from other provinces. The provincial governments are bound to give full protection to all the comers from outside their provinces. "Use what you consider as yours so as not to injure others", is a famous maxim of equity. It is also a grand moral code of conduct. How apposite today?

> *The bane of our life is our exclusive provincialism, whereas my province must be co-extensive with the Indian boundary so that ultimately it extends to the boundary of the earth. Else it perishes*

"Live in Rome as the Romans do", is a sound commonsense maxim so long as it does not apply to Roman vices. The process of progressive blending must be one of rejecting the bad and absorbing the good....The bane of our life is our exclusive provincialism, whereas my province must be co-extensive with the Indian boundary so that ultimately it exteds to the boundary of the earth. Else it perishes.[3]

In his opinion an Indian was a citizen of India enjoying equal rights in every part of India. Therefore, a Bengali had every right in Bihar as a Bihari. But he wished to emphasize that a Bengali must merge in the Bihari. He must never be guilty of exploiting Biharis or feeling a stranger or behaving as a stranger in Bihar.... All rights flowed from duties previously and duly performed. One thing he must stress that in both the Dominions of India, the use of force for the assertion of rights must be eschewed altogether if they were to make any progress. Thus neither the Bengalis nor the Biharis could assert themselves at the point of the sword, nor could the Boundary Commission Award similarly be changed. It was the first lesson to be learnt in a democratic independent India....Liberty never meant the licence to do anything at will. Independence meant voluntary restraint and discipline, voluntary acceptance of the rule of law in the making of which the whole of India had its hand through its elected representatives. The only force at the disposal of democracy was that of public opinion. Satyagraha, civil disobedience and fasts had nothing in common with the use of force, veiled or open. But even these had restricted use in democracy. They could not even think of them whilst the Governments were settling down and the communal distemper was still stalking from one province to another.[4]

Dravidistan?

Gandhiji then referred to the movement for Dravidistan— Southern India comprising the population speaking the four Dravidian languages—Telugu, Tamil, Malayalam and Kanarese. Why should this portion of India speaking the four languages be separated from the rest? Had not these languages, rich as they were, drawn largely upon Sanskrit for their richness? He had travelled through the four provinces and he found no difference between them and the rest of the provinces. It was a myth to consider that those living in the south of the Vindhya Range were non-Aryans and in the north Aryans—Whatever they might have been at one time, they were so intermixed that they were one people from Kashmir to Cape Comorin, notwithstanding that India was cut into two. It would be folly to make further divisions. If they did not stop at that division, there would be no end to independent sovereign States which would be useless for India and the world. Let it not be said of them that they were fit for one political system only under bondage and as freemen, savage-like they would split up into as many groups as they liked, each group going its own way. Or would they be held in bondage by one despotic State possessing an army large enough to bring them under subjection? He adjured them and especially the people of the South to give up the thraldom of the English language which was good as a language of international commerce and diplomacy. It could never become the language of the millions of India. The century or more of British rule had failed to make English spoken by more than a few millions in this ocean of Indian humanity. If they looked at the census they would discover that more millions spoke Hindustani, a mixture of Hindi and Urdu, written in the Nagari or Urdu scripts. Sanskritized Hindi or Persianized Urdu was confined to far fewer. He was asked whether they could learn it in their own provincial script. He had no objection. As a matter of fact the Hindustani Prachar Sabha allowed the boys of the South to learn Hindustani in their provincial script. They later on learnt the two scripts, so that they could become easily acquainted with the literature in the North. Patriotism demanded that much from them. There was a grave danger of their becoming pettily provincial-minded. If all became petty, where would be the India of their love? He freely admitted that if it was, as it was, wrong for the Southerners not to learn Hindustani, it was equally wrong for the Northerners not to learn one or more of the Southern languages which had very rich literature. He appealed to members from the South to resolve never to ask for English speech in an Indian audience. They would then soon pick up Hindustani. Let them remember that India free could cohere as one, only if it accepted moral government. Congress as a fighting machine against bondage was held together by its moral force. Should it be different when it had almost attained political freedom?[5]

66

THE PROBLEM OF MINORITIES

Hindus if they want unity among different races must have the courage to trust the minorities. Any other adjustment must leave a nasty taste in the mouth. Surely the millions do not want to become legislators and municipal councillors. And if we have understood the proper use of Satyagraha, we should know that it can be and should be used against an unjust administrator whether he be a Hindu, Musalman or of any other race or denomination, whereas a just administrator or representative is always and equally good whether he be a Hindu or a Musalman. We want to do away with the communal spirit. The majority must therefore make the beginning and thus inspire the minorities with confidence in their bona fides. Adjustment is possible only when the more powerful take the initiative without waiting for response from the weaker.

So far as employment in the Government departments is concerned, I think it will be fatal to good government, if we introduce there the communal spirit. For *Hindus if they want unity among different races must have the courage to trust the minorities* administration to be efficient, it must always be in the hands of the fittest. There should be certainly no favouritism. But if we want five engineers we must not take one from each community but we must take the fittest five even if they were all Musalmans or all Parsis. The lowest posts must, if need be, be filled by examination by an impartial board consisting of men belonging to different communities. But distribution of posts should never be according to the proportion of the numbers of each community. The educationally backward communities will have a right to receive favoured treatment in the matter of education at the hands of the national Government. This can be secured in an effective manner. But those who aspire to occupy responsible posts in the Government of the country, can only do so if they pass the required test.[1]

Independent India cannot afford to have communal representation and yet it must placate all communities, if the rule of independence is not based on coercion of minorities.[2]

> *Free India will be no Hindu raj, it will be Indian raj based not on the majority of any religious sect or community but on the representatives of the whole people without distinction of religion*

Hindustan belongs to all those who are born and bred here and who have no other country to look to. Therefore, it belongs to Parsis, Beni Israels, to Indian Christians, Muslims and other non-Hindus as much as to Hindus. Free India will be no Hindu *raj*, it will be Indian *raj* based not on the majority of any religious sect or community but on the representatives of the whole people without distinction of religion. I can conceive of a mixed majority putting the Hindus in a minority. They would be elected for their record of service and merits. Religion is a personal matter which should have no place in politics. It is the unnatural condition of foreign domination that we have unnatural divisions according to religion. Foreign domination going, we shall laugh at our folly in having clung to false ideals and slogans.[3]

I swear by my religion. I will die for it. But it is my personal affair. The State has nothing to do with it. The State would look after your secular welfare, health, communications, foreign relations, currency and so on, but not your or my religion. That is everybody's personal concern.[4]

Anglo-Indians and Foreigners

All foreigners will be welcome to stay here, only if they look upon themselves as one with the people. India cannot tolerate foreigners who wish to remain here with safeguards for their rights. This would mean that they want to live here as superior persons and such a position must lead to friction.[5]

> Religion is a personal matter which should have no place in politics

If this is true of the European, how much more true must it be for those Anglo-Indians and others who have adopted European manners and customs in order to be classed as Europeans demanding preferential treatment? All such people will find themselves ill at ease if they expect continuation of the favoured treatment hitherto enjoyed by them. They should rather feel thankful that they will be disburdened of preferential treatment to whcih they had no right by any known canon of reasoning and which was derogatory to their dignity.[6]

His political right is in no danger. It is his social status which is non-existent. He frets over his Indian parentage and he is disowned by the European race. He is therefore, between Scylla and Charybdis. I often meet him. He is washed out in the process of living above his means and trying to live the European life and look like Europeans. I have pleaded with him to make his choice and to throw in his lot with the vast multitude. If these men and women will have the courage and the foresight to appreciate this very simple and natural position, they will serve themselves, they will serve India and they will be spared the galling position in which they find themselves. The greatest problem before the dumb Anglo-Indian is that of determining his social status. He is saved, the moment he recognizes himself as an Indian and lives like one.[7]

67

AN INDIAN GOVERNOR

1. An Indian Governor should, in his own person, and in his surroundings, be a teetotaller. Without this, prohibition of the fiery liquid is wellnigh inconceivable.

2. He and his surroundings should represent hand-spinning as a visible token of identification with the dumb millions of India, a token of the necessity of 'bread labour' and organized non-violence as against organized violence on which the society of today seems to be based.

3. He must dwell in a cottage accessible to all, though easily shielded from gaze, if he is to do efficient work. The British Governor naturally represented the British might. For him and his was erected a fortified residence—a palace to be occupied by him and his numerous vassals who sustained his empire. The Indian prototype may keep somewhat pretentious buildings for receiving princes and ambassadors of the world. For these, being guests of the Governor, should constitute an education in what "Even Unto This Last"—equality of all—should mean in concrete terms. For him no expensive furniture, foreign or indigenous. Plain living and high thinking must be his motto, not to adorn his entrance but to be exemplified in daily life.

4. For him there can be no untouchability in any form whatever, no caste or creed or colour distinction. He must represent the best of all religions and all things Eastern or Western. Being a citizen of India, he must be a citizen of the world. Thus simply, one reads, did the Khalif Omar, with millions of treasure at his feet, live; thus lived Janaka of ancient

times; thus lived, as I saw him, the Master of Eton in his residence in the midst of, and surrounded by, the sons of the Lords and Nabobs of the British Isles. Will the Governors of India of the famished millions do less?

5. He will speak the language of the province of which he is the Governor and Hindustani, the lingua franca of India written in the Nagari or Urdu script. This is neither Sanskritized Hindi nor Persianized Urdu. Hindustani is emphatically the language which is spoken by the millions north of the Vindhya Range.

This does not pretend to be an exhaustive list of the virtues that an Indian Governor should represent. It is merely illustrative.[1]

68

THE PRESS

The sole aim of journalism should be service. The newspaper press is a great power, but just as an unchained torrent of water submerges whole country sides and devastates crops, even so an uncontrolled pen serves but to destroy. If the control is from without, it proves more poisonous than want of control. It can be profitable only when exercised from within. If this line of reasoning is correct, how many of the journals in the world would stand the test? But who would stop those that are useless? And who should be the judge? The useful and the useless must, like good and evil, go on together, and man must make his choice.[1]

The superficiality, the one-sidedness, the inaccuracy and often even dishonesty that have crept into modern journalism, continuously mislead honest men who want to see nothing but justice done.[2]

I have before me extracts from journals containing some gruesome things. There is communal incitement, gross misrepresentation and incitement to political violence bordering on murder. It is of course easy enough for the Government to launch out prosecutions or to pass repressive ordinances. These fail to serve the purpose intended except very temporarily, and in no case do

> *The newspaper press is a great power, but just as an unchained torrent of water submerges the whole country-side and devastates crops, even so an uncontrolled pen serves but to destroy*

they convert the writers, who often take to secret propaganda, when the open forum of the press is denied to them.

The real remedy is healthy public opinion that will refuse to patronize poisonous journals. We have our journalists' Association. Why should it not create a department whose business it would be to study the various journals and find objectionable articles and bring them to the notice of the respective editors? The function of the department

> The real remedy is healthy public opinion that will refuse to patronize poisonous journals

will be confined to the establishment of contact with the offending journals and public criticism of offending articles where the contact fails to bring about the desired reform. Freedom of the press is a precious privilege that no country can forego. But if there is, as there should be, no legislative check save that of the mildest character, an internal, check such as I have suggested should not be impossible and ought not to be resented.[3]

I hold that it is wrong to conduct newspapers by the aid of... immoral advertisements. I do believe that if advertisements should be taken at all there should be a rigid censorship instituted by newspaper proprietors and editors themselves and that only healthy advertisements should be taken....The evil of immoral advertisements is overtaking even what are known as the most respectable newspapers and magazines. That evil has to be combated by refining the conscience of the newspaper proprietors and editors. That refinement can come not through the influence of an amateur editor like myself but it will come when their own conscience is roused to recognition of the growing evil or when it is superimposed upon them by a Government representing the people and caring for the people's morals.[4]

My plea is for due regard for truth in advertising. It is a habit with people...to treat the printed word in a book or a newspaper as gospel truth. There is need, therefore, for extreme caution in drawing up advertisements. Untruths are most dangerous.[5]

69

PEACE BRIGADES

Some time ago I suggested the formation of a Peace Brigade whose members would risk their lives in dealing with riots, especially communal. The idea was that this Brigade should substitute the police and even the military. This reads ambitious. The achievement may prove impossible. Yet, if the Congress is to succeed in its non-violent struggle, it must develop the power to deal peacefully with such situations. Let us therefore see what qualifications a member of the contemplated Peace Brigade should possess.

- He or she must have a living faith in non-violence. This is impossible without a living faith in God. A non-violent man can do nothing save by the power and grace of God. Without it he won't have the courage to die without anger, without fear and without retaliation. Such courage comes from the belief that God sits in the hearts of all and that there should be no fear in the presence of God. The knowledge of the omnipresence of God also means respect for the lives of even those who may be called opponents or *goondas*. This contemplated intervention is a process of stilling the fury of man when the brute in him gets the mastery over him.
- This messenger of peace must have equal regard for all the principal religions of the earth. Thus if he is a Hindu, he will respect the other faiths current in India. He must therefore possess a knowledge of the general principles of the different faiths professed in the country.
- Generally speaking this work of peace can only be done

by local men in their own localities.

- The work can be done singly or in groups. Therefore no one need wait for companions. Nevertheless one would naturally seek companions in one's own locality and form a local Brigade.
- This messenger of peace will cultivate through personal service contacts with the people in his locality or chosen circle, so that when he appears to deal with ugly situations, he does not descend upon the members of a riotous assembly as an utter stranger liable to be looked upon as a suspect or an unwelcome visitor.
- Needless to say, a peace bringer must have a character beyond reproach and must be known for his strict impartiality.
- Generally there are previous warnings of coming storms. If these are known, the Peace Brigade will not wait till the conflagration breaks out but will try to handle the situation in anticipation.
- Whilst, if the movement spreads, it might be well if there are some whole-time workers, it is not absolutely necessary that there should be. The idea is to have as many good and true men and women as possible. These can be had only if volunteers are drawn from those who are engaged in various walks of life but have leisure enough to cultivate friendly relations with the people living in their circle and otherwise possess the qualifications required of a member of the Peace Brigade.

> *It is a mistake to blame the goondas. They never do mischief unless we create an atmosphere for them*

- There should be a distinctive dress worn by the members of the contemplated Brigade so that in course of time they will be recognized without the slightest difficulty.

These are but general suggestions. Each centre can work out its own constitution on the basis here suggested.[1]

Ordinarily, the efficient running of a large volunteer corps based on force implies the possibility of the use of force in the event of breach of discipline. In such bodies little or no stress is laid on a man's character. Physique is the chief factor. The contrary must obtain in non-violent bodies in which character or soul force must mean everything and physique must take second place. It is difficult to find many such persons. That is why non-violent corps must be small, if they are to be efficient. Such brigades may be scattered all over, there may be one each for a village or a mohalla. The members must know one another well. Each corps will select its own head. All the members will have the same status, but where everyone is doing the same work there must be one person under whose discipline all must come, or else the work will suffer. Where there are two or more brigades the leaders must consult among themselves and decide on a common line of action. In that way alone lies success. If non-violent volunteer corps are formed on the above lines, they can easily stop trouble. These corps will not require all the physical training given in *akhadas*, but a certain part of it will be necessary.

One thing, however, should be common to members of all such organizations and that is implicit faith in God. He is the only companion and doer. Without faith in Him these Peace Brigades will be lifeless. By whatever name one calls God, one must realize that one can only work through His strength. Such a man will never take another's life. He will allow himself if need be, to be killed and thereby live through his victory over death.

The mind of the man in whose life the realization of this law has become a living reality will not be bewildered in crisis. He will instinctively know the right way to act.

In spite, however, of what I have said above I would like to give some rules culled from my own experience:

- A volunteer may not carry any weapons.
- The members of a corps must be easily recognizable.
- Every volunteer must carry bandages, scissors, needle and thread, surgical knife etc., for rendering first aid.
- He should know how to carry and remove the wounded.
- He should know how to put out fires, how to enter a fire area without getting burnt, how to climb heights for rescue work and dscend safely with or without his charge.
- He should be well acquainted with all the residents of his locality. This is a service in itself.

- He should recite Ramanama ceaselessly in his heart and persuade others who believe to do likewise.

Man often repeats the name of God parrot-wise and expects fruit from so doing. The true seeker must have that living faith which will not only dispel the untruth of parrot-wise repetition from within him but also from the hearts of others.[2]

Goondas

It is a mistake to blame the *goondas*. They never do mischief unless we create an atmosphere for them. I was eye-witness to what happened in Bombay on the Prince's day in 1921. We sowed the seed and the *goondas* reaped the harvest. Our men were at their back....We must resolutely discountenance the practice of absolving the respectable class from blame.... The Bania and the Brahmana must learn to defend himself even violently, if not non-violently, or surrender his womenfolk and possessions to the *goondas*. They are a class apart, whether they are labelled Musalman or Hindu.[3]

The remedy against cowardice is not physical culture but the braving of dangers. So long as the parents of the middle class Hindus, themselves timid, continue to transmit their timidity by keeping their grown-up children in cotton-wool so long will there be their desire to shun danger and run no risks. They will have to dare to leave their children alone, let them run risks and even at times get killed in so doing. The puniest individual may have a stout heart. The most muscular

> *The remedy against cowardice is not physical culture but the braving of dangers*

Zulus cower before English lads. Each village has to find out its stout hearts.[4]

The would-be member of a Peace Brigade should come into close touch and cultivate acquaintance with the so-called *goonda* element in his vicinity. He should know all and be known to all and win the hearts of all by his living and selfless service. No section should be regarded as too contemptible or mean to mix with. *Goondas* do not drop from the sky, nor do they spring from the earth like evil spirits. They are the product of social disorganization, and society is, therefore, responsible for their existence. In other words, they should be looked upon as a symptom of corruption in our body politic. To remove the disease we must first discover the underlying cause. To find the remedy will then be a comparatively easy task.[5]

70
INDIAN NATIONAL CONGRESS

Indian National Congress which is the oldest national political organization and which has after many battles fought her non-violent way to freedom cannot be allowed to die. It can only die with the nation. A living organism ever grows or it dies. The Congress has won political freedom, but it has yet to win economic freedom, social or moral freedom. These freedoms are harder than the political, if only because they are constructive, less exciting and not spectacular. All-embracing constructive work evokes the energy of all the units of the millions.

The Congress has got the preliminary and necessary part of her freedom. The hardest has yet to come. In its difficult ascent to democracy, it has inevitably created rotten boroughs leading to corruption and creation of institutions, popular and democratic only in name. How to get out of the weedy and unwieldy growth?

> The Congress has won political freedom, but it has yet to win economic freedom. These freedoms are harder than the political, if only because they are constructive, less exciting and not spectacular

The Congress must do away with its special register of members, at no time exceeding one crore, not even then easily identifiable. It had an unknown register of millions who could never be wanted. Its register should now be co-extensive with all the men and women on the voters' rolls in the country. The Congress business should be to see that no faked name gets in and no legitimate name is left out. On its own register it will have a body of servants of the nation who would be workers doing the work allotted to them from time to time.

Unfortunately for the country they will be drawn chiefly for the time being from the city dwellers, most of whom would be required to work for and in the villages of India. The ranks must be filled in increasing numbers from villagers.

These servants will be expected to operate upon and serve the voters registered according to law in their own surroundings. Many persons and parties will woo them. The very best will win. Thus and in no other way can the Congress regain its fast ebbing unique position in the country. But yesterday the Congress was unwittingly the servant of the nation, it was Khuda-i-Khidmatgar—God's servant. Let it now proclaim to itself and the world that it is only God's servant— nothing more, nothing less. If it engages in the ungainly skirmish for power, it will find one fine morning that it is no more. Thank God, it is now no longer in sole possession of the field.

I have only opened to view the distant scene. If I have the time and health, I hope to discuss in these columns what the servants of the nation can do to raise themselves in the estimation of their masters, the whole of the adult population, male and female.[1]

His Last Will and Testament

[The following draft of a new constitution for the Indian National Congress was prepared by Gandhiji on 29th January, 1948, a day before his death. Being his last piece of writing it may be taken as his "Last Will and Testament".]

Though split into two, India having attained political Independence through means provided by the Indian National Congress, the Congress in its present shape and form, i.e., as a propaganda vehicle and parliamentary machine, has outlived its use. India has still to attain social, moral and economic independence in terms of its seven hundred thousand villages as distinguished from its cities and towns. The struggle for the ascendency of civil over military power is bound to take place in India's progress towards its democratic goal. It must be kept out of unhealthy competition with political parties and communal bodies. For these and other similar reasons, the A.I.C.C. resolves to disband the existing Congress organization and flower into a Lok Sevak Sangh under the following rules with power to alter them as occasion may demand.

Every Panchayat of five adult men or women being villagers or village-minded shall form a unit.

Two such contiguous Panchayats shall form a working party under a leader elected from among themselves.

When there are one hundred such Panchayats, the fifty first grade leaders shall elect from among themselves a second leader and so on, the first grade leaders meanwhile working under the second grade leader. Parallel groups of two hundred Panchayats shall continue to be formed till they cover the whole of India, each succeeding group of Panchayats electing second grade leader after the manner of the first. All second grade leaders shall serve jointly for the whole of India and severally for their respective areas. The second grade leaders may elect, whenever they deem necessary, from among themselves a chief who will, during pleasure, regulate and command all the groups.

(As the final formation of provinces or districts is still in a state of flux, no attempt has been made to divide this group of servants into Provincial or District Councils and jurisdiction over the whole of India has been vested in the group or groups that may have been formed at any given time. It should be noted that this body of servants derive their authority or power from service ungrudgingly or wisely done to their master, the whole of India.)

- Every worker shall be habitual wearer of Khadi made from self-spun yarn or certified by the A.I.S.A. and must be a teetotaller. If a Hindu, he must have abjured untouchability in any shape or form in his own person or in his family and must be a believer in the ideal of inter-communal unity, equal respect for all religions and equality of opportunity and status for all irrespective of race, creed or sex.

- He shall come in personal contact with every villager within his jurisdiction.
- He shall enrol and train workers from amongst the villagers and shall keep a register of all these.
- He shall keep a record of his work from day to day.
- He shall organize the villages so as to make them self-contained and self-supporting through their agriculture and handicrafts.
- He shall educate the village folk in sanitation and hygiene and take all measures for prevention of ill health and disease among them.
- He shall organize the education of the village folk from birth to death along the lines of Nai Talim, in accordance with the policy laid down by the Hindustani Talimi Sangh.
- He shall see that those whose names are missing on the statutory voters' roll are duly entered therein.
- He shall encourage those who have not yet acquired the legal qualification, to acquire it for getting the right of franchise.
- For the above purposes and others to be added from time to time, he shall train and fit himself in accordance with the rules laid down by the Sangh for the due performance of duty.

The Sangh shall affiliate the following autonomous bodies: A.I.S.A., A.I.V.I.A., Hindustani Talimi Sangh, Harijan Sevak Sangh, and Goseva Sangh.

Finance

The Sangh shall raise finances for the fulfilment of its mission from among the villagers and others, special stress being laid on the collection of poor man's pice.[2]

71

INDIA, PAKISTAN AND KASHMIR

It is our misfortune that the country was divided into two parts. The division was avowedly by reason of religious cleavage. Behind it might be economic and other causes. They could not have brought out the cleavage. The poison that fills the air arose also from the same communal cause. Irreligion masquerades as religion. It sounds nice to say that it would have been better if there had been no communal question. But how could the fact be undone?

It has been repeatedly asked whether in the event of a war between the two, the Muslims of the Union will fight against the Muslims of Pakistan and the Hindus of one against those of the other. However unlikely it may appear at present, there is nothing inherently impossible in the conception. There is any day more risk in distrusting the profession of loyalty than in trusting it and courageously facing the danger of trusting. The question can be more convincingly put in this way: Will the Hindus ever fight the Hindus and the Muslims their co-religionists for the sake of truth and justice? It can be answered by a counter question: Does not history provide such instances?

> *There is any day more risk in distrusting the profession of loyalty than in trusting it and courageously facing the danger of trusting*

In solving the puzzle the great stumbling block in the way is that truth is at a discount. Let us hope that in this holocaust some there are who will stand firm in their faith in the victory of truth.[1]

Partition was demanded on religio-communal grounds and it is therefore the duty of Pakistan, as its name implies, to remain clean in all its dealings. Both Hindus and Muslims had resorted to cruel acts and made grievous blunders, but that does not mean that this mad race should go on, culminating in war. A war would bring the Dominions under the sway of a third power and nothing can be worse.[2]

If there is a war (between India and Pakistan), the Hindus in Pakistan cannot be fifth columnists there. No one would tolerate that. If their loyalty lies not with Pakistan, they should leave it. Similarly, the Muslims whose loyalty is with Pakistan should not stay in the Indian Union. To secure justice for the Hindus and Sikhs is the function of the Government. The people can make the Government do their will.... The Muslims are reported to have said *hanske liya Pakistan, larke lenge Hindustan....* Some dream of converting the whole of India to Islam. That never will happen through war. Pakistan can never destroy Hinduism. The Hindus alone can destroy themselves and their faith. Similarly, if Islam is destroyed, it will be destroyed by the Muslims in Pakistan, not by the Hindus in Hindustan.[3]

The universal way to have proper adjustment is for both the States to make a frank and full confession of guilt on either side and come to terms, failing agreement to resort to arbitration in the usual manner. The other and rude way is that of war.... There is no escape from it if there is neither agreement nor arbitration. Meanwhile... Muslims, who had not of their own free will chosen to migrate to Pakistan, should be asked by their neighbours to return to their homes with a perfect feeling of safety. This cannot come about with the aid of the military. It can be done by return to sanity by the people concerned.[4]

To drive every Muslim from India and to drive every Hindu and Sikh from Pakistan would mean war and eternal ruin for the country. If such a suicidal policy is followed in both the States, it would spell the ruin of Islam and Hinduism in Pakistan and the Union. Good alone can beget good. Love breeds love. As for revenge, it behoves man to leave the evil-doer in God's hands.[5]

Death for me would be a glorious deliverance rather than that I should be a helpless witness of the destruction of India, Hinduism, Sikhism and Islam. That destruction is certain if Pakistan ensures no equality of status and security of life and property for all professing the various faiths of the world and if India copies her. Only then Islam dies in the two Indias, not in the world. But Hinduism and Sikhism have no world outside India.[6]

Surely, it is cowardly on the part of the majority to kill or banish the minority for fear that they will all be traitors. Scrupulous regard for the rights of minorities well becomes a majority. Disregard of them makes of a majority a laughing stock. Robust faith in oneself and brave trust of the opponent, so-called or real, is the best safeguard.[7]

Those who have felt driven from Pakistan should know that they are citizens of the whole of India, not merely of the Punjab or N.W.F.P. or Sind. The condition is that wherever they go, they should mix with the inhabitants there, as sugar with milk. They should be industrious and honest in their dealings. They must realize that they were born to serve India and add to her glory, never to degrade her. They should refuse to waste their time in gambling or drinking or quarrelling among themselves. It is human to err, but it is also given to human beings to learn from their mistakes and not to repeat them. If the refugees follow this advice, they would be an asset wherever they go and the people in every province would welcome them with open arms.[8]

If Pakistan would be a purely Muslim State and the Indian State a purely Hindu and Sikh state, with no rights for the minorities on either side, it would mean ruin for both the States.[9]

Had not the Quaid-i-Azam said that Pakistan was not a theocratic State and that it was purely a secular State? That the claim cannot always be justified in action is, unfortunately, too true. Is the Union to be a theocratic State and are the tenets of Hinduism to be imposed on non-Hindus?....The Indian Union will then cease to be a land of hope and promise, a land to which all Asiatic and African races look, indeed the whole world. The world expects not littleness and fanaticism from India whether as the Union or Pakistan. It expects greatness and goodness from which the whole world can derive a lesson and light in its prevailing darkness.[10]

Kashmir

Neither the Maharajasaheb in Kahsmir nor His Exalted Highness the Nizam had any authority to accede to either Dominion, without the known consent of their people. This was, so far as he knew, made clear in the case of Kashmir. If the Maharaja alone had wanted to accede, Gandhiji could not defend such accession. The accession was provisionally agreed to by the Union Government because both the Maharaja and Sheikh Abdulla, speaking for the people of Kashmir and Jammu, wanted it. Sheikh Abdulla came on the scene because he claimed to represent the people of Kashmir and Jammu, not merely the Muslims but the whole of the people.

He had heard whispers that Kashmir could be divided into two parts, Jammu going to the Hindus and Kashmir to the Muslims. He could not think of such divided loyalties and splitting up of Indian States into so many parts. He hoped, therefore, that wisdom would rule all India and an ugly situation would be avoided without delay if only for the sake of the lakhs of Indians who felt compelled to become helpless refugees.[11]

72
FOREIGN SETTLEMENTS IN INDIA

Goa

In Free India, Goa cannot be allowed to exist as a separate entity in opposition to the laws of the free State. Without a shot being fired, the people of Goa will be able to claim and receive the rights of citizenship of the free State.[1]

Surely there is not much to choose between French and Portuguese imperialism. The hands of imperialism are always dyed red. The sooner imperialistic powers shed their imperialism like Ashoka the Good, the better it will be for the groaning world.... It is ridiculous for the Head of the Government Information Bureau to write of Portugal as the motherland of the Indians of Goa. Their mother country is as much India as mine. Goa is outside British India but it is within geographical India as a whole. And there is very little, if anything, in common between the Portuguese and the Indians of Goa.[2]

French Settlements

It is not possible for the inhabitants of these small foreign settlements to remain under servility in the face of the millions of their countrymen who have become free from the British rule....I hope...the great French nation would never identify itself with the suppression of people, whether black or brown, in India or elsewhere.[3]

73

INDIA AND WORLD PEACE

The better mind of the world desires today not absolutely independent States warring one against another, but a federation of friendly interdependent States. The consummation of that event may be far off. I want to make no grand claim for our country. But I see nothing grand or impossible about our expressing our readiness for universal interdependence rather than independence.[1]

My ambition is much higher than independence. Through the deliverance of India, I seek to deliver the so-called weaker races of the earth from the crushing heels of Western exploitation. India's coming to her own will mean every nation doing likewise.[2]

This I know that if India comes to her own demonstrably through non-violent means, India will never want to carry a vast army, an equally grand navy and a grander air force. If her self-consciousness rises to the height necessary to give her a non-violent victory in her fight for freedom, the world values will have changed and most of the paraphernalia of war would be found to be useless. Such an India may be a mere dream, a childish folly. But such in my opinion is undoubtedly the implication of an India becoming free through non-violence. When that freedom comes...it will have come through a gentlemanly understanding with Great Britain. But then it will not be an imperialistic, haughty Britain manoeuvring for world supremacy, but a Britain humbly trying to serve the common end of humanity.[3]

India will no longer then be helplessly driven into Britain's wars of exploitation, but hers will be the voice of a powerful nation seeking to keep under restraint all the violent forces of the world.[4]

I venture to suggest, in all humility, that if India reaches her destiny through truth and non-violence, she will have made no small contribution to the world peace for which all the nations of the earth are thirsting and she would also have, in that case, made some slight return for the help that those nations have been freely giving to her.[5]

When India becomes self-supporting, self-reliant, and proof against temptations and exploitation, she will cease to be the object of greedy attraction for any power in the West or the East and will then feel secure without having to carry the burden of expensive armaments. Her internal economy will b the strongest bulwark against aggression.[6]

If I want freedom for my country, believe me, if I can possibly help it, I do not want that freedom in order that I, belonging to a nation which counts one-fifth of the human race, may exploit any other race upon earth, or any single individual. If I want that freedom for my country, I would not be deserving of that freedom if I did not cherish and treasure the equal right of every other race, weak or strong, to the same freedom.[7]

I feel in the inmost recesses of my heart... that the world is sick unto death of blood-spilling. The world is seeking a way out, and I flatter myself with the belief that perhaps it will be the privilege of the ancient land of India to show that way out to the hungering world.[8]

> *If I want freedom for my country, believe me, if I can possibly help it, I do not want that freedom in order that I, belonging to a nation which counts one-fifth of the human race, may exploit any other race upon earth, or any single individual. If I want that freedom for my country, I would not be deserving of that freedom if I did not cherish and treasure the equal right of every other race, weak or strong, to the same freedom*

What policy the National Government will adopt I cannot

say. I may not even survive it much as I would love to. If I do, I would advise the adoption of non-violence to the utmost extent possible and that will be India's great contribution to the peace of the world and the establishment of a new world order. I expect that with the existence of so many martial races in India, all of whom will have a voice in the government of the day, the national policy will incline towards militarism of a modified character. I shall certainly hope that all the efforts to... show the efficacy of non-violence as a political force will not have gone in vain and a strong party representing true non-violence will exist in the country.[9]

74

THE MESSAGE OF THE EAST

If India fails, Asia dies. It has been aptly called the nursery of many blended cultures and civilizations. Let India be and remain the hope of all the exploited races of the earth, whether in Asia, Africa or in any part of the world.[1]

(In the course of his address to the concluding session of the Inter-Asian Relations Conference held at Delhi on 2-4-1947 Mahatma Gandhi, stating that the wisdom had come to the West from the East, remarked as follows:)

The first of these wise men was Zoroaster. He belonged to the East. He was followed by Buddha who belonged to the East—India. Who followed Buddha? Jesus, who came from the East. Before Jesus was Moses who belonged to Palestine though he was born in Egypt. After Jesus came Mohammad. I omit any reference to Krishna and Rama and other lights. I do not call them lesser lights, but they are less known to the literary world. All the same I do not know a single person in the world to match these men of Asia. And then what happened? Christianity became disfigured when it went to the West. I am sorry to say that. I would not talk any further.... What I want you to understand is the message of Asia. It is not to be learnt through the Western spectacles or by imitating the atom bomb. If you want to give a message to the West, it must be the message of love and the message of truth.... In this age of democracy, in this age of awakening of the poorest of the poor, you can redeliver this message with the greatest emphasis. You will complete the conquest of the West not through vengeance because you have been exploited, but with real understanding.

The Message of the East **281**

I am sanguine if all of you put your hearts together...not merely heads...to understand the secret of the message these wise men of the East have left to us, and if we really become worthy of that great message, the conquest of the West will be completed. This conquest will be loved by the West itself. The West today is pining for wisdom. It is despairing of a multiplication of the atom bombs, because atom bombs mean utter destruction not merely of the West but of the whole world, as if the prophecy of the Bible is going to be fulfilled and there is to be a perfect deluge. It is up to you to tell the world of its wickedness and sin.... That is the heritage your teachers and my teachers have taught Asia.[2]

75

OBITER DICTA

Adivasis

The Adivasis are the original inhabitants whose material position is perhaps no better than that of Harijans and who have long been victims of neglect on the part of the so-called high classes. The Adivasis should have found a special place in the constructive programme. Non-mention was an oversight. They provide a vast field of service for Congressmen. The Christian missionary has been more or less in sole occupation of the field. Great as his labour has been, it has not prospered as it might have, because of his ultimate aim being the Adivasis' conversion to his fold and their becoming de-Indianised. Anyway no one who hopes to construct Swaraj on the foundation of non-violence can afford to neglect even the least of India's sons. Adivasis are too numerous to be counted among the least.[1]

> *The highest form of freedom carries with it the greatest measure of discipline and humility*

Discipline

The highest form of freedom carries with it the greatest measure of discipline and humility. Freedom that comes from discipline and humility cannot be denied, unbridled licence is a sign of vulgarity alike to self and one's neighbours.[2]

There will have to be rigid and iron discipline before we achieve anything great and enduring and that discipline will not come by mere academic argument and appeal to reason and logic. Discipline is learnt in the school of adversity. And when zealous young men will train themselves to responsible work without any shield, they will learn what responsibility and discipline are.[3]

Doctors

The fact remains that the doctors induce us to indulge, and the result is that we have become deprived of self-control and have become effeminate.[4]

My quarrel with the medical profession in general is that it ignores the soul altogether and strains at nothing in seeking merely to repair such a fragile instrument as the body. Thus ignoring the soul, the profession puts men at its mercy and contributes to the diminution of human dignity and self-control.[5]

Dress

The national dress...is the most natural and the most becoming for an Indian. I believe that our copying of the European dress is a sign of our degradation, humiliation and our weakness, and that we are committing a national sin in discarding a dress which is best suited to the Indian climate and which, for its simplicity, art and cheapness, is not to be beaten on the face of the earth and which answers hygienic requirements.[6]

> There will have to be rigid and iron discipline before we achieve anything great and enduring. Discipline is learnt in the school of adversity

My narrow nationalism rebels against the hat, my secret internationalism regards the sola hat as one of the few boons from Europe. But for the tremendous national prejudice against the hat, I would undertake to become president of a league for popularizing sola hats.

Educated India has erred in taking to (in this climate) unnecessary, unhygienic, inelegant trousers and betraying general hesitation to take up the sola hat. But I know that national likes and dislikes are not governed by reason.[7]

Flag

A flag is a necessity for all nations. Millions have died for it. It is no doubt a kind of idolatry which it would be a sin to destroy. For a flag represents an ideal. The unfurling of the Union Jack evokes in the English breast sentiments whose strength it is difficult to measure. The Stars and Stripes mean a world to the Americans. The Stars and the Crescent will call forth the best bravery in Islam. It will be necessary for us Indians—Hindus, Mohamedans, Christians, Jews, Parsis and all others to whom India is their home—to recognize a common flag to live and to die for.[8]

Lawyers

The duty of a lawyer is always to place before the judges, and to help them to arrive at, the truth, never to prove the guilty as innocent.[9]

Leadership

Those who claim to lead the masses must resolutely refuse to be led by them, if we want to avoid mob law and desire ordered progress for the country. I believe that mere protestation of one's opinion and surrender to the mass opinion is not only not enough but in matters of vital importance, leaders must *act*

> *Those who claim to lead the masses must resolutely refuse to be led by them*

contrary to the mass opinion, if it does not commend itself to their reason.[10]

A leader is only first among equals. Some one must be put first, but he is and should be no stronger than the weakest link in the chain. Having made our selection we must follow him or the chain is broken and all is loose.[11]

Music

Music, truly speaking, is an ancient and sacred art. The hymns of Samaveda are a mine of music, and no *ayat* of the Koran can be recited unmusically. David's Psalms transport you to raptures and remind you of the hymns from Samaveda. Let us revive this art and patronize the school of music.

We see Hindu and Musalman musicians sitting cheek by

> A leader is only first among equals

jowl and partaking in musical concerts. When shall we see the same fraternal union in other affairs of our life? We shall then have the name of Rama and Rahman simultaneously on our lips.[12]

Parties

If we have no charity, and no tolerance, we shall never settle our differences amicably and must therefore always submit to the arbitrament of a third party, *i.e.* to foreign domination.[13]

No school of thought can claim a monopoly of right judgment. We are all liable to err and are often obliged to revise our judgments. In a vast country like this, there must be room for all schools of honest thought. And the least, therefore, that we owe to ourselves as to others is to try to understand the opponent's viewpoint and, if we cannot accept it, respect it as fully as we would expect him to respect ours. It is one of the indispensable tests of a healthy public life and, therefore, fitness for Swaraj.[14]

Politics

To see the universal and all-pervading spirit of Truth face to face one must be able to love the meanest of creation as oneself. And a man who aspires after that cannot afford to keep out of any field of life. That is why my devotion to Truth has drawn me into the field of politics; and I can say without the slightest hesitation and yet in all humility, that those who say that religion has nothing to do with politics do not know what religion means.[15]

Priests

It is a painful fact, but it is a historical truth, that priests who should have been the real custodians of religion have been instrumental in destroying the religion of which they have been custodians.[16]

Public Funds

If we do not account for every single pie we receive and do not make judicious use of the funds, we shall deserve to be blotted out of public life.[17]

Public money belongs to the poor public of India than whom there is none poorer on earth. We have to be more wakeful, more cautious, more careful; and let us be ready to account for every pie that we receive from the public.[18]

Public Institutions

...After considerable experience with the many public institutions which I have managed, it has become my firm conviction that it is not good to run public institutions on permanent funds. A permanent fund carries in itself the seed of the moral fall of the institution. ... Institutions maintained on permanent funds are often found to ignore public opinion, and are frequently responsible for acts contrary to it. In our country we experience this at every step. Some of the so-called religious trusts have ceased to render any accounts. The trustees have become the owners and are responsible to none. I have no doubt that the ideal is for public institutions to live, like nature, from day to day. The institution that fails to win public support has no rights to exist as such.[19]

It is my settled conviction that no deserving institution ever dies for want of support. Institutions that have died have done so either because there was nothing in them to commend them to the public or because those in control lost faith, or which is perhaps the same thing, lost stamina.[20]

It is not our financial position, but our moral position that is precarious. No movement or activity that has the sure foundation of the purity of character of its

> *No school of thought can claim a monopoly of right judgment. In a vast country like this, there must be room for all schools of honest thought*

workers, is ever in danger to come to an end for want of funds.... We have to tap humbler resources. Our middle classes and even poor classes support so many beggars, so many temples, why will they not support a few good workers? We must beg from door to door, beg grain, copper coins, do as they do in Bihar and Maharashtra.... But remember that everything will depend on the singleness of your purpose, your devotion to the task and the purity of your character. People won't give for such work unless they are sure of our selflessness.[21]

Public Opinion

Public opinion alone can keep a society pure and healthy.[22] Legislation in advance of public opinion if often worse than useless.[23]

Healthy public opinion has an influence of which we have not realized the full significance. Public opinion becomes intolerable when it becomes violent and aggressive.[24]

Public Workers

There is in modern public life a tendency to ignore altogether the character of a public worker so long as he works efficiently as a unit in an administrative machinery. It is said that everybody's character is his own private concern. Though I have known this view to have been often taken I have never been able to appreciate, much less to adopt it. I have known the serious consequences overtaking organizations that have counted private character as a matter of no consequence.[25]

> *If we do not account for every single pie we receive and do not make judicious use of the funds, we shall deserve to be blotted out of public life. Public money belongs to the poor public of India*

Punctuality

It would be a distinct gain to the national cause if the leaders and workers strictly keep their hours.... No man is expected to do more than he really can. If at the end of the day there is surplus work left or he cannot get through it without missing a meal or encroaching upon the hours of sleep or recreation, there is mismanagement somewhere. I have no doubt that if we cultivate the habit of punctuality and acting according to programme, the index of national efficiency will go up, our advance towards our goal will be rapid, and the workers will be healthier and longer lived.[26]

Races

It is wholly unnecessary for the sake of the love of horse flesh to have horse races and all their attendant excitement. They pander to the vices of humanity and mean a waste of good cultivable soil and good money. Who has not witnessed as I have, the ruin of fine men caused by the gamble on the race-courses? It is time to leave alone the vices of the West and to strive to adopt the best that it has to give.[27]

> *I have known the serious consequences overtaking organizations that have counted private character as a matter of no consequence*

Refugees

They should learn the art of humility which demands a rigorous self-searching rather than a search of others and consequent criticism, often harsh, oftener undeserved and sometimes only deserved. Searching of self ennobles, searching of others debases. The sufferers should learn the art and virtue of corporate life, in which the circumference of co-operation is ever widening till at last it encircles the whole human race. If they did this, no sufferer will live in isolation. All of them, no matter to which province they belong, will hold together and would be considering not the welfare of self but that of all. This does not mean that all of them will live or insist on living at one place, an impossible feat at any time, more so today, when lakhs and lakhs of people have been torn from their homes, not knowing where to lay their heads upon. But this humble spirit of co-operation does mean that wherever they are placed, they will feel one with all the sufferers, no matter from what strata of society they are drawn or to which province they belong. Insistence on being accommodated in a particular place of one's choice there will be none. The sufferers will never grumble.

Moreover, every sufferer who is not a cripple will do his or her full share of work against bread, clothing and shelter in a becoming manner. Thus they will realize the dignity of labour and feel dependent upon no one. All will be equal to one another irrespective of sex. Some labour will be shared by all, *e.g.* sanitary work including latrine-cleaning and scavenging. No labour will be considered too low or too high. In this society there will be no room for drones, idlers or loafers.[28]

Rivers

We have more Ganges and Jamunas than the two. They remind us of the sacrifices we must make for the sake of the land we are living in. They

> *It would be a distinct gain to the national cause if the leaders and workers strictly keep their hours....*

remind us of the process of purification that we must continuously go through as the rivers themselves are going through from moment to moment. In the modern rush, the chief use we have for our rivers is to empty our gutters in them and navigate our cargo vessels, and in the process make them dirtier still. We have no time... to stroll down to these rivers, and in silent meditation listen to the message they murmur to us.[29]

END NOTES

1. INDIA OF MY DREAMS

1. *Young India*, 21-2-1929; 2. *Young India*, 5-2-1925; 3. *Young India*, 6-8-1925; 4. *Speeches and Writings of Mahatma Gandhi*, p. 405; 5. *Young India*, 11-8-1920; 6. *Yound India*, 6-4-1921; 7. *Young India*, 17-9-1925; 8. *Young India*, 11-8-1927; 9. *Young India*, 7-10-1926; 10. *Young India*, 30-4-1931; 11. *Young India*, 10-9-1931

2. THE MEANING OF SWARAJ

1. *Young India*, 19-3-1931; 2. *Young India*, 29-1-1925; 3. *Young India*, 1-12-1927; 4. *Young India*, 6-8-1925; 5. *Young India*, 26-6-1924; 6. *Young India*, 28-7-1921; 7. *Young India*, 26-3-1931; 8. *Young India*, 16-4-1931; 9. *Young India*, 23-1-1930; 10. *Young India*, 5-3-1931; 11. *Young India*, 5-3-1931; 12. *Young India*, 26-3-1931; 13. *Young India*, 26-3-1931; 14. *Young India*, 18-6-1931; 15. *Harijan*, 2-1-1937; 16. *Harijan*, 27-5-1939; 17. *Harijan*, 25-3-1939; 18. *Harijan*, 25-3-1939

3. IN DEFENCE OF NATIONALISM

1. *Young India*, 16-3-1921; 2. *Gandhiji in Indian Villages*, p. 170; 3. *Young India*, 12-3-1925; 4. *Young India*, 1-6-1921; 5. *Young India*, 18-6-1925; 6. *Young India*, 18-6-1925; 7. *Young India*, 4-4-1929; 8. *Young India*, 16-4-1931; 9. *Harijan*, 17-11-1933

4. DEMOCRACY IN INDIA

1. *Young India*, 3-6-1926; 2. *Young India*, 7-5-1931; 3. *Young India*, 30-7-1931; 4. *Young India*, 17-4-1924; 5. *Harijan*, 11-1-1936; 6. *Harijan*, 12-11-1938; 7. *Harijan*, 22-4-1939; 8. *Harijan*, 27-5-1939; 9. *Harijan*, 23-9-1939; 10. *Harijan*, 18-5-1940; 11. *Harijan*, 27-5-1939; 12. *Harijan*, 27-5-1939; 13. *Delhi Diary*, p. 18; 14. *Delhi Diary*, p. 86; 15. *Harijan*, 18-1-1948; 16. *Young India*, 28-7-1920; 17. *Young India*, 8-9-1920; 18. *Young India*, 22-9-1920; 19. *Young India*, 23-2-1921; 20. *Young India*, 2-2-1921; 21. *Young India*, 26-1-1922; 22. *Young India*, 2-3-1932; 23. *Harijan*, 1-2-1942

5. INDIA AND SOCIALISM

1. *Harijan*, 20-2-1937; 2. *Harijan*, 2-1-1937; 3. *Harijan*, 20-4-1940; 4. *Harijan*, 20-4-1940; 5. *Harijan*, 13-7-1947

6. INDIA AND COMMUNISM

1. *Young India*, 15-11-1928; 2. *Amrita Bazar Patrika*, 2-8-1934; 3. *Harijan*, 13-3-1937; 4. *Harijan*, 13-3-1937; 5. *Harijan*, 31-3-1946; 6. *Harijan*, 6-10-1946

7. THE CURSE OF INDUSTRIALISM

1. *Young India*, 25-7-1929; 2. *Harijan*, 2-11-1934; 3. *Young India*, 5-11-1925; 4. *Young India*, 17-6-1926; 5. *Harijan*, 14-9-1935; 6. *Harijan*, 29-8-1936; 7. *Harijan*, 1-9-1946

8. CLASS WAR

1. *Young India*, 26-11-1931; 2. *Amrita Bazar Patrika*, 2-8-1934; 3. *Amrita Bazar Patrika*, 3-8-1934; 4. *Harijan*, 5-12-1936; 5. *Harijan*, 19-10-1935

9. STRIKES

1. *Speeches and Writings of Mahatma Gandhi*, p. 1049; 2. *Young India*, 16-2-1921; 3. *Harijan*, 11-8-1946; 4. *Harijan*, 11-8-1946

10. CHOICE BEFORE LABOUR

1. *Young India*, 11-2-1920; 2. *Speeches and Writings of Mahatma Gandhi*, p. 1046; 3. *Young India*, 14-1-1932

11. RIGHTS OR DUTIES?

1. *Harijan*, 6-7-1947

12. THE PROBLEM OF UNEMPLOYMENT

1. *Young India*, 6-10-1921; 2. *Young India*, 3-11-1921; 3. *Harijan*, 11-5-1935; 4. *Harijan*, 19-12-1936; 5. *Harijan*, 3-7-1937

13. DARIDRANARAYAN

1. *Young India*, 4-4-1929; 2. *Young India*, 5-5-1927; 3. *Young India*, 15-9-1927; 4. *Young India*, 3-4-1931; 5. *Young India*, 15-10-1931; 6. *Harijan*, 11-3-1939; 7. *From Yeravda Mandir*, Chap. VI; 8. *From Yeravda Mandir*, Chap. VI; 9. *Young India*, 24-6-1926; 10. *Speeches and Writings of Mahatma Gandhi*, p. 353

14. THE GOSPEL OF BREAD LABOUR

1. *Young India*, 11-4-1929; 2. *From Yeravda Mandir*, Chap. IX; 3. *Young India*, 8-1-1925; 4. *Young India*, 26-3-1931; 5. *Harijan*, 29-6-1935; 6. *Harijan*,

1-6-1935; 7. *Harijan*, 29-6-1935; 8. *Young India*, 13-8-1925; 9. *Harijan*, 11-5-1935

15. SARVODAYA

1. *Hind Swaraj*, Chap. XIII; 2. *From Yeravda Mandir*, Chap. XII; 3. *Young India*, 25-11-1926; 4. *Young India*, 9-12-1926; 5. *Young India*, 20-9-1928; 6. *Young India*, 20-12-1928; 7. *From Yeravda Mandir*, Chap. I; 8. *Young India*, 4-9-1930; 9. *Young India*, 17-7-1924; 10. *Young India*, 17-7-1924; 11. *Harijan*, 13-7-1947

16. THEORY OF TRUSTEESHIP

1. *Harijan*, 3-6-1939; 2. *The Modern Review*, 1935, p. 412; 3. *Harijan*, 3-12-1938; 4. *Harijan*, 7-1-1939; 5. *Harijan*, 16-12-1939; 6. *Harijan*, 22-2-1942

17. NON-VIOLENT ECONOMY

1. *Speeches and Writings of Mahatma Gandhi*, p. 384; 2. *Young India*, 13-10-1921; 3. *Young India*, 15-11-1928; 4. *Harijan*, 9-10-1937; 5. *Harijan*, 15-1-1938; 6. *Constructive Programme*, pp. 20-21; 7. *Harijan*, 30-12-1939; 8. *Harijan*, 1-6-1947

18. THE WAY TO EQUAL DISTRIBUTION

1. *Harijan*, 25-8-1940; 2. *Young India*, 23-3-1921

19. INDIA'S RECORD OF NON-VIOLENCE

1. *Young India*, 11-8-1920; 2. *Young India*, 22-6-1921; 3. *Young India*, 26-1-1922; 4. *Young India*, 4-7-1929

20. THE SARVODAYA STATE

1. *Young India*, 2-1-1930; 2. *Young India*, 2-7-1931; 3. *The Modern Review*, 1935, p. 412; 4. *Harijan*, 15-9-1946; 5. *Harijan*, 1-9-1940

21. SATYAGRAHA AND DURAGRAHA

1. *Young India*, 15-12-1921; 2. *Young India*, 24-3-1920; 3. *Young India*, 3-11-1921; 4. *Young India*, 5-1-1922; 5. *Young India*, 20-10-1927; 6. *Harijan*, 15-4-1933; 7. *Speeches and Writings of Mahatma Gandhi*, p. 474; 8. *Speeches and Writings of Mahatma Gandhi*, p. 476; 9. *Young India*, 28-4-1920; 10. *Young India*, 2-2-1921; 11. *Young India*, 2-4-1931; 12. *Harijan*, 18-3-1939; 13. *Harijan*, 18-3-1939; 14. *Harijan*, 13-10-1940; 15. *Harijan*, 21-4-1946; 16. *Harijan*, 6-5-1933

22. The Tillers of the Soil

1.*Young India*, 5-12-1929; 2. *The Bombay Chronicle*, 28-10-1944; 3. *The Bombay Chronicle*, 12-1-1945; 4. *The Bombay Chronicle*, 12-1-1945

23. Back to the Village

1. *Harijan*, 4-4-1936; 2. *Harijan*, 4-4-1936; 3. *Speeches and Writings of Mahatma Gandhi*, p. 323; 4. *Young India*, 30-3-1931; 5. *Harijan*, 1-3-1935; 6. *Young India*, 11-9-1924; 7. *Harijan*, 1-3-1935; 8. *Harijan*, 1-3-1935; 9. *Harijan*, 7-3-1936; 10. *Harijan*, 11-4-1936; 11. *Harijan*, 16-3-1936; 12. *Harijan*, 27-2-1937; 13. *Harijan*, 19-10-1937; 14. *Harijan*, 16-5-1936; 15. *Harijan*, 28-1-1939; 16. *Harijan*, 28-1-1939

24. Every Village a Republic

1. *Harijan*, 26-7-1942; 2. *Harijan*, 26-7-1942; 3. *Harijan*, 10-11-1946; 4. *Harijan*, 4-8-1946; 5. *Mahatma*, Vol. IV, p. 144

25. Panchayat Raj

1. *Harijan*, 28-7-1946; 2. *Harijan*, 1-7-1947

26. Village Industries

1. *Harijan*, 16-11-1934; 2. *Harijan*, 23-11-1934; 3. *Harijan*, 29-8-1936; 4. *Harijan*, 20-1-1940; 5. *Costructive Programme*, p. 12; 6. *Constructive Programme*, p. 15; 7. *Harijan*, 28-12-1947; 8. *Harijan*, 7-9-1934; 9. *Harijan*, 25-1-1935

27. What the Government can do

1. *Harijan*, 28-4-1946

28. Village Exhibitions

1. *Gram Udyog Patrika*, July 1946

29. The Music of the Spinning Wheel

1. *Young India*, 20-5-1926; 2. *Young India*, 21-7-1920; 3. *Young India*, 20-10-1921; 4. *Young India*, 8-12-1921; 5. *Young India*, 21-8-1924; 6. *Young India*, 11-11-1926; 7. *Harijan*, 13-4-1940

30. The Mill Industry

1. *Young India*, 16-2-1921; 2. *Harijan*, 23-10-1937; 3. *Harijan*, 25-8-1946; 4. *Harijan*, 31-3-1946; 5. *Harijan*, 25-8-1946; 6. *Young India*, 24-7-1924; 7. *Young India*, 17-9-1925

31. THE GOSPEL OF SWADESHI

1. *Speeches and Writings of Mahatma Gandhi*, pp. 336-44; 2. *From Yeravda Mandir*, Chap. XVI

32. COW PROTECTION

1. *Young India*, 6-10-1921; 2. *Harijan*, 15-9-1940; 3. *Young India*, 6-10-1921; 4. *Young India*, 7-7-1927; 5. *Harijan*, 31-8-1947; 6. *Harijan*, 8-2-1942

33. CO-OPERATIVE CATTLE-FARMING

1. *Harijan*, 15-2-1942; 2. *Delhi Diary*, pp. 270-71

34. VILLAGE SANITATION

1. *Constructive Programme*, p. 15; 2. *Harijan*, 8-2-1935; 3. *Harijan*, 9-1-1937

35. VILLAGE HEALTH

1. *Harijan*, 26-5-1946; 2. *Harijan*, 2-6-1946; 3. *Harijan*, 1-9-1946; 4. *Harijan*, 15-9-1946; 5. *Harijan*, 15-6-1947; 6. *Harijan*, 11-8-1946

36. VILLAGE DIET

1. *Harijan*, 26-10-1944; 2. *Harijan*, 1-2-1935; 3. *Harijan*, 1-2-1935; 4. *Harijan*, 15-2-1935

37. THE VILLAGE WORKER

1. *Young India*, 17-4-1924; 2. *Harijan*, 23-11-1935; 3. *Harijan*, 20-2-1937; 4. *Harijan*, 18-8-1940; 5. *Harijan*, 25-3-1939

38. ALL-ROUND VILLAGE SERVICE

1. *Harijan*, 17-3-1946; 2. *Harijan*, 2-3-1947

39. A CALL TO YOUTH

1. *Young India*, 9-7-1925; 2. *Young India*, 9-7-1925; 3. *Young India*, 22-12-1927; 4. *Harijan*, 6-5-1933; 5. *Harijan*, 21-9-1935; 6. *Young India*, 21-2-1929; 7. *Young India*, 29-12-1927; 8. *With Gandhiji in Ceylon*, p. 109; 9. *Young India*, 7-11-1929; 10. *Harijan*, 1-3-1935; 11. *Harijan*, 19-12-1936

40. THE NATION'S HEALTH, HYGIENE AND DIET

1. *Constructive Programme*, pp. 18-9; 2. *Harijan*, 25-1-1942; 3. *Young India*, 18-7-1929; 4. *Young India*, 15-8-1929; 5. *Autobiography*, p. 270; 6. *Young*

India, 8-8-1929; 7. *Harijan*, 5-8-1933; 8. *India's Case for Swaraj*, p. 402; 9. *Young India*, 7-10-1926; 10. *Young India*, 17-12-1925; 11. *Harijan*, 5-1-1934; 12. *Delhi Diary*, p. 108; 13. *Delhi Diary*, p. 111

41. DRINK AND DRUGS

1. *India's Case for Swaraj*, p. 403; 2. *Young India*, 8-6-1921; 3. *Young India*, 12-1-1928; 4. *Harijan*, 3-6-1939; 5. *Harijan*, 9-3-1934; 6. *Young India*, 3-3-1927; 7. *Young India*, 15-9-1927; 8. *Young India*, 4-4-1929; 9. *Young India*, 25-6-1931; 10. *Key to Health*, pp. 32-4; 11. *Young India*, 12-1-1921; 12. *Young India*, 4-2-1926; 13. *Key to Health*, pp. 39-42

42. URBAN SANITATION

1. *Young India*, 26-12-1924; 2. *Young India*, 19-11-1925; 3. *Young India*, 26-11-1925; 4. *Speeches and Writings of Mahatma Gandhi*, pp. 375-76; 5. *Young India*, 28-3-1929; 6. *Harijan*, 18-2-1939; 7. *Satyagraha in South Africa*, p. 240

43. EVIL WROUGHT BY THE FOREIGN MEDIUM

1. *Hind Swaraj*, 1908; 2. *Young India*, 27-4-1921; 3. *Young India*, 1-6-1921; 4. *Young India*, 1-9-1921; 5. *Young India*, 5-7-1928

44. MY OWN EXPERIENCE

1. *Harijan*, 9-7-1938

45. INDIA'S CULTURAL HERITAGE

1. *Young India*, 1-9-1921; 2. *Young India*, 17-11-1920; 3. *Harijan*, 9-5-1936

46. THE NEW EDUCATION

1. *Young India*, 1-9-1921; 2. *Harijan*, 8-3-1935; 3. *Harijan*, 8-5-1937; 4. *Harijan*, 8-5-1937; 5. *Harijan*, 8-5-1937; 6. *Harijan*, 31-7-1937; 7. *Harijan*, 28-8-1937; 8. *Harijan*, 11-9-1937; 9. *Harijan*, 9-10-1937; 10. *Harijan*, 9-10-1937

47. BASIC EDUCATION

1. *Constructive Programme*, pp. 15-16; 2. *Harijan*, 6-4-1940; 3. *Harijan*, 2-11-1947; 4. *Young India*, 1-9-1921

48. HIGHER EDUCATION

1. *Harijan*, 31-7-1937; 2. *Harijan*, 2-10-1937; 3. *Harijan*, 2-11-1947; 4. *Constructive Programme*, pp. 16-17; 5. *Harijan*, 22-6-1940; 6. *Young India*,

25-8-1927; 7. *Harijan*, 23-3-1947; 8. *Young India*, 6-12-1928; 9. *Harijan*, 1-12-1933; 10. *Young India*, 6-8-1925; 11. *Young India*, 2-8-1928

50. NATIONAL LANGUAGE AND SCRIPT

1. *Young India*, 27-8-1925; 2. *Constructive Programme*, p. 20

51. PROVINCIAL LANGUAGES

1. *Constructive Programme*, pp. 19-20; 2. *Harijan*, 25-8-1946; 3. *Harijan*, 21-9-1947; 4. *Young India*, 13-5-1926

52. HINDI IN THE SOUTH

1. *Young India*, 16-6-1920; 2. *Young India*, 2-2-1921; 3. *Young India*, 2-2-1921; 4. *Young India*, 18-6-1931; 5. *Harijan*, 10-9-1938

53. A CODE FOR STUDENTS

1. *The Bombay Chronicle*, 9-1-1946; 2. *Young India*, 9-6-1927; 3. *Young India*, 26-12-1929; 4. *Young India*, 5-11-1931; 5. *Harijan*, 2-10-1937; 6. *To The Students*, p. 283

54. REGENERATION OF INDIAN WOMEN

1. *Constructive Programme*, pp. 17-18; 2. *Speeches and Writings of Mahatma Gandhi*, p. 424; 3. *Speeches and Writings of Mahatma Gandhi*, p. 425; 4. *Young India*, 17-10-1929; 5. *Harijan*, 2-12-1939; 6. *Young India*, 27-9-1928; 7. *Harijan*, 22-3-1942; 8. *Young India*, 3-2-1927; 9. *Young India*, 25-11-1926; 10. *Harijan*, 23-5-1936; 11. *Young India*, 21-6-1928; 12. *Young India*, 5-8-1926; 13. *Young India*, 8-10-1925; 14. *Young India*, 21-10-1926; 15. *Harijan*, 14-1-1940; 16. *Harijan*, 1-3-1942; 17. *Young India*, 28-5-1925

55. WOMEN'S EDUCATION

1. *Speeches and Writings of Mahatma Gandhi*, pp. 426-8; 2. *Harijan*, 27-2-1937; 3. *Amrita Bazar Patrika*, 12-1-1935; 4. *Harijan*, 9-11-1947

56. BIRTH-CONTROL

1. *Young India*, 12-3-1925; 2. *Key to Health*, pp. 52-54; 3. *Harijan*, 28-3-1936; 4. *Harijan*, 2-5-1936; 5. *Amrita Bazar Patrika*, 12-1-1935; 6. *Young India*, 2-4-1925; 7. *Harijan*, 14-9-1935; 8. *Harijan*, 31-3-1946

57. SEX EDUCATION

1. *Harijan*, 21-11-1936

58. CHILDREN

1. *Autobiography*, p. 312; 2. *Young India*, 29-10-1931; 3. *Young India*, 19-11-1931

59. COMMUNAL UNITY

1. *Constructive Programme*, p. 8; 2. *Young India*, 24-12-1931; 3. *Young India*, 29-10-1931

60. VARNASHRAMA DHARMA

1. *The Modern Review*, Oct. 1935, p. 413; 2. *Young India*, 27-10-1927; 3. *Young India*, 8-12-1920; 4. *Harijan*, 25-3-1933; 5. *Young India*, 4-6-1931; 6. *Harijan*, 11-2-1933; 7. *Young India*, 5-1-1921; 8. *Harijan*, 16-11-1935

61. THE CURSE OF UNTOUCHABILITY

1. *Speeches and Writings of Mahatma Gandhi*, p. 387; 2. *Harijan*, 11-2-1933; 3. *Young India*, 25-5-1921; 4. *Young India*, 29-7-1926; 5. *Young India*, 5-1-1922; 6. *From Yeravda Mandir*, Chap. IX; 7. *Harijan*, 11-2-1933

62. RELIGIOUS TOLERANCE IN INDIA

1. *Young India*, 20-10-1927; 2. *Young India*, 24-11-1927; 3. *Young India*, 24-11-1927; 4. *Harijan*, 6-3-1937; 5. *Young India*, 8-9-1920; 6. *Young India*, 20-1-1927; 7. *Young India*, 21-3-1929; 8. *Young India*, 22-12-1927; 9. *Young India*, 28-8-1924; 10. *Harijan*, 18-3-1933; 11. *Young India*, 28-8-1924; 12. *Young India*, 26-9-1929

63. PROSELYTIZATION

1. *Young India*, 29-5-1924; 2. *Young India*, 17-12-1925; 3. *Young India*, 23-4-1931; 4. *Harijan*, 30-1-1937

64. PROBLEMS OF ADMINISTRATION

1. *The Nation's Voice*, p. 71; 2. *Harijan*, 21-12-1947; 3. *Harijan*, 29-9-1946; 4. *Harijan*, 23-4-1938; 5. *Harijan*, 8-9-1946; 6. *Harijan*, 5-5-1946; 7. *Delhi Diary*, pp. 113-14; 8. *Young India*, 8-10-1931; 9. *Harijan*, 31-7-1937; 10. *Young India*, 30-6-1927; 11. *Young India*, 8-12-1927; 12. *Young India*, 12-8-1926; 13. *Young India*, 27-8-1931; 14. *Young India*, 6-10-1926; 15. *Young India*, 22-12-1927; 16. *Young India*, 19-1-1930; 17. *Harijan*, 7-12-1947; 18. *Young India*, 9-3-1922

65. REORGANIZATION OF PROVINCES

1. *Delhi Diary*, pp. 378-80; 2. *Harijan*, 30-11-1947; 3. *Harijan*, 21-9-1947; 4. *Harijan*, 7-9-1947; 5. *Harijan*, 27-7-1947

66. THE PROBLEM OF MINORITIES

1. *Young India*, 29-5-1924; 2. *Young India*, 19-1-1930; 3. *Harijan*, 9-8-1942; 4. *Harijan*, 22-9-1946; 5. *Harijan*, 29-9-1946; 6. *Harijan*, 7-4-1946; 7. *Young India*, 29-8-1929

67. AN INDIAN GOVERNOR

1. *Harijan*, 24-8-1947

68. THE PRESS

1. *An Autobiography*, p. 287; 2. *Young India*, 12-5-1920; 3. *Young India*, 28-5-1931; 4. *Young India*, 25-3-1926; 5. *Harijan*, 24-8-1935

69. PEACE BRIGADES

1. *Harijan*, 18-6-1938; 2. *Harijan*, 5-5-1946; 3. *Young India*, 29-5-1924; 4. *Young India*, 29-5-1924; 5. *Harijan*, 15-9-1940

70. INDIAN NATIONAL CONGRESS

1. *Harijan*, 1-2-1948; 2. *The Last Phase*, Vol. II, pp. 819-20

71. INDIA, PAKISTAN AND KASHMIR

1. *Harijan*, 26-10-1947; 2. *Delhi Diary*, pp. 307-08; 3. *Delhi Diary*, pp. 40-41; 4. *Delhi Diary*, p. 19; 5. *Delhi Diary*, p. 26; 6. *Delhi Diary*, p. 332; 7. *Delhi Diary*, pp. 31-32; 8. *Delhi Diary*, p. 82; 9. *Delhi Diary*, p. 91; 10. *Delhi Diary*, p. 140; 11. *Delhi Diary*, pp. 163-64

72. FOREIGN SETTLEMENTS IN INDIA

1. *Harijan*, 30-6-1946; 2. *Harijan*, 8-9-1946; 3. *Harijan*, 16-11-1947

73. INDIA AND WORLD PEACE

1. *Young India*, 26-12-1924; 2. *Young India*, 12-1-1928; 3. *Young India*, 9-5-1929; 4. *Young India*, 9-5-1929; 5. *Young India*, 12-3-1931; 6. *Young India*, 2-7-1931; 7. *Young India*, 1-10-1931; 8. *India's Case for Swaraj*, p. 209; 9. *Harijan*, 21-6-1942

74. The Message of the East

1. *Delhi Diary*, p. 31; 2. *Harijan*, 20-4-1947

75. Obiter Dicta

1. *Harijan*, 18-1-1942; 2. *Young India*, 3-6-1926; 3. *Young India*, 19-5-1927; 4. *Hind Swaraj*, p. 83; 5. *Young India*, 11-6-1925; 6. *Speeches and Writings of Mahatma Gandhi*, p. 393; 7. *Young India*, 6-6-1929; 8. *Young India*, 13-4-1921; 9. *Young India*, 11-6-1925; 10. *Young India*, 14-7-1920; 11. *Young India*, 8-12-1921; 12. *Young India*, 15-4-1926; 13. *Young India*, 17-4-1924; 14. *Young India*, 17-4-1924; 15. *An Autobiography*, p. 504; 16. *Young India*, 20-10-1927; 17. *Young India*, 6-7-1921; 18. *Young India*, 16-4-1931; 19. *An Autobiography*, p. 198; 20. *Young India*, 15-10-1925; 21. *Harijan*, 28-11-1936; 22. *Young India*, 18-12-1920; 23. *Young India*, 29-1-1921; 24. *Young India*, 7-5-1931; 25. *Harijan*, 7-11-1936; 26. *Harijan*, 24-9-1938; 27. *Harijan*, 18-1-1948; 28. *Harijan*, 14-12-1947; 29. *Young India*, 23-12-1926